THE MAKING OF A MUSEUM: PERSONAL RECOLLECTIONS

THE MAKING OF A MUSEUM: PERSONAL RECOLLECTIONS

(भोपाल स्थित इंदिरा गांधी राष्ट्रीय मानव संग्रहालय के नृशास्त्रीय विवरण पर आधारित)

Edited by

Ravindra K. Jain

AAKAR

The Making of A Museum: Personal Recollections
Edited by Ravindra K. Jain

ISBN 978-96-5002-220-7

First Published, 2013

Published by
AAKAR BOOKS
28 E Pocket IV, Mayur Vihar Phase I, Delhi 110 091
Phone : 011 2279 5505 Telefax : 011 2279 5641
info@aakarbooks.com; www.aakarbooks.com

Printed at
Mudrak, 30 A, Patparganj, Delhi 110 091

Contents

Preface and Acknowledgements

The present collection of essays and interviews forms a part of my project on 'Process and the Product: Anthropology, Museology and Community' undertaken by me as the Tagore National Fellow for Culture Research, Ministry of Culture, Government of India from A.D. 2011 to 2013. My nodal office for the fellowship was the Indira Gandhi Rashtriya Manav Sangrahalaya (IGRMS)/National Museum of Mankind, Bhopal, Madhya Pradesh. Having been trained as an anthropologist but with no specialist background in museology, I decided to embark on an ethnography of IGRMS. While sifting through the various dimensions represented in IGRMS, I singled out the activities and opinions of the curators of the museum as a significant lacuna in the public perception of the institution. This book is projected as an initial effort to fill that lacuna.

A few words about the structure of this volume. I begin with an overview of the 'Museum and Its Communities' that serves as a general Introduction. Part One consists of six essays in Hindi and in English to sensitize the reader about personal explorations in museum fieldwork by the respective authors. Part Two consists of interviews, again in Hindi and English, transcribed in a manner so as to retain the original flavour of the interaction between myself as the interviewer and thirteen curators as the interviewees. Part Two is preceded by a brief Preface to the interviews.

In preparing the following text I have incurred many debts. First and foremost, I am immensely grateful to all my contributors whose enthusiasm and candour were outstanding features of our collaboration. For the photographs accompanying the text and the cover, my thanks go to Mr. Tapas Biswas. Timely advice by Shri Vikas Bhatt and Shri

A.K. Tiwari came in handy under trying circumstances. Aakar Books did an extremely competent and efficient job of publishing. I extend my sincere thanks. Smt. Rachna Shrivastava provided valuable office assistance. Finally, this work would not have been possible without the unstinted cooperation of the Director, IGRMS, Prof. K.K. Misra.

R. K. J.

Introduction: Museum and Its Communities

Ravindra K. Jain

"It happens that the poor are not economic machines. They live in communities. If there are social norms that expect them to spend on funerals and weddings, etc., then these claim higher priority on their income". Ajit Sinha, 'An Anthropological Way of Doing Economics', *Economic and Political Weekly*, December 24, 2011, p. 33.

"For Weber, what creates community is a social relationship based on the subjective feeling of belonging to the same community. I add that this belief is sustained by the existence of an objective community that is socially constituted and symbolized by institutions, spokespeople, emblems, and myths." S. Dufoix, *Diasporas*, 2003, p. 70

The Anthropological Museum

The logo of Indira Gandhi Rashtriya Manav Sangrahalaya (IGRMS), Bhopal, is the depiction of a prehistoric person on a local rock shelter *in situ* with chest thrust outwards, making a dynamic move forward. It nicely sums up the saga of human community in a Museum of Mankind. Anthropology, as the holistic study of humankind, with its tangible and intangible heritage, could not have been better represented. As I just said, the logo of IGRMS is based on an authentic *in situ* representation and one has to travel only some fifty kilometres north to Bhimbedka to experience the artistic depiction on huge rock shelters of the entire saga of prehistoric human communities' hunting, warfare, movements, and assembly and sundry rituals. When one enters the sprawling campus of the IGRMS open museum the visitor encounters what a founding father of Anthropology, E.B. Tylor wrote in 1871 while defining 'culture' in a descriptive sense: "Culture or civilization, taken in its wide ethnographic sense, is that complex whole which includes knowledge, belief, art, morals, law, custom, and any other capabilities and habits acquired by man as a member of society". Here I wish to fasten on two aspects of this classic definition of culture: one, its nature as "a complex whole" and, two, its character as "capabilities and habits acquired by man as a member of society". The relationship between tangible and intangible heritage constitutes the "complex whole" which anthropologists have attempted to decipher either in bio-cultural terms or in cultural-structural terms. In the former perspective the primate beginnings and biological evolution of humanity and the continuing ethological/ behavioural affinities between human beings and higher primates have been the major focus. In this direction of anthropological research, the classical notion of cultural relativism has been seriously interrogated and a common denominator of bio-psychological-cultural humanity has been postulated (see Freeman 1965, 1966; Fox 1975; Jain 1989). In cultural-structural terms, Claude Levi-Strauss has gone the farthest in not only relating tangible to intangible heritage ("the logic of the concrete") but in subsuming this relationship in the nature of phenomenal reality itself. For him the decoding of human Culture/cultures rests on the interface between the apparent and the real, a discovery that he characterizes as common to the epistemologies of geology, Marxism and psychoanalysis—his "three mistresses" (see Levi-Strauss 1966; also Leach 1970). I shall not here go into the finer points of Levi-Strauss's epistemology and the derivation he makes in his journey to structural anthropology from structural linguistics and Boolean algebra. But let me here itself make the point that the anthropological concept of culture as a "complex whole" of human heritage in its two *avatars* mentioned above comes alive in the venue and display of the Museum of Mankind that is IGRMS.

This brings me to the second leg of Tylor's famous definition, viz. that the capacities and habits of man in creating culture are acquired by him as a member of society. Let me here recount what Ludwig Wittgenstein, the eminent philosopher, told his student Rush Rees; that "the most important thing he gained from talking to Straffa (the Cambridge economist) was an 'anthropological' way of looking at philosophical problems" (Monk 1991: 260-261). What did Wittgenstein mean by "an anthropological way"? To put it simply, he meant "look and see". Now I ask, could there be anything more vivid to illustrate this proposition than the museum collection, the repository of diverse and concrete visual culture? And could there be anything more elementary in making the transition from "looking" to the "seeing" of museum displays than the 'communities' of human beings where humankind acquires culture, to paraphrase Tylor, as members of society? When one reflects on the virulent debate between the erstwhile proponents of 'culture' (the American anthropologists) and of 'society' (the British anthropologists) one is left wondering in amazement how the feuding parties could have overlooked the necessary complementarity between the two concepts which Tylor enunciated so early in the history of anthropology. Coming to our own era, globalization of the mind which must accompany globalization of infrastructures necessitates a view of the unity of the social sciences and, in the case at hand, between anthropology, sociology and museology. In simpler terms if we do not only look but 'see' the interfaces between the three disciplines, any concept of the museum and its anthropological repository would be incomplete without its sociological matrix, namely, the communities that undergird this heritage.

The Sociological Matrix: Museum Communities

In their order of importance the three communities that I discuss are: firstly, the creators of heritage, namely, the artists, artistes and craftsmen; secondly, the museum curators and collectors who are the backbone of the presentation and dissemination of this heritage; and, finally, the publics that 'consume' this heritage. As will be obvious there are overlaps between the three, neatly epitomized in the 'community museum' movement (see UNESCO 2010). The conceptual umbrella under which this movement is seen has been noted to be the "identity" of the communities concerned (Bandarin 2010). In my view this concern with 'identity' may not capture the sociological meat of products and processes, may turn out to be a red herring, and might indeed be pernicious in emphasizing exclusion and exclusivity in the life-worlds of communities as they exist in modern times (see Brubaker and Cooper 2000). At this stage of the discussion, however, I would retract my steps in this direction and would rather delineate the broad contours of each of the three communities distinguished by me above.

The Creators

I shall have little to say about the lives of these communities in the conventional ethnographic sense; the Notes and Queries approach (Royal Anthropological Institute 1874) makes clear what the ethnographer in the field attempts to capture in a descriptive-cum-holistic sense. This itself is a very wide and rich field of study, collection and representation in a museum. More to the point of my interest and prognostication is the livelihood aspect of the communities of the creators and, to anticipate somewhat, the crises of livelihood which these communities are embroiled in.

Let me begin with a simple example. The humble 'broom' has been the fulcrum of a whole desert museum called Arna Jharna 23 kilometres outside Jodhpur city in Rajasthan (Bharucha 2010). On display are 200 varieties of brooms from the State of Rajasthan. The interdisciplinary research on the broom, an object so ordinary, if not inconspicuous, has catalyzed the museum's growth. The museum came into contact with diverse communities—notably, professional broom-making communities like the Banjara, the Koli and the Harijans, in addition to many other rural communities that make brooms for their own use from whatever material is available in their environments. Along with broom-makers, both professional and non-professional, the research on brooms has also necessitated close dialogue with multiple users of brooms, from rural and urban areas, who have alerted the museum staff about the myriad values, beliefs, and customs surrounding brooms. Let us note that unlike the District Six Museum in Cape Town, South Africa, which evolved out of a social movement that brought together a larger number of people living in District Six, who were displaced by the apartheid regime, this museum (Arna Jharna) is based on the craft of diverse communities. The few families living in hutments surrounding the Arna Jharna museum from the Bhil and Meghwal communities are itinerate and are linked to the temporary labour market of the local mining industry. Caste, patriarchy, and gender defines many of the variables; the Harijan community monopolizes the use of bamboo (*bans*), the Koli community works almost exclusively with date-palm (*khajur*), and the Banjara, now dispersed and impoverished, works primarily with different components of grass (*panni, munjh, sarkanda, sirhi*). Further, the majority community of broom-makers is that of Harijans (rather than politically active *dalits*) who are largely employed by the municipality as sweepers. They are the most socially stigmatized as "untouchables" but produce the most expensive brooms in the market made of bamboo. In contrast, the Banjara community, which comes from a relatively higher caste group, produces the poor man's broom of grass. From such examples we learn that economic mobility does not get translated into social status. The schisms remain across traditional divides despite contradictory economic realities.

I alluded to Arna Jharna as a simple example, but paradoxically this museum based on the humble broom provides an organic base, as it were, for the further evolution of the museum. Once the museum curator enters the field of plants, bushes and shrubs for the materials of the broom-making process it seems logical to extend one's sights to other cultural uses of wood. In the case of Arna Jharna, and in keeping with the object (like broom), its communities and its surrounding significance one comes to wooden musical instruments and musicians. This "nascent intervention in the field of grass-roots museology in the Indian context" (Bharucha

2010) leads forward to building of a new structure for its collection of 130 folk musical instruments. Thanks to the vision of the pioneer of the broom museum, Komal Kothari, he has also initiated from the early 1960s research, collection and organizing the vast musical repertoire of traditional musicians from the Langa, Manganiar, and Kalbelia communities, among others. Without this initiative there would not have been a resurgence in 'Rajasthani folk music' both at the national and international levels. And, as Bharucha (2010) expresses it, "a temperature-controlled and acoustically-sound building would be an ideal addition to the Arna Jharna Museum" located as it is in a harsh and stony landscape marked by cavernous sandstone mines and waste deposits.

In discussing Arna Jharna, I have given the example of caste communities focused around particular material objects, brooms and musical instruments. The anthropologist has always had a strong professional and humanitarian interest in tribal communities. The synergy between land and its produce both in the cultivated and natural state has been a special feature of tribal life. Indeed one of the *differentium specificum* between Caste and tribe in the anthropological (rather than in the administrative) sense would be in the perceptions and attachments to land. In this respect, speaking early about Village Studies of caste in the 1950s and 1960s, Dumont and Pocock (1957) had observed with insight, "The architectural and demographic fact that is the Indian village lures us away from a structural perspective." The obverse of this is true about the tribal village: here the structural perspective is provided in the first place by the *terra firma*, the land and its inhabitants. This is not the occasion for me to enter into the complex question of tribal land tenure systems in India but if there is one generalization that holds true for the land systems of the country as a whole, it is that the idea of "commons" in land tenure is intrinsic to tribal polity, economy, society and cosmology. Or, to put the matter in another way, in contrast to caste villages, the attachment of tribal groups to the land they inhabit and use is not fragmented qualitatively in an absolute sense and juridically in a relative sense in the same way as in the former. There are accounts of the political leadership around land enjoyed by hereditary chiefs and headmen in tribal villages all over India. To cut a long story short, the question of ethnic conflict, both intra-tribal and inter-tribal, is based on the "commons" concept and practice of the tribals both in the stability and population movements in their villages. Examples are the Naga-Meitei and Naga-Kuki conflagrations in the Northeastern tribal belt and endemic conflicts between the tribals and outsiders throughout the Chotanagpur (now Jharkhand) region since the 19th century era of colonial hegemony. The land question or sovereignty over territory is in the forefront of inter-tribal and intra-tribal conflicts in the Northeast (see Bose and Manchanda 2011) and it would pay sociologists to compare and contrast the tribal pattern of violence with factional conflicts in caste villages of the country. What may be seen in the context of conflict has its counterpart in the context of tribal cooperation and exchange. The point I wish to make is that land and its products define parameters of structural relationships in tribal villages.

The above is an important datum for the tribal museologist. When the issue is that of relating objects to their museum representations, it is important to bear in mind the anthropological framework of interpretations. Surely the tribal museologist of India would have to reckon with the facts that forest and mineral products in the vast central Indian belt and specific forms of processes and products (for example, swidden agriculture) in the valleys and hills of Northeast India are the most salient features of tribal habitats. Further, it is precisely in these tribal regions that both poverty and insurgency are rampant in a virulent form. In the widest anthropological terms for live interpretation this is the framework we have to adopt. Till now the tribal museum displays have been based on descriptive classifications of the Notes and Queries type. Interpretations arise when historical ecology of inter and intra-tribal conflict and cooperation is attempted. Examples are the cultural ecological symbiosis of exchange between the Toda, the Kota, the Badaga and the Kurumba tribes of the Nilgiri

Hills. Visual representations of these tribal cultures must be accompanied by interpretative exegeses. Similarly, as pointed out before, the material bases of inter and intra-tribal conflicts in the Northeast and the conflict of interest between tribals and the outsiders (for example, the Pasco Corporation in Odisha) have to be explored and visually represented. Then and only then would the pedagogical-cum-cognitive functions of a tribal museum alert the publics to an understanding of the concatenation between natural resources (mines and forests for example), poverty, and insurgency in tribal areas. It is through such displays that the understanding of the nexus between livelihoods and material culture would be framed in the wider dynamics of socio-political processes affecting the tribals today. The armory of museum displays in addition to objects would include photos, texts, videos and many reference materials for the researchers. Photos and videos will be used to show the real lives of the tribes. There would be mannequins, maps, graphs, hardcover books, audiotapes, models and dioramas. An exemplary museum depicting a major crisis in the life history of a nation and its people is the Apartheid (1948 to 1994) Museum at Freedom Park in Johannesburg, South Africa, founded in 1995. Along similar lines, would it be asking too much to have a display devoted to the Bhopal Gas Tragedy in the IGRMS, Bhopal?

The Curators

Next to the caste and tribal communities, creators of tangible and intangible heritage displayed in the museums, I would give pride of place to the curators of the museum who constitute an indispensable middle-rung of communities associated with it. The curators are usually the unsung heroes among museum stakeholders but as I propose to show their labour, dedication and commitment to the collection, display, preservation, and dissemination in the museum constitutes its life-blood. I present my findings in the form of the conclusions of a case study based on interviews with curators of the IGRMS, Bhopal. The full study is the subject of this book consisting of the detailed interview transcripts and sundry written contributions by this section of the museum community; here I present my findings in the perspective of their unique middle class position located in the evolution of IGRMS.

First a few words about the middle class, the new middle class in India and the particular characteristics of the typical middle class character of our IGRMS museum curating community. Apropos the middle class, J.M. Barbalet (1986: 567) observes: "Changes in economic organization and the division of labour since the turn of the century pose questions about social class which Marxist and Weberian theories have not been able to answer satisfactorily. Developments in productive organization have increased the number of clerical, supervisory, administrative and managerial jobs; the growth of commodities markets has given rise to a large number of sales, service and accounts jobs; the increasing application of scientific technologies to production has generated new categories of scientific and technical work; the expanded role of the state has increased the numbers of administrative, managerial, professional and semi-professional jobs". These developments are more specific to the industrial West and, in fact, presage post-industrial growth in those countries, but they also indicate contemporary and future trends for industrializing, manufacturing, and servicing concerns in countries like India. There undoubtedly is the growth of a rapidly increasing "new middle class" in India representing "a social group that operates as a proponent of economic liberalization", says Fernandes (2006, xviii). Further she adds that "This middle class is not "new" in terms of its structural or social basis. In other words, its "newness" does not refer to upwardly mobile segments of the population entering the middle class. Rather, its newness refers to a process of production of a distinctive social and political identity that represents and lays claim to the benefits of liberalization." My point in discussing IGRMS curators as a middle class is precisely that their own identity construction (if such a construction could indeed be scientifically captured) is not that of the "new" middle class of Fernandes' description. They signify, on the other hand, a newly educated, highly motivated, upwardly mobile middle class emerging from the regional (rather than metropolitan) urban, peri-urban (small town) and rural environments in our country. It is difficult to say that, like in the West, there has been "disappearance of status" (Barbalet, 1986) considerations among them because caste, regional and linguistic loyalties persist in the processes of social stratification and mobility of this class within the new context, but a distinctively salient tendency needs to be highlighted. This tendency is a heightened commitment to the new jobs, viewed essentially as an opportunity to be cashed in as a consequence of newly acquired education and mobility. To take a very different contextual parallel, the same tendency is found among many of the Indian information technology specialists working abroad who work extra hours, much beyond the statutory requirements for their jobs, often to the chagrin of their native co-workers! (Lakha 2005).

When one says that these middle class curators wish to 'cash in' the newly acquired opportunity bestowed by education and mobility, it is not always the higher income incentive (a point on which the parallel with IT workers abroad breaks down) but something more and else, the motivation to 'prove' themselves as dedicated members of a 'building team' headed by a worthy leader. Time and again in my interviews with curators at IGRMS this motivation came to the fore so much so that one could almost delineate a paradigm as follows:

(a) Roots in a rural or peri-urban area
(b) Low level of income and education
(c) Acceptance of a job in the museum at a low level in both income and status
(d) Gaining mobility (not necessarily through promotion to a higher post in the museum itself) but by acquiring higher educational qualifications while still in job.
(e) Field trips in different parts of the country to enrich museum collections as well as their own 'anthropological' experience
(f) Moving around in different sections of the museum

thus accumulating 'holistic' experience of the institution

(g) Encounters with and finding solutions to problems that the curators faced due to insurgency in tribal areas.

(h) Continuing associations with catchment areas partly as a compensation for being stuck in stagnant professional positions within the museum itself.

(i) It may not be an exaggeration to say that the museum curators whose life stories I have narrated are the unsung heroes of IGRMS. None of them believed that their career trajectories were worth being found out, but once stimulated into recalling their life in the museum and beyond, there were revelations and lessons which no amount of top-downward history would convey.

To be able to contextualize the work of the curators it would be instructive to follow the sequence in which IGRMS was developed at its present site. In 1979, when the site of the Museum was occupied for infrastructure development, the landscape was arid and devoid of any vegetation. There were no water sources in the area, nor any link road to approach the site. The campus was to be landscaped within these

IGRMS overlooking the Bhopal lake

constraints. The site offered by the Madhya Pradesh Government was on the slope of the Shamla Hills overlooking the famous Bhopal Lake. It was an extraordinary site for museum-making with over thirty rock shelters with rock paintings on the shelves of many shelters datable back to prehistoric period. By the end of 1979 the Museum was in possession of a total area of 196.95 acres. The main facet of the Museum display was planned to highlight (a) the bio-cultural evolution and variation of mankind, (b) the culture and society in pre-and-proto historic period, and (c) the contemporary patterns of culture from different ecological zones of the country. The exhibitions were to be developed in the form of proto-types of community habitats from desert zones, coastal regions, river basins, hilly terrains of the Himalayas, the central Indian plateau etc. as open air components. An elaborate indoor museum on 28,056 sq. metres area was also planned. By January 1988 a few components of the first open air exhibition in the museum campus titled 'Tribal Habitat' was opened for the public. The exhibits of life-size housing dwellings of selected groups of tribal communities were built by concerned tribal groups with materials from their own villages. This exhibition was strengthened from time to time, and by 2006 A.D. there were about thirty house types.

To begin with, priority was given to build a few temporary structures in the Shamla Hills campus, pending construction of permanent buildings. Construction of a temporary exhibition structure, Avratti Bhavan, was completed by May 1990 and the first indoor periodical exhibition, Vastu Prasang, was opened. Soon after this the various establishment units were shifted from the temporary accommodation in Arera Colony, except the Library and Specimen Storage units which required special care and security. Work on the development of an approach road to the Museum Campus, internal road networks and pathways were speeded up and a large collection of ethnographic specimens was also achieved. Special mention should be made of the collection of nearly a thousand objects from Kerala, including a 110 ft long *palliyodam* (snake boat), and a few traditional house types. The 'coastal village' open air exhibition was established with these collections, and more house-types of fishermen communities from Andhra Pradesh, Odisha, and Kerala. Work on the 'desert village' complex also started with a cluster of house-types of Rabari community of Gujarat and Rajput community of Rajasthan. Some of the thirty odd rock shelters with prehistoric rock-paintings have been formed into another open air exhibition titled 'Rock Art Heritage' opened to the public in 1991.

As mentioned earlier incumbents of curatorial jobs in IGRMS considered themselves members of teams headed by leaders worthy of emulation. More often than not these leaders were Directors of the Museum. Many are the stories of the sharing in privation and hardships (working late at night, even sleeping in the open, eating rudimentarily cooked food in construction sites) between these leaders and ordinary workers during the time that the Museum was being raised.

The Publics

In a recent article (Jain 2011: 1-8) I have articulated the vision of a mini-cultural revolution in India to be backed by a communication initiative on a novel and, prospectively, on a massive scale. The take-off points and platforms for the initiative, I suggest, would be our museums. We shall need to rope in imagination and motivation of our youth and school children in the first place. Rather than a hemmed-in and four-walled visit to a museum, the young and adult visitors would be exposed to a combination of tangible and intangible cultural heritage by a dramatization (tableaux) of festivals and demonstration of traditional but ever-changing arts and crafts. As has been happening in the popular annual 'Balrang' festival in Jawahar Bal Bhavan, Bhopal, from 1996 to 1999 and in Bharat Bhavan, Bhopal, from 2000 to 2004, the occasion is replete with ingratiating narratives in songs, stories and dances etc. It is heartening to see that since 2005 to date its organization has been taken over on a bigger scale by IGRMS. The festival is a joint undertaking of IGRMS and the Folk Educational Secretariat of Education Department, Government of Madhya Pradesh. Children from faraway regions of India participate and present glimpses of their habitat, culinary habits, folk songs and dances. By visiting *pandals* of their own state and other states, the children get a sense of oneness which goes a long way in uniting the country. Needless to say, the event is marked by competitions of artistic, written, and oral compositions by children and prizes are given to the best performers. As Rajeev Lochan, Director of the Gallery of Modern Art, New Delhi, recently pointed out, like in all art, the accent here is on 'experience' rather than abstract 'understanding'. Much can be written on the impact on the museum public represented by advanced school children and accompanying adults, including their teachers. Another relevant step taken in the same direction by IGRMS recently was to hold a National Workshop on 'Anthropology and Museums' (December 14-16, 2011) attended by post-graduate students of anthropology from 14 departments all over the country. The pedagogical, training and inspirational impact of such a Workshop, and popular lectures organized along side, cannot be overestimated. The participants were asked to give feedback on various aspects of their visit to IGRMS and when these responses are analysed, a way could be paved for designing an open-air museum 'movement' in the regions along lines successfully pursued at IGRMS. A third exhibition held recently at my suggestion was the bringing together of students of vernacular architecture at the School of Planning and Architecture, Bhopal, with their sketches and models, and the curatorial staff of IGRMS. The latter had provided the former with detailed information and visual experience of life-sized models of tribal habitat on campus upon which their exercises were based. The exhibition was open to the public with a view to apprising interested parties about commercial and general applications of vernacular architecture.

I do not wish to conclude this account as a report- card on the achievements of IGRMS in relation to its present and potential publics, but I must also mention two significant departures which this Museum has made from the conventional format: one, travelling exhibitions and cultural performances that mark a two-way truck between Bhopal in central India and other socio-cultural-ecological regions of the country, and, two, the founding and facilitation of cultural interpretation centres in different parts of India. Two such interpretation centres are at the Kamlabari *satra* located in the World Heritage site of Vaishnavite temple-cum-monastic complex at Majuli and the Ashon cultural interpretation centre in Manipur. It is of utmost significance that the IGRMS nexus with both these sites is founded upon the existence of indigenous museums. It has been claimed, rightly or wrongly, that the Dakshinapath *satra* in Majuli founded some 357 years ago can be regarded as the first museum in the world!

Concluding Remarks

In the advanced science and art of museology today one hears and reads a lot about eco-museums, mobile museums and, above all, about community museums. My own impression is that most community museums in Asia, apart from the ones in classical civilizations like the Hindu, Buddhist and Islamic ones in countries like Thailand, Indonesia and India itself, are by and large small, localized and pre-literate ones (for example, in Laos, Gajadhur et al. 2010; the bamboo museum in northeast Thailand, Carina zur Strassen and Jakhadte Jayo 2010). To mobilize local communities for a museum movement in these circumstances may be relatively easy. When one turns to cultural centres in the great civilizational complexes of Asia, it is imperative that there be a marriage between the literati who would manage the research and preservation sides and the other curators who would deal specifically with display and dissemination for the general publics. Furthermore the relevance and justification of a community museum movement for purposes of preserving and fostering cultural identity of groups and communities may again be a motive and provide sustenance for the smaller localized museums. When it comes to the management of cultural heritage in a diverse, multi-faceted, historical, literate, and fast-changing country like ours, the parameters of preservation and dissemination must rise above ethnic and cultural identity alone. It is no small matter that in India the global vision of Santiniketan (for art and literature) and Sriniketan (for crafts) was concretized by the poet Rabindranath Tagore nearly a century ago. What we have to imagine for our day and age in the present globalized world is the integration of the metropolis and the rural areas, of tribe and caste, of machine and the post-machine. The task of preservation and augmentation of cultural heritage, the unique creation of man and his works with its indelible mark of humanity, beckons us in this direction.

References

Bandarin, F. 2010. Preface in UNESCO. *Community-based Approach to Museum Development in Asia and the Pacific for Culture and Sustainable Development.* Paris: UNESCO.

Barbalet, J.M. 1986. Limitations of Class Theory and the Disappearance of Status: The Problem of the New Middle Class. *Sociology* 20(4): 557-575.

Bharucha, R. 2010. Arna-Jharna: The Desert Museum of Rajasthan. IN UNESCO. *Community-based Approach to Museum Development in Asia and the Pacific for Culture and Sustainable Development.* Paris: UNESCO.

Bose, Tapan and Rita Manchanda 2011. Expanding the middle space in the Naga peace process. *Economic and Political Weekly* XLVI (53): 51-60.

Brubaker, R. and Frederick Cooper 2000. Beyond "Identity". *Theory and Society* 29: 1-47.

Cara zur Strassen and Jakhadte Jayo 2010. The Lahu Bamboo Museum. In UNESCO. *Community-based Approach to Museum Development in Asia and the Pacific for Culture and Sustainable Development.* Paris: UNESCO.

Dufoix, Stéphane 2003. *Diasporas.* Berkeley, Los Angeles, London: University of California Press.

Dumont, L. and David F. Pocock 1957. Village Studies. *Contributions to Indian Sociology* (old series) 1: 23-41.

Fernandes, Leela 2007. *India's New Middle Class.* New Delhi: Oxford University Press.

Fox, Robin 1975. *Encounter with Anthropology.* London: Peregrine Books.

Freeman, Derek 1966. Social Anthropology and the Scientific Study of Human Behaviour. *Man* (new series) 1(3): 330-342.

Gajadhur, Tara et al. 2010. Working with Source Communities in a Developing Country – The Traditional Arts and Ethnology

Centre. In UNESCO. *Community-based Approach to Museum Development in Asia and the Pacific for Culture and Sustainable Development*. Paris: UNESCO.

Jain, R. K. 1989. The Concept of Man in Anthropology: Beyond Cultural Relativism. *Eastern Anthropologist* 42(2): 137-149.

Jain, R. K. 2011. Anthropology and a Mini Cultural Revolution: A Vision. *Humankind* 7: 1-8.

Lakha, Salim 1999. The State of Globalization and Indian Middle Class Identity. In Michael Pinches (ed.) *Culture and Privilege in Capitalist Asia*. New York: Routledge. Pp. 251-274.

Leach, Edmund 1970. *Levi-Strauss*. London: Fontana/Collins.

Levi-Strauss, C. 1966. *The Savage Mind*. London: Weidenfeld and Nicolson.

Monk, R. 1991. *Ludwig Wittgenstein: The Duty of Genius*. London: Vintage.

Royal Anthropological Institute (RAI) 1874 (1964). *Notes and Queries in Anthropology*. London: RAI.

Sinha, Ajit 2011. An Anthropological Way of Doing Economics. *Economic and Political Weekly* XLVI (52): 33-35.

Tylor, E. B. 1871 (1903). *Primitive Culture: Researches into the Development of Mythology, Philosophy, Religion, Art and Custom*. Volume 1. London: John Murray.

UNESCO 2010. *Community-based Approach to Museum Development in Asia and the Pacific for Culture and Sustainable Development*. Paris: UNESCO.

PART ONE :
ESSAYS

बेलापाट, तोकसिंह अगरिया और भेंगराज पक्षी

शम्पा शाह

एक दूसरे का हाथ पकड़े, पेड़ों का साज पहने, गोल घेरे में नृत्यरत पहाड़ियां? या आदिवासी युवक-युवतियां? या कि दोनों ही? पहाड़ों की इस अंतहीन श्रृंखला में चढ़ते-उतरते अचानक मुझे बैगा युवक-युवतियों के मांदर की थाप पर सैला नृत्य करते, जुड़े-जुड़े हाथों की गूँथ दिखी। लहर की तरह ऊपर जाते फिर नीचे आते हाथों की गूंथ। ढीली चोटी सी यह गूंथ, जो न खुलती है और न जिसका ओर-छोर ही मिलता है।

कल रात भर बारिश होती रही, आज सबेरे से भी रह-रह कर हो रही है। जंगल के रास्ते में कीचड़ मचा है। गाड़ी का पहिया रह-रहकर इसमें फँस कर बेदम हो जाता है। चार लोग उतर कर ठेलते हैं और तब गाड़ी आगे बढ़ती है। यूं तो नई फ़ोर-स्ट्रोक गाड़ी है, डरने की कोई बात नहीं लेकिन इसी रास्ते से अँधेरे में लौटने का खयाल डरा रहा है। ईश्वर कहता है कि यदि ऐसा हुआ तो चाडा या छिलपिटा में ही रुक लेंगे। अभी तो तीन ही बजे हैं। मन को तसल्ली हो जाती है। उतरती-चढ़ती गाड़ी का हिण्डोला है और तुका तसल्ली से हथेली पर गाल टिकाये सो रहा है। जिस जगह की या जिस चीज़ की तलाश में हम जा रहे हैं उसके सचमुच में यानी ठोस पदार्थ रूप में होने की मुझे कतई उम्मीद नहीं है। मैं यह लगभग मान कर चल रही हूं कि हजारों वर्षों से निष्कंप खड़े इन जंगल, पहाड़ों और यहां बसने वाले अगरिया लोगों के मिथकों के संधिस्थल पर कोई सीता की रसोई या भीम की बैठक सी शिला होगी, जिसे देख मन बरबस यह मान लेगा कि सैंकड़ों बरस पहले पनकू राम मरावी, तोकसिंह मरावी, लक्ष्मण टेकाम के परदादा के परदादा इस जगह पर पत्थर से लोहा गला रहे थे और उनकी परदादी की परदादी अपनी एड़ियों से धौंकनी चला रही थीं। "आ गया बैलापाट, बस यहीं उस पिकरी के झाड़ के पास गाड़ी रोक दो" तोकसिंह जी की आवाज़ आई। पहाड़ के ऊपर जंगल से घिरी एक छोटी सी गुहाड़ी या मैदान। सड़क की बांई ओर कोई पचास फीट लम्बी, मेरुदण्ड-सी मिट्टी की एक

ढूह। पास जाकर देखा तो मैं हत्प्रभ रह गई–ढूह मिट्टी की नहीं, लौह अयस्क को गला कर लोहा बनाने की प्रक्रिया में निकलने वाले गेरा या कि स्लेग की थी। तोक सिंह जी जैक कीन को बता रहे थे ''यहीं हमारे आजा, परदादे रहते थे, यहीं एक कतार में उनकी कोठियां (लोहा गलाने की मिट्टी की भट्टी) बनी थी, जिसमें वे रात-दिन लोहा पिघलाते थे और गेरा (स्लैग) को फेंकते जाते थे, वहां सामने उनके घर रहे होंगे और सड़क के उस पार घना जंगल देखती हैं ना माताजी, (वे स्वयं 65 बरस के तो होंगे, लेकिन बंगाल की तरह यहां भी लड़की को मां कह कर संबोधित करने का चलन है)। बस दस कदम नीचे उतरने पर साफ पानी की झिरी है–सोनाझिरी, वहीं से वे लोग पानी लाते रहे होंगे।'' जैक कीन बौराये से गेरा के टुकड़े उठा रहे थे और चुम्बक से उन टुकड़ों में रह गये लोहे की जांच-पड़ताल करने में जुटे थे। बाकी सारे लोग जिनमें हम सब और तोक सिंह जी के भाई हीरा और गोपाल भी शामिल थे उन्हें कभी नली, तो कभी कटोरी के आकार में जम गये गेरा के टुकड़े ला-ला कर दे रहे थे। जंगल के उस निविड़ सन्नाटे में यकायक कई धोंकनियां सांस लेने लगी थीं। मानव सभ्यता के विकास की बुनियाद जिन चन्द आविष्कारों पर टिकी है उनमें से एक लोहे की खोज है। लौह पत्थर को पिघलाकर उसमें से लोहा प्राप्त करने और फिर उससे नाना वस्तुएँ गढ़ने की प्रक्रिया को सधने में कितने वर्ष लगे होंगे, कितने शरीर दझे होंगे?

बूंद स्वाती की भले हो
बेधती है मर्म की सीपी का उसी निर्मम त्वरा से
वज्र जिससे फोड़ता चट्टान को
भले ही फिर व्यथा के तम में
बरस पर बरस बीतें एक मुक्ता-रूप को पकते।

तभी न लुहारों की कथाओं में ऐसा ज़िक्र आता है कि पहले लुहारों के पास कोई औज़ार नहीं थे। वे हथौड़े की जगह अपनी मुट्ठी, संडसी की जगह हाथ और निहाई की जगह अपने घुटनों का इस्तेमाल करते थे। वह तो बाद में जाकर एक के ऊपर एक पांव धर कर बैठे कुत्ते को देख सण्डसी, कठफोड़वे की चोंच को देख हथौड़ा और जिस शाख को वह ठोकता रहता है उसे देख निहाई बनाने का विचार बारह भाई अगरियाओं में से सबसे छोटे के दिमाग में आया था। कितने तन कितनी भट्ठियों में झुँके होंगे तब कहीं विकास की एक दहलीज़ पार हुई होगी। उस पचास फीट लम्बी मिट्टी की ढूह पर खड़े हम न जाने किस प्राचीन इतिहास की प्राचीर पर खड़े थे।

विशाल पिकरी के झाड़ (बरगद, पीपल से मिलता-जुलता कुछ उनके अधबीच

का पेड़) तले जिस पर महुलाइन या माहुल की घनी बेल चढ़ी थी, बेलापाट देवी का थान है। नहीं कोई मूर्ति नहीं है, पर सब जानते हैं और यहां से गुज़रते समय सभी, खासकर अगरिया लोग अगरबत्ती-नारियल अवश्य चढ़ाते हैं। बादल न जाने कब और कैसे छंट गये थे।

बरसात के बाद की कोमल धुली-धुली धूप खिल आई थी, हम सभी ने बेलापाट देवी को प्रणाम किया। बहुत लम्बे समय के बाद मन में ऐसी शांति की अनुभूति हुई कि जिसकी चाह में लोग मंदिर जाते होंगे पर जो अब दिनोंदिन वहां से गायब है।

छिलपिटा में गाड़ी रुकी तो एक जाने-पहचाने चेहरे को देख मैं चकित रह गई, ''आप? पनकूरामजी क्या यहीं हैं?'' बताया गया कि पनकूराम जी तो अपने दामाद रामा टेकाम के साथ मवई में रहते हैं और ये रामा टेकाम के जुड़वां भाई लक्ष्मण टेकाम हैं! यह भी पता चला कि मैं अभी दस दिन पहले भोपाल में लोकरंग कार्यक्रम में इन्हीं से मिली थी लेकिन मैं तब भी उन्हें रामा टेकाम समझ कर ही मिली थी और मैंने तब भी उनसे पनकू राम जी के हाल-समाचार पूछे थे और पूरी जानकारी ली थी। मुझे बड़ी झेंप लगी। मुझे झेंपता देख तोक सिंह जी बोले ''राम-लक्ष्मण की जोड़ी है, इन्हें कौन अलग कर पाया है, माताजी?'' छिपपिटा के पास के जंगल से नवल और लक्ष्मण लोहा-पत्थर बीन कर ले आये थे। बोरियां गाड़ी में रख दी गईं और यहां से लक्ष्मण और उनकी पत्नी भी हमारे साथ हो लिये। रात घिर आई थी। बारिश तो थमी हुई थी लेकिन जंगल, पहाड़ों के अंधेरे रास्ते में गाड़ी चलाना कोई खेल-मज़ाक नहीं था। गाड़ी 10-15 कि.मी. प्रतिघण्टा की रफ्तार से चल रही होगी। बीच-बीच में अँधकार में डूबे गांव गुज़रते जाते थे। --चाड़ा...।

शाम को आते वक्त हमने चाड़ा में चाय पी थी। चाय की दुकान दरअसल घर के बरामदे का हिस्सा थी और चाय बनाकर पिलाने वाले भी घर के सदस्य ही थे इसलिये दुकान में न होकर घर में ही चाय पीने का अनुभव हुआ था। अधेड़ उम्र की एक बैगा स्त्री लगातार मेज़ पर से जूठे गिलास-प्लेटें उठा उन्हें धोने में जुटी थी, एक जवान स्त्री जो शायद उसकी बहू होगी चूल्हे पर चाय बना रही थी। एक युवक जो उसका बेटा जान पड़ता था, लोगों को चाय, मटर-भजिये देने और पैसे लेने में जुटा था। हालांकि यह दूसरा काम वह शायद ठीक न ही कर पाता होगा। हमारे ही सामने कुछ सरकारी से आदमी लड़के को आधी रकम दे गये और उनके ''ठीक है न'' कह कर निकल जाने में ऐसा भाव था, जैसे कह रहे हों कि एक तो हमने तुम्हारी दुकान में चाय पी, तुम्हें उसी से खुश होना चाहिये, तिस पर हम पैसे भी दे रहे हैं, अपना भाग्य समझो। युवक तो कुछ नहीं बोला पर चाय बनाती स्त्री चिल्लाती रही

कि यह तो आधा पैसा भी नहीं है। कि दुपहर, आफिस में भी छः चाय गई थीं। पर वह सरकारी इल्लियों की फौज फूहड़ ठहाके लगाती, सुना-अनसुना करती चली गई। दुकान की एक मेज़ और बैन्च पर बस्ता और ट्रांजिस्टर लिये उसी घर की एक दस बरस की बच्ची बैठी कॉपी में बड़े मनोयोग से लिख रही थी। ट्रांजिस्टर पर कोई कुछ बोले जा रहा था। मुझे लगा कि बच्ची ने ट्रांजिस्टर सुनने की गरज से नहीं बल्कि इसलिये लगा रखा था ताकि उसे दुकान में आने वाले लोगों की बातें न सुनाई दें। ट्रांज़िस्टर से निकलता शोर बच्ची के लिये एक आड़ थी, जिसकी ओट में बैठी वह गणित की कोई गुत्थी हल कर रही थी। मध्यप्रदेश में रहने वाले आदिवासी समूहों में बैगा प्रिमिटिव जनजाति में आते हैं। सदियों से जंगलों में रहते आये इन लोगों को सरकार, आज़ादी के बाद से हल-बक्खर पकड़ा किसान बनाने, उन्हें मैदानों में बसाने के प्रयास में जुटी है। जंगलों पर अपने अधिकार के छिने जाने से आहत-परेशान ये लोग अब मजबूरन गांवों में रह रहे हैं। जोड़-हिसाब तो न बच्ची के पिता का खराब है न उसकी मां का, पर वे क्या उपाय करें कि जिससे उनकी आवाज़ इस देश को चलाने का दावा करने वाले (सरकारी) लोग सुनें। बच्ची की तरह कभी उनके पास भी जंगल की ओट थी। यह नहीं कि जीवन की कठिनाइयां तब कम थीं पर कम से कम एक आड़ तो थी, अब तो वे बिल्कुल खुले में पड़े हैं।

ड्राईवर हार्न बजा रहा है। चाय की घरनुमा दुकान में जुटे बैगा परिवार के चित्र में सबकुछ यथावत है, अधेड़ स्त्री गिलास-प्लेट धो रही है, उसकी बहू फिर चाय बना रही है, लड़का बिना गिने पैसे ले रहा है, ट्रांज़िस्टर की ओट में बच्ची गणित के सवाल पर झुकी है। क्या बच्ची का हिसाब कभी इतना पक्का हो पायेगा? क्या ट्रांजिस्टर के शोर के पीछे से वह वो आवाज़ पा सकेगी कि जिसमें वह किन्हीं सरकारी अफसरों से कहे कि सैंतालीस रुपये बने हैं और उन्हें यह बाटा की दुकान के कैश काउण्टर के पीछे से आई आवाज़ की तरह सुनाई दे जहां एक रुपया भी कम चुकाने का सवाल ही नहीं बनता?

लौटते समय सब कुछ अँधेरे की ओट था, न चाय की दुकान दिखी, न कोई लोग दिखे। झोंपड़ियों पर गाड़ी की लाईट पड़ती तो पता चलता कि किसी गांव से गुज़र रहे हैं अन्यथा न किसी तरह की कोई रोशनी दिखाई देती थी न कोई आवाज़ें। तभी गाड़ी की हेडलाईट से बोर्ड पर लिखा एक नाम क्षण भर को रौशन हुआ "रजनी सरई"। इस नाम को तो मैं जानती हूं। किसका गांव है यह? स्मृति के काले पानी से तैर कर एक नाम ऊपर आया और रात जो पहले ही बहुत काली थी उसे और स्याह कर गया। रामजी राम मरावी जो बमुश्किल पच्चीस-छब्बीस का रहा होगा जब तपेदिक उसे लील गया था। वो और उसके पिता पनकूराम मरावी भोपाल

आये थे तब एक महीने तक मानव संग्रहालय में उन्होंने मेरे ही सेक्शन में काम किया था। मैंने पनकूराम जी से पहले कभी संसार की उत्पत्ति से जुड़ा अगरिया-मिथक सुना था। इस बार हमारा आग्रह उनसे उसी मिथक को उनके पारंपरिक लौह शिल्प में रुपायित करने का था। पहले तो बाप-बेटे दोनों ने साफ़ इन्कार कर दिया, कहने लगे यह कथा ही हमें नहीं आती। मैंने कहा, ''अच्छा ठीक है, रहने दीजिये लेकिन आज रात नींद में ज़रूर याद करियेगा!'' दूसरे दिन सबेरे रामजी राम बोला ''मैडम बहुत सारा लोहा लाना पड़ेगा पूरी सृष्टि जो बनानी है।'' एक महीने तक रात-दिन मेहनत करने के बाद वह अद्‌भुत म्युरल तैयार हुआ था जिसके शिखर पर रामजी राम ने बड़े मन से भेंगराज पक्षी को बिठाया था। उस पूरे महीने हथौड़े की ठकठक के बीच रामजी राम की खांसी गूंजती रहती थी। एक दिन बुखार आने पर डॉक्टर को बुलाया था और तभी पता चला कि उसे तपेदिक है। डॉक्टर और मैंने खूब समझाया था कि अब यह जानलेवा बीमारी नहीं है और नियमित दवा लेने से इससे पूरी तरह से छुटकारा पाया जा सकता है। उसी दौरान उसे क्राफ्ट म्यूज़ियम दिल्ली से भी न्यौता मिला था और उसने कहा था कि गांव जाकर वह भोपाल और दिल्ली के पैसों से कुछ ज़मीन खरीदेगा और फिर निश्चित ही भोपाल आकर इलाज करवायेगा। इस बात को डेढ़-दो साल बीत गए वह भोपाल नहीं आया और फिर एक मेले में पनकूराम जी मिले तो यह भयानक खबर लेकर कि रामजीराम नहीं रहा। पसीने से चमकती उसकी दुबली-पतली देह, लगातार घन चलाते हुए उठती-गिरती उसके हाथों की मांस-पेशियां बावजूद धौंकनी-सी चलती खांसी के मुझे यह अंदाज़ा नहीं लगा था कि वह देह इतनी खोखली हो चुकी थी। डॉक्टरी विद्या और दवाइयों के अब लोगों तक पहुँचने पर अपने भरोसे के कारण भी शायद चिंता वैसी नहीं हुई जैसी होनी चाहिये थी। हालांकि अब मुझे अपनी कमअक्ली पर बहुत कोफ़्त होती है। देश के विकास की कहानी तो शहरों से कस्बों की ओर जाती सड़कों पर ही चरमराने लगती है और गांव, विशेषकर जंगल-पहाड़ों के गांवों में तो पंक्चर टायर की तरह बैठ जाती है। कई गांवों के बीच एक स्वास्थ्य केंद्र जिसमें प्राय: एक डॉक्टर की नियुक्ति। न पर्याप्त दवाइयां न सुविधाएं, और तिस पर मंहगी एम.बी.बी.एस. की पढ़ाई कर आज कोई युवा डॉक्टर गांव में रहना नहीं चाहता है। लिहाज़ा वह महीने में दो-चार दिन से ज़्यादा उपस्थित नहीं रहता। किसी कंपाउण्डर या उससे भी कम ट्रेनिंग पाये आदमी के भरोसे स्वास्थ्य केंद्र चल रहे होते हैं। स्कूलों में हम बदस्तूर उनके बच्चों को पढ़ा रहे हैं कि टोना-टोटकाए झाड़-फूंक अंधविश्वास हैं और बीमार होने पर डॉक्टर के पास जाना चाहिये। कोई पूछे कि किस डॉक्टर के पास जाना चाहिये? क्या इन्हीं स्वास्थ्य केंद्रों के दम पर हम देश को तपेदिक मुक्त

करने का स्वप्न देखते हैं? वैसे पिछले कुछ समय से तो देश का मतलब पूरी तरह से शहर बल्कि मेट्रो शहर हो गया है। अब यह वाक्य पाठ्य पुस्तकों में भी पढ़ने को नहीं मिलता कि असल भारत गांवों में बसता है। उँगलियों पर गिने जा सकने वाले शहरों का मतलब ही यदि भारत है तो निश्चित ही स्वास्थ्य विभाग देश को तपेदिक मुक्त करने का तमगा लगा सकेगा। पर यदि गांवों को सम्मिलित किया जाये तो वहां आज भी हर पांचवें घर में कोई युवा रामजी राम तपेदिक का निवाला बन रहा है। गाड़ी में बैठे साथियों से मैंने उसके परिवार की खोज-खबर चाही। पता चला कि उसकी पत्नी अकेली अपने तीन बच्चों के साथ रह रही है। थोड़ी-बहुत खेती है उसे दूसरों को आधे हिस्से पर करने के लिये दे रखा है। बच्चों को पढ़ा रही है। बड़ी लड़की 10वीं में है, बेटा अभी बहुत छोटा है, न हल सम्भाल सकता है न ही घन चला सकता है। अंधेरी रात जंगल के रपटीले रास्ते और हमारे गन्तव्य की दूरी के चलते मैं गाड़ी रोकने को नहीं कह पाई। रजनी सरई का घर अन्धेरे में पीछे छूट गया। हठात् किसी पक्षी का स्वर सन्नाटे को बेधता बड़े पास से गुज़रा। किसी ने कहा, ''भेंगराज पक्षी है।'' मैंने मन ही मन दिवंगत रामजी राम को प्रणाम किया।

अगले दिन उठे तो आसमान साफ़ था, हवा बहुत ठण्डी थी लेकिन धूप में ताप था। कमरे में बँधी बछिया रह रहकर रंभा उठती थी और तुका पीछे पड़ा था कि बछिया को उसकी अम्मा के पास ले जाओ उसे भूख लगी है! किसी के हाथ खाली हों तब तो वो बछिया को उसकी अम्मा के पास ले जाये। तोक सिंह जी की पत्नी की आंखों की रोशनी लगभग जा चुकी है, वो बेचारी बहू-बेटों या बच्चों को रह रहकर पुकारती हैं। घर के बच्चे सुबह-सुबह ही ढोर-डंगर को चराने ले गये हैं। बहू रमतिया हम सब के लिये दाल-भात पका रही है क्योंकि आज हमें जंगल में कोयला गिराने जाना है।

शायद अब यह बता देना वाजिब होगा कि हम कहां, क्यों और किसलिये आये हैं? इस पूरे किस्से का सूत्रपात लगभग पन्द्रह बरस पहले भिलाई में हुआ था। हमारे संग्रहालय ने इस इस्पात नगरी में एक लौह कार्यशाला आयोजित की थी जिसमें देश के तीन प्रमुख आदिवासी समुदाय, जो पारंपरिक रूप से लौह अयस्क से लोहा गलाने का काम करते आये हैं, अपनी प्राचीन देशज पद्धतियों से लोहा तैयार करने वाले थे। मैं उनकी पद्धतियों के प्रलेखन का काम कर रही थी और वहीं जैक कीन से मुलाकात हुई। वे लन्दन के निकट किसी गांव में बच्चों के लिये एक संस्था चलाते थे जहां बच्चों को मिट्टी-बांस-बल्लियों से घर बनाने, डबल रोटी बनाने, लोह अयस्क से लोहा गलाने आदि की दुनिया की प्राचीन पद्धतियों से परिचित कराया जाता था। उन्हें हिन्दी नहीं आती थी लिहाज़ा मैंने उनके और लोहा गलाने

वालों के बीच भिलाई में एक भाषाई सेतु का काम किया था। कार्यशाला खत्म होने के बाद सब अपनी-अपनी राह गये। इस बीच चौदह बरस बीत गये। एक माह पूर्व अचानक जैक कीन संग्रहालय में प्रकट हुए। वे किसी तोक सिंह अगरिया का पता पूछ रहे थे जो हमारी भिलाई वाली कार्यशाला में सम्मिलित हुए थे। पता तो मेरी नोटबुक में मिल गया पर चेहरा आदि कुछ याद नहीं आया। इस बीच कई अन्य लौह शिल्पियों के साथ परिचय व मिलना-जुलना होता रहता था लेकिन तोक सिंह उनमें से एक नहीं थे। जैक कीन अब तक उस संस्थान से रिटायर हो चुके थे और इस बार वे लोहे की कहानी को पुस्तकाकार लिखने की गरज से दुनिया के भ्रमण पर निकले थे और चीन, कोरिया, भूटान होते हुए भारत पहुँचे थे। तोक सिंह व उनके साथियों द्वारा भिलाई में गलाये गये लोहे का सेम्पल उनके पास था और परीक्षण के बाद उन्हें पता चला था कि वह बहुत अच्छी किस्म का लोहा था लिहाज़ा वे उनके साथ एक बार फिर लोहा गिराने की प्रक्रिया दोहराना चाहते थे। वे ऐसे किसी दुभाषिया की तलाश में थे जिसे अंग्रेजी-हिंदी भाषाओं के ज्ञान के अलावा पारंपरिक ज्ञान पद्धतियों को जानने-समझने में रुचि हो और खासकर उन लोगों के प्रति मन में आदर भाव हो। लेकिन ऐसा व्यक्ति मिलना आसान नहीं था, और कुल मिलाकर वे अकेले ही डिण्डोरी जिले में गौरा-कन्हारी नामक गांव ढूंढ़ते-ढूंढ़ते पहुंच गये और दस दिन वहां ठहरे। बिना भाषा के जो कुछ हो सकता था सब हुआ और वह वाकई बहुत था—लोहा गिराने की कोठी तैयार करने से लगाकर लोहा गिराने तक की प्रक्रियाएं हुईं। दोनों के द्वारा जो कुछ भी देख कर या मूकाभिनय द्वारा देखा-समझा जा सकता था समझा गया। प्रश्न सब के सब अतिप्रश्न थे। उन्हें उच्चारित यदि किया भी गया तो वे गौरा कन्हारी के पहाड़ों-जंगलों में अनुत्तरित तैरते रहे, किसी ने पलट कर उनका जवाब देने की कोशिश नहीं की।

लौट कर जैक कीन ने बताया कि वे दस दिन अविस्मरणीय थे पर यदि सम्भव हुआ तो वे एक महीने बाद वहां किसी दुभाषिये के साथ वापस जाना चाहेंगे। गौरा-कन्हारी नाम और उसका वर्णन मेरे ज़हन में अटका रहा—नदी किनारे का, जंगल के निकट का 15-20 घरों का अगरिया गांव, जहां न बिजली है, न हैंडपंप और न कोई सरकारी इमारत। एक महीने बाद जब जैक कीन का फोन आया तब तक ठण्ड उतार पर थी, लगा कि तुका को लेकर जाया जा सकता है और इस तरह जैक कीन के साथ मैं, ईश्वर और तुका गौरा-कन्हारी के लिये निकल पड़े।

भोपाल से जबलपुर की ट्रेन की यात्रा का तो पता नहीं चला लेकिन जबलपुर से डिण्डोरी जाने वाली सड़क निर्माणाधीन थी। तिस पर दो-तीन दिनों की बेमौसम तेज़ बरसात ने तो उसे चौपट ही कर डाला था। जबलपुर से डिण्डोरी पहुँचने में छः

घण्टे लगे और यह तय किया गया कि रात वहीं रुकना ठीक रहेगा। डिण्डोरी नर्मदा के तट पर है। शाम हम नर्मदा पर बने पुल पर टहलते रहे। बहुत दूर किसी ने घाट पर दिया जलाया। नदी के समूचे विस्तार में इकलौता एक दिया, हम से इतनी दूर फिर भी एक बच्चे की सी अनझिप आंख से हमें टुकुर-टुकुर ताकता हुआ...। फिर दूसरा, तीसरा, पांचवा दिया जला...।

हम डिण्डोरी बाज़ार की तरफ़ लौट चले। जगह-जगह चूल्हों पर चाय बन रही थी, हमने तीन चाय तो पी ही होंगी। चूल्हे की चाय का स्वाद चायपत्ती में नहीं उसमें बस गई लकड़ी के धुंए की गन्ध में होता है और एक हद तक इन चाय की दुकानों में पसरे इत्मीनान में भी, जहां से उठने का मन ही नहीं करता। साप्ताहिक बाज़ार का दिन था—कांवर मेंं ताज़ी सब्ज़ियों के डाले, मिट्टी, एल्यूमिनियम के बर्तन भर कर लोग आ रहे थे। कोदो, कुटकी, धान, हल्दी, मिर्ची, नमक की डलियों के ढेर, गुड़, लाई के लड्डु, सिंगार-पिटार, कपड़े, छाते, नए जूते-चप्पल...। क्या नहीं था उस सड़क के दोनों ओर लगे छोटे से बाज़ार में। चार बैगा लड़कियां सिर पर लकड़ी के गट्ठर उठाये उस दुकान में आईं जहां हम चाय पी रहे थे। उनमें से दो की पीठ पर छोटा बच्चा था। लड़कियों ने गट्ठर उतार कर खड़े कर दिये तो मेरा ध्यान गट्ठर को बांधने के तरीके पर गया। गट्ठर इस तरह से बँधा था कि रस्सी हर लकड़ी के चारों ओर भी बँधी थी, इस तरह से कि गट्ठर को बिना लकड़ी गिराये आसानी से खड़ा किया जा सकता था। दुकानदार ने चारों गट्ठर खरीद लिये और बीस-बीस रुपये उन्हें दिये। जाने कितनी दूर से वे लड़कियां चल कर आ रही थीं कितनी बार गट्ठर खड़ा कर वे कुछ पलों के लिए सुस्ताई होंगी। पीठ पर सोते हुए बच्चे को ठीक किया होगा और अब बीस रुपये में सप्ताह भर की गृहस्थी खरीद वे वापिस घर जायेंगी।

डिण्डोरी से गौरा-कन्हारी करीब तीन घण्टे की यात्रा थी। जैक कीन ने बताया था कि पिछली बार जब वे वहां गये थे तो अपना तम्बू ले जाना भूल गये थे और इसलिये कन्हारी स्थित किसी लड़कों के आश्रम में रुके थे जो गौरा से तीन कि.मी. दूर था। उनका कहना था कि इस बार हम उनके तम्बू में रह सकते हैं और वे उसी आश्रम में ठहर जायेंगे। बारिश के बाद ज़मीन बहुत गीली थी और तुका के साथ होने के कारण तम्बू में रहने को लकर मन में कुछ चिन्ता थी। लेकिन देश के कई भागों में गांव-गांव जाने के बाद मुझे कहीं यह भी मालूम था कि गांवों का भारत अभी भी रुडयार्ड किपलिंग के 'किम' नामक उपन्यास से ज़्यादा भिन्न नहीं है, जिसमें नायक कहता है, "इस देश में तुम्हें यदि किस्से-कहानी कहने आते हैं तो खाने-रहने की चिन्ता करने की कोई ज़रूरत नहीं है"। इसलिये मन में कहीं यह आस भी थी कि रहने का इंतज़ाम हो ही जायेगा। अचानक जीप 360 का मोड़ मुड़ी और ढलान पर

उतरने लगी, देखा तो सामने नदी थी। नदी का पाट उस जगह उथला ही होगा क्यों कि लोगों की एक छोटी सी टोली सायकिल पर सामान बांधे वहां से पैदल नदी पार कर रही थी, जीप भी उनके पीछे-पीछे पार हो गई। जीप को वहीं खड़ा कर दिया गया और हम सब पैदल किनारा चढ़ने लगे। ऊपर एक मंदिर था और उससे लगी एक धर्मशालानुमा सीमेन्ट की इमारत। गांव के घर कुछ दूर खेतों के बीच थे। सबसे पहले जो छोटा सा घर दिखा वही तोक सिंह अगरिया का घर था, देखा तो दरवाज़े पर ताला लटक रहा था। तभी दूर खेत की मेड़ पर से बच्चे और कई अन्य लोग आते दिखे--वे आये और बड़ी गर्मजोशी से जैक व हम सबसे मिले। परिचय कराया-तोक सिंह और उनकी पत्नी। हम ने परस्पर एक दूसरे को पहचाना, तोक सिंह बोले ''भिलाई!'' मैंने कहा, ''भिलाई!'' इस बीच तोक सिंह के बेटे, बहू, भाई उनके बच्चों आदि से परिचय हो गया। हमने आने का उद्देश्य बताया तो सब बोले, 'बहुत अच्छा हुआ माताजी आप आ गयीं, वर्ना पिछली बार तो हम इनके लिये भूत थे और ये हमारे लिये भूत!' मंदिर से लगी धर्मशालानुमा इमारत में हमारे रुकने का इंतज़ाम होने लगा, कोई झाडू लगाने लगा तो कोई खटिया लेने दौड़ा। यह इमारत गांव के घरों से दूर थी और इसकी खिड़कियों और रोशनदान के शीशे नदारद थे। दिन में ही अच्छी खासी ठंड थी, रात की ठण्डी हवा की कल्पना कर मैंने तोक सिंहजी और उनकी पत्नी से पूछा कि क्या यह सम्भव है कि हम सब उनके घर में ही रहें? वे बोले ''यह तो सबसे अच्छा रहेगा। हम दोनों यही चिन्ता कर रहे थे कि यहां खाना भी लाते-लाते ही ठण्डा हो जायेगा और फिर यहां ठण्ड भी बहुत होगी।'' तोक सिंह और उनकी पत्नी भी इन दिनों अपने छोटे बेटे के घर में ही रह रहे थे, उनकी पत्नी की आंखों की रोशनी जब से गयी तब से घर के कामकाज में दिक्कत होती है। मुझे यह सुन कर बड़ी हैरानी हुई क्योंकि उन्हें देखकर यह कतई आभास नहीं होता है कि वे इतना कम देखती हैं। हम सब अपना बोरिया बिस्तर लेकर उनके छोटे बेटे नवल के घर आ गये। कमरे के एक कोने में एक बछिया बंधी थी और दीवार में तम्बूरा, ढोलक, मंजीरे की दो जोड़ लटकी थी। घर में आते ही हम सब के चेहरे पर खुशी और सुकून देखे जा सकते थे। लेकिन तुका के तो जैसे पौ बारह हो गये थे। घर के आंगन में कभी मुर्गा चला आता तो कभी पिल्ले। कमरे में आओ तो बछिया उसने और हम सबने जम कर गरम गरम दाल-भात खाया। बातें चल पड़ीं। पता चला कि गौरा कन्हारी से 20 कि.मी. दूर किवाड़ नामक गांव में हाल ही हस्तशिल्प विकास निगम द्वारा उस इलाके के लौह शिल्पियों की एक कार्यशाला आयोजित की गई थी जिसमें तोक सिंह भी हिस्सा लेकर कल ही गांव लौटे थे। पता यह भी चला कि शिविर आरम्भ करवा कर हस्तशिल्प निगम वाले

अधिकारी बिना हिसाब-किताब किये दस दिन से नदारद हैं, लिहाज़ा सारे कलाकार भी अपने अपने घर चले गये थे। किवाड़ गाँव जाकर तैयार की गई वस्तुओं को देखा तो समझ में आया कि शिविर का उद्देश्य यह जानना नहीं था कि उस इलाके के लोगों को क्या आता है अथवा वे कौन से रूपाकार बनाते हैं बल्कि उसका उद्देश्य उन्हें डिज़ाइन देकर उनसे काम करवाकर देखना था कि वे उनके काम के हैं या नहीं। मार्केटिंग इत्यादि के दबावों के चलते आज कई संस्थाएं ऐसा कर रही हैं। अच्छे-बुरे, नैतिक-अनैतिक की बहस से परे इसमें एक तरफ होमोजिनाईज़ेशन का खतरा है जिसमें बस्तर और बांकुरा के काम में फ़र्क नहीं रह जायेगा और जिससे अंततः इनका मार्केट सिकुड़ेगा क्यों कि एक ही जैसी चीज़ें लोग क्यों और कब तक लेंगे? दूसरा, अपने डिज़ाइनों को जब हम कलाकारों को देते हैं तो उनके द्वारा अब तक बनाये जा रहे रूपाकारों और उनमें निहित संभावनाओं से भी खुद को काट ही लेते हैं।

शाम होते न होते चारों ओर से बादल घिर आये थे। चूंकि गौरा चारों ओर से पहाड़ों से घिरा है इसलिये ऐसा लग रहा था मानो पहाड़ ही बादल उगल रहे हों। बाहर बहुत ठंड थी, हम सब कमरे में जा दुबके। भीतर एक कोने में आग जल रही थी और कमरे की स्निग्ध गर्माहट का बाहर के तूफानी मौसम से कोई लेना-देना नहीं था। तुका ने तम्बूरे और ढोलक का राग छेड़ा। तोक सिंह जी की पत्नी तम्बूरे पर गाने लगीं, तोक सिंह जी ढोलक बजाने लगे और बाहर के लोगों से बिदकने-शर्माने वाले तुका ने जो नाचना शुरू किया तो दो घण्टे तक रुकने का नाम ही नहीं लिया। घर के सारे बच्चे उसे देख हँसते-हँसते लोट-पोट थे। उजाले में और अपनी शहरी नाप तोल से देखें तो वह कमरा कतई बड़ा नहीं था लेकिन ढिबरी और जलते अलाव की मद्धिम रोशनी में कमरे की दीवारें गायब हो गई थीं उसमें तोक सिंह, उनके दो भाई, पत्नी, बहू, दो बेटे, हम तीनों, सात बच्चे और एक बछिया सब आराम से पैर फैलाकर बैठे थे और हमारे बीच पर्याप्त जगह थी जिसमें घूम-घूम कर तुका नाच रहा था, नाचते-नाचते गिर रहा था, गिरते-गिरते नाच रहा था। मुझे उस लेख का स्मरण हो आया जिसमें अज्ञेयजी ने लिखा था कि जब हम किसी बदलाव के आने का इंतज़ार कर रहे होते हैं तब अक्सर यह अंदाज़ा नहीं लगा पाते कि उसके साथ और क्या-क्या आयेगा। मसलन बिजली आई तो घर के कमरे अचानक छोटे दिखने लगे, रात में बाहर पेड़ों या तारों को देखना छूट गया।

यह कमरे का मद्धिम उजाला ही था जिसने तुका की धड़क खोल दी थी और वह इतना उन्मुक्त होकर नाच पा रहा था। सबके चेहरे नज़र आ रहे थे पर उजाला इतना नहीं था कि आपको सिकुड़कर सिमटकर बैठना पड़े। मन हो तो आप सबके

साथ हो सकते थे, मन हो तो अकेले, और चाहें तो बिना शर्मिन्दा हुए एक झपकी भी ले सकते थे! बाहर पानी बरसने लगा था और घर में भी दो एक जगह पानी टपकने लगा था लेकिन बातों का सिलसिला देर रात तक चलता रहा। गौरा में उनका परिवार कब आकर बसा, उनके आजा-परदादा कहां से आये, लुहारों की कथा इत्यादि-इत्यादि। रह-रहकर कमरे में बैठा कोई न कोई कह उठता अच्छा हुआ कि उस मंदिर की इमारत में नहीं रहे-यहां सब साथ हैं तो कितना अच्छा लग रहा है, बकौल तुका के "सब मुलाकात कर रहे हैं कितना मजा आ रहा है ना?' रात भर बारिश होती रही, अलाव के बावजूद बहुत ठंड थी और जगह जगह से छत टपक भी रही थी। अगला दिन बरसाती होने के बावजूद हम छिलपिटा होते हुए बेलापाट गये। शाम बेलापाट में जो बादल छँटे तो फिर दुबारा नहीं आये और उस रात आसमान में आकाश गंगा ऐसे उफनती रही कि मानो धरती पर छलांग ही लगा देगी।

सुबह उठे तो साल की दातून और गरम पानी तैयार रखे थे। साल की दातून नीम की तुलना में कहीं मुलायम होती है और तिस पर कड़वी भी नहीं होती। रमतिया ने खाना रोज़ से जल्दी बना दिया था क्योंकि आज सब जंगल में कोयला गिराने जाने वाले थे।

चार-छः खेत पार करते ही जंगल शुरू हो गया। इसं पूरे इलाके में जंगल कहते ही पहाड़ की भी कल्पना करनी होगी क्योंकि जहां मैदान है वहां खेत हैं, जहां दादर हैं वहां जंगल हैं। नवल, लक्ष्मण, तोक सिंह इतना तेज चल रहे थे कि मुझे लगभग भागना पड़ रहा था। यह मुख्यतः साल का जंगल थाः कच्च् हरा। उसके पारदर्शी हरे, चमकते पत्तों से छन छन कर आती सूरज की किरणें भी मुलायम हरे रंग की थीं। नीचे पीले-भूरे पत्तों का ढेर था और उसके नीचे गीली काली मिट्टी। रंगों को अलग-अलग करके देख पाना यहां असम्भव था। मिट्टी को काला मैंने लिख तो दिया पर यदि उसे रंगों में बनाना हो तो काला रंग हर्गिज़ नहीं लगेगा, जाने कौन से रंग लगाने होंगे। मुझे वेन गॉग द्वारा अपने भाई थियो को लिखे उस पत्र का ख्याल हो आया जिसमें उसने मिट्टी तथा जंगल में पड़ रही खास रोशनी को चित्र में बनाने की कठिनाई के बारे में बहुत विस्तार से लिखा है। जब किसी चीज़ को ठहरकर देखने-समझने की कोशिश करो तो पता चलता है कि आंख खुली होने के बावजूद हम अक्सर तो चीज़ों को देखते ही नहीं हैं केवल उसके स्वरूप की जो मान्य छवि हमारे दिमाग में पहले से मौजूद है, उसी को बार-बार देखते हैं। बहुत से लोग जो जीवन में बोरियत की शिकायत करते हैं वे भी एक हद तक कुछ नया न देख पाने की विवशता के चलते ही बोर होते होंगे। चीज़ों को हर बार नई तरह से देखने के लिये एक बच्चे की नज़र चाहिये होती होगी। हम बड़ी तेज़ी से पहाड़ पर चढ़ रहे थे,

अचानक बायें मुड़कर हम कुछ नीचे उतरे जहां एक छोटी-सी खुली जगह थी। वहीं पास में साल का एक लम्बा ठूंठ भी खड़ा था। नवल कुल्हाड़ी से उसे गिराने लगा। लक्ष्मण सिंह और तोक सिंह जी जंगल में गायब हो गये और कुछ ही देर में साल के मोटे मोटे लट्ठे लेकर लौटे। जंगल में पेड़ की शाखायें कई बार अपने आप ही टूट कर गिरती हैं, वे लोग उन्हें ही खोज रहे थे। बड़ी ज़ोर की आवाज़ के साथ साल का वह सूखा ठूंठ गिरा जिस पर नवल कुल्हाड़ी भांज रहा था। बड़े-बड़े लट्ठे काट कर उन्हें फिर आड़ी और खड़ी कतार में एक के ऊपर एक जमा दिये गये जैसे चिता सजाई जाती है। और तब नीचे से आग लगा दी गई। इस तरह लकड़ियों को जलते हुए देखना अजीब बेचैन करने वाला अनुभव था। हम कुछ दूर हट कर ढलान पर बैठे थे। सुलगती लकड़ियों से रह-रहकर चटकने का स्वर उठता था। पर भभक वे ऐसे रही थीं मानो इतने वर्षों के संचय के पीछे साध यही हो। आकाश के नीले जल में छलांग लगाती लपटें...अधीर।

कोयला बनने में एक-डेढ़ घण्टा लगना था, तोक सिंहजी बोले "माताजी, जब पानी पर धरती का हिलना किसी तरह से नहीं थमा तब बड़ादेव ने मीटिंग बुलाई और सारे देवता मिलकर वैसे ही चिन्ता करने लगे जैसे आज यहां पर बैठ कर आप-हम कर रहे हैं! तब फिर उन्होंने बारह भाई अगरिया, तेरह भाई तामासुर, चौदह भाई कांसासुर को बुलाया कि भई कीलें बनाओ और ऐसा उपाय करो कि धरती का पानी पर डगडिग-डगडिग होना थम जाये...कथा चलती रही, मन की डगडिग-डगडिग भी थम गई और उधर कोयला तैयार हो चुका था और अब उसे छितरा कर ठण्डा करने का उपाय करना था। एक लम्बी गीली लकड़ी से उसे छितरा दिया गया। अब हमारे आगे लकड़ी की जगह कोयला था। साल की लकड़ी या कोयला जलने पर राख बहुत कम देती है इसलिये भी इसका कोयला लोहा गलाने के लिये बहुत उपयुक्त होता है। पेड़ भी क्या अद्‌भुत चीज़ है, जीता है तब तक तो जीवन लुटाता ही है और मर कर भी इतनी आंच कि पत्थर पिघला दे! कितनी 'पूस की रातों' में किसी हल्कू और किसी जबरा की जान बचा ले!

कोयला बोरों में भर हम घर को लौट चले। घर में ज़बरदस्त तैयारियां चल रही थीं। औरतों की टोली मिट्टी की कोठी (फर्नेस) की मरम्मत में जुटी थीं। रमतिया मिट्टी की बनी बेहद सुंदर चक्की में कोदो दल रही थी क्योंकि कोदो की भूसी को मिट्टी में मिलाकर ही कोठी और नरी यानी मिट्टी की नलीनुमा दो संरचनाएं बनाई जाती हैं जो कोठी के तले में जोड़ी जाती हैं। इसमें फिर बांस की नलियां जुड़तीं जिनका दूसरा सिरा भाँते या चमड़े की एक जोड़ी धौंकनियों से जुड़ा होता है। कोदो और कुटकी नामक दो छोटे अनाजों को धान और गेहूं के बड़े भाई-बहन जैसा माना

जाता है और यह भी कि अमीरों ने तो उन्हें बहुत पहले घर से निकाल दिया और अब वे गरीबों के घर में ही आसरा पाते हैं। कोदो-कुटकी ऐसे अनाज हैं कि वर्षों घर में पड़े रहें तब भी सड़ते नहीं हैं, इसीलिये अकाल के समय के लिये इसे विशेष रूप से रखा जाता है। लोग तो यहां तक बताते हैं कि पुराने समय में स्त्रियां कोदो को मिट्टी में मिलाकर घर की दीवार बनाती थीं ताकि घोर अकाल की अवस्था में, दीवार तोड़कर अन्न प्राप्त किया जा सके। बहरहाल लोहे के काम में कोदो की महिमा यह कि इसकी भूसी यदि मिट्टी में मिली हो तो भट्टी बहुत मज़बूत हो जाती है और ऊँचे तापमान पर जब लोहा पिघलने लगता है तब भी नहीं दरकती।

लोहा गिराने की तैयारी में जुटी तीसरी टोली समनापुर बाज़ार से पूजा पाठ की सामग्री लाने गई थी जिसमें दारू के अलावा सुअर और चूज़े भी शामिल थे। आपको ध्यान ही होगा कि लोहा पत्थर (लौह अयस्क) पिछले ही दिन छिलपिटा से लाया जा चुका था।

समनापुर से आने वाली टोली लौटी नहीं थी और इसलिये समय पाकर मैं बुढनेर नदी के किनारे बने शिव मंदिर की तरफ़ चली गई। शाम के झुटपुटे में आज वहां खासी चहल पहल दिखी। अभी-अभी ठसाठस भरी एक जीप और दो ट्रैक्टर-ट्रॉलियां आकर रुकीं और देखते ही देखते नदी किनारे कोई तीस-एक चूल्हे जल उठे। आनन-फानन में लोगों ने नहाया, कपड़े धोये, खाना बनाया और अपने कनस्तर-पोटली समेट कर ट्रालियों में अगले पड़ाव की तरफ़ चल दिये। दो दिन बाद शिवरात्रि थी और ये सब अमरकंटक जा रहे थे। पता चला कि नर्मदा के परकम्मावासियों का भी बुढनेर के किनारे गौरा में पड़ाव डालना लगभग तय रहता है और इसीलिये किसी ने मंदिर से लगी वह सीमेन्ट की पक्की इमारत भी बनाई है। एक घण्टा ही मैं वहां बैठी थी और उतने में ही जीवन का एक पूरा मेला-ठेला आया और चला गया। बच्चे-बूढ़े, ढोल-मंजिरा, लोटा-डुरिया, कम्बल-हण्डिया सब कुछ तो था वहां। 70-80 किलोमीटर दूर के गांवों से आये ये लोग जिनके पास न पैसा है न फुर्सत कि वे अपने बच्चों को छुट्टियों में सैर सपाटे के लिये कहीं ले जायें या बूढ़ों को कोई बड़ा तीरथ करवा पायें पर साल में एक दो अवसर ऐसे ज़रूर होते हैं जब वे निकल पड़ते हैं—सायकिलों पर, पैदल या ट्रैक्टर ट्रॉलियों में और खासी लम्बी यात्राएं करते हैं।

तमाम अभावों के बावजूद-पेप्सी और अंकल चिप्स के बिना भी बच्चों को यात्रा का रोमांच और बूढ़ों को तीरथ का जो संतोष शायद यहां मिलता होगा वह शहर के बच्चों-बूढ़ों को नसीब नहीं होता होगा।

शिवरात्रि पर गौरा में भी बड़ा मेला भरता है, आसपास के गांवों से खूब लोग

आते हैं ऐसा तोक सिंह जी ने बताया। दुर्भाग्य से हमें अगले दिन यानी शिवरात्रि से एक दिन पूर्व ही वहां से वापिस लौट जाना था।

समनापुर गई टोली लौट आई थी और अब काम शुरू करना था। दो बार लोहा गलाया जाना था और इसीलिये अनुमान था कि पूरा रतजगा होगा। उस कत्ल की रात का वर्णन तो क्या किया जाये, ऐसी ठण्ड थी कि दो स्वेटरों और भट्टी में जलती आग के बावजूद नाक-कान का पता नहीं चल रहा था और वे सब के सब एक छोटी सी धोती और ऊपर एक कुर्ता डाले थे। भला हो उस नियम कानून का कि जिसके चलते लोहासुर की पूजा अर्चना दारू-मांस आदि से की जाती है और प्रसाद के रूप में काम करने वाले सभी स्त्री-पुरुष उसे ग्रहण भी करते हैं। उन दोनों के प्रताप से ही वे लोग रात भर इतनी कड़ी मेहनत कर पाये होंगे। दुर्भाग्य से उस रात की गई दोनों भट्ठियों में लाख कोशिशों के बावजूद गेरा (स्लैग) अपने आप नहीं बहा और इसलिये लोहा बहुत अच्छी किस्म का नहीं प्राप्त हो सका। लेकिन इस अत्याधुनिक युग में जब भारी भरकम तकनीकी का इस्तेमाल कर बड़े-बड़े अंतर्राष्ट्रीय कल कारखानों में लोहा गलाया जा रहा है तब मिट्टी और कोदो की भूसी और पैरा को मिलाकर तैयार की गई करीब ढाई फुट की भट्टी में, गौरा नामक एक छोटे से गांव में जहां अभी बिजली भी नहीं पहुँची है वहां हजारों वर्ष पुरानी तकनीक से कोई आठ-दस लोग आज भी लोहा गला रहे हैं यह अपने में ही क्या गज़ब की बात नहीं है?

दूसरे दिन जब जाने से पहले जैक कीन उन्हें इस प्राचीन ज्ञान को बचाये रखने और उसे हमारे साथ साझा करने के लिए धन्यवाद दे रहे थे तब तोक सिंह जी रो पड़े और बोले, 'ज्ञान तो हमारे आजा-दादाओं ने हमें दिया लेकिन आज हमारे इस ज्ञान का मोल मिट्टी के बराबर भी नहीं है।' रोना आता है अपने इस अभागे देश पर जिसने आज़ादी पाकर तरक्की का कुछ ऐसा स्वप्न देखा कि जिसके चलते हमारे सबसे हुनरमंद, ज्ञानी और मेहनती लोग छिटक कर हाशिये पर फिंका गये और अनपढ़, गँवार कहला रहे हैं। जिन्हें आई.आई.टी. या ऐसे ही किसी वैज्ञानिक अनुसंधान केन्द्र में अध्यापक के पद पर होना चाहिये था उन्हें आज कोई नाम से भी नहीं जानता। साधारण मिट्टी और कोदो की भूसी को मिलाकर बनी कोठी या फर्नेस इतना ऊँचा तापमान कैसे ले पाती है? इस सिलिन्ड्रिकल भट्टी का ऊपर से करीब 20 के कोण पर झुके होने का क्या अर्थ है आदि प्रश्न क्या हमारे इंजीनियर्स के लिये महत्त्व के नहीं होने चाहिये? क्या इस बात की हल्की-सी भी संभावना नहीं है कि यदि हमने इन देशज तकनीकों पर काम कर उन्हें विकसित किया होता तो शायद आज कई गांवों में बेहतर गुणवत्ता और कम लागत में लोहा पिघलाने के छोटे-छोटे

उत्पादक कारखाने होते और जो कम से कम गांवों की ज़रूरत को तो पूरा कर ही सकते थे? गाँवों में आज भी ऐसे कई किसान परिवार मिलेंगे जिनके पास इन पारंपरिक भट्टियों में गले लोहे के बने बाप-दादा के जमाने के खेती के कोई न कोई उपकरण हैं। वे इसे बहुत सम्हाल कर रखते हैं क्योंकि बकौल उनके यह लोहा बहुत मज़बूत होता है और इस पर बार-बार सान भी नहीं चढ़वानी पड़ती। पर एक ओर घोर अनदेखी और दूसरी ओर जंगल से लकड़ी, खनिज आदि लेने के बाबत नियमों की लम्बी फेहरिस्त ने इस प्राचीन पद्धति को पूरी तरह से चौपट कर दिया है। अब किसी अगरिया घर के बाहर कोठी देखने को नहीं मिलती। वे बाज़ार से लोहा खरीद कर उसके औजार आदि बनाकर जीवन यापन करते हैं।

जब नई कोठी या फर्नेस बनती है और उसमें पहली बार लोहा गलाया जाता है तो उस लोहे को कुँवारी लोहा कहते हैं और इसकी बड़ी मान्यता है। इस लोहे की अंगूठी पहन लो तो समझो तमाम तरह की बाधाओं के खिलाफ कवच पहन लिया और खास कर बिजली गिरने के भय से तो पूरी तरह से मुक्त हुआ जा सकता है। सुबह हम सबको रात गलाये गये लोहे से बनी एक एक अंगूठी मिली...।

बुढ़नेर के किनारे तम्बू वाली दुकानें लगने लगी थीं। सभी, विशेषकर रमतिया और तोक सिंहजी की पत्नी हमसे अगले दिन यानी शिवरात्रि तक रुकने का आग्रह कर रहे थे। वहां से जाने का मन तो हममें से किसी का नहीं था। चारों ओर से पहाड़ियों से घिरा गौरा धरती का केंद्र मालूम होता था वहां से भला कोई क्यों कर जाना चाहेगा

दिया मन को दिलासा, पुनः आऊँगा भले ही
बरस दिन, अनगिन युगों के बाद
क्षितिज ने पलक से खोली, तमक कर दामिनी बोली
अरे यायावर रहेगा याद?

Traditional Salt Making Among the Meiteis of Manipur: A Study of Intangible Cultural Heritage

N. Shakmacha Singh and K.K. Basa***

ABSTRACT

Salt as an important ingredient of food is obtained from different sources of nature like sea water, salt springs, domes or rock bed, etc. It is indispensably required both by humans and animals. Salt not only flavours our meal but also serves as an item for preserving food and seasoning. This mineral substance has played a very vital role in the socio-religious and economic spheres of human cultures round the globe. The present paper is an outcome of the field investigation conducted at Ningel village in the Thoubal district of Manipur. Ningel is the only surviving village in Manipur, where the traditional method of salt making is still in practice. Participant observation and interview methods were adopted during the field investigation. Findings from the local publications and other secondary sources like books of history, institutional reports, monographs, etc. are also incorporated here to analyse both the textual and contextual data in the historical development of salt making in Manipur. The present study not stresses the traditional knowledge system of the community but an attempt has also been made to explore some of the intangible aspects and their relevance to the socio-economic and religious sphere of both the hillsmen and plainsmen in Manipur. The

* Museum Assistant, Indira Gandhi Rashtriya Manav Sangrahalaya, Bhopal, Madhya Pradesh

** Former Director, Indira Gandhi Rashtriya Manav Sangrahalaya, Bhopal, Madhya Pradesh

religious beliefs and practices, concerning the use of salt among them have been incorporated in this paper to know the importance of these practices in maintaining strong and peaceful social relations. To salvage this age-old tradition, steps were taken by the government organization Indira Gandhi Rashtriya Manav Sangrahalaya to develop the paraphernalia of a salt-making site, as an exhibit in its open air exhibition premises. A demonstrative workshop was organized by inviting some skilled members of the village in the museum campus. The paper examines the parameters of those problems faced out of change of context, when these traditional salt makers were displaced from their own working environment to a new environment (museum campus) for making salt.

Introduction

Manipur with a landmass of 22,327 sq. kms, covered with ninety per cent of hill area, is centred by a flat-oval shaped valley. It is situated in the eastern corner of the Indian sub-continent and bordered with the neighbouring country Myanmar in the east. The State is bounded on the north by Nagaland, Assam on the west and Mizoram on the south. The land is inhabited by three major ethnic groups, the Meitei, Nagas and the Kuki-chin. The valley of Manipur is predominantly inhabited by the Meiteis who speak the Meitei dialect which belongs to the Tibeto-Burman family of languages. Meities are the larger ethnic fold comprising seven major clan-groups that ruled under their respective chiefdoms and principalities. During the historical period, there were seven clans of the Meiteis but there were five principalities ruled by five clan chieftains who were also both political and social heads of the respective clans (Kabui 1991: 146). Meitei as a nationality came into existence by the amalgamation of these seven clans or *Salais* under which many other social ethnic groups were also merged. Successive growth of immigrants in this kingdom was reported from the reign of King *Kyamba* (1467-1508 A.D.) onwards among which some of them were war captives. They were given a permanent settlement and further absorbed into different clan groups and thus into the larger social fold of the Meiteis.

The land has witnessed a sizeable number of immigrants from different geographical areas. Some sections of the western immigrants are reported to be well acquainted with the work of making salt. Historical account on the immigration and settlement of the *Mayang Kalishas*[1] (a sect of western immigrants) links them to the early period of salt making in Manipur. The *Mayang Kalichas* entered the territory of Manipur from the west by crossing the *Jiri, Barak* and *Iril river* and made their first settlement on the bank of *Leimatak* river. According to Sharma (1991: 61)" the Meiteis called them *Pangal Maar*. Their villages were often raided by the *Khumal* king *Adon Thinkolhanba* during 930 A.D. to collect salt from them. Their forefathers belonged to the fishermen community, who used to supplement their economy by manufacturing salt at the sea shore and the tradition of salt making continued to exist when they entered the territory of Manipur." According to Chandrasingh (as quoted in Sharma 1991: 62), "these people first came into contact with the *Khuman* king *Adon Thinkolhanba* in the year 930 A.D. who raided their villages and brought some of them as war captives and they were given land to settle in the area presently known as *Meeyang yumpham*." The settlements of the *Mayang Kalishas* were not confined to a particular place but extended to certain areas of Manipur where they were entrusted to work for the manufacture of salt. They were further shifted to settle at *Yawakhong* (presently Waikhong), and engaged for manufacturing salt. This place of their settlement still exists under the name of *Waikhong Laimanai* (Sharma 1991: 62). *Waikhong* is considered one of the prime locations where salts were manufactured mainly for the royal family. The production of salt under the patronage of the king in the *Meiteileipak* (the land of Meiteis) began during the reign of King Paikhomba (1666-97). After the discovery of naturally existing salt sites in the eastern foothills and valley of Manipur like *Chikhong* and *Ningel*, the *Meeyang Kalishas* from the *Waikhong* were engaged for the production of salt in these areas too. During the reign of Maharaja Bhagyachandra, when the salt site *Chandrakhong* was discovered, they were further allowed to make their settlement at *Chandrakhong*, for the production of salt (Sharma 1991: 63).

According to the Pemberton Report, 1835 (quoted in Sanajaoba 1993: 29-30), "The valley, however, is particularly rich in the far more valuable mineral of salt, the principal springs of which are found on its eastern side, not far from the foot of the hills. The best are those of *Wueekhong*, *Ningyal*, *Sengmiee* and *Chundrukhong*, where salt is manufactured in quantities not only sufficient for the consumption of the inhabitants of the valley, but to be made an article of traffic with the surrounding tribes, who barter for it their tobacco, ginger, cloth and cotton. The salt obtained from the springs of *Wueekhong*, is far superior to that of the other localities named, and supply for the use of the royal family is always obtained from thence. The spots containing these springs are said to be discovered by a very subtle vapour, which is always found hovering over them at an early hour of the morning; as soon as the fact is clearly ascertained, a shaft is sunk down to the spring, and cylinders, formed of the hollowed trunks of a large tree, let perpendicularly into the opening, are preserved in an erect position, by ramming earth between them and the sides of the well; the diameter of the cylinders is seldom more than six feet, and the depth varies from forty to sixty feet. All the wells are considered the property of the Rajah, who levies a tax of 1/5th upon the quantity of water drawn; from the remainder the wages of the manufacturers are defrayed, each of whom receives per mensem two baskets of salt containing one hundred circular pieces each, amounting in weight to 12½ seers, the bazaar price of which varies from three to four rupees. The villagers engaged in this manufacture cultivate but to a very limited extent, and barter their salt for the products of the agriculturists and fishermen. The quantity of salt, obtained by artificial evaporation, is about 1/19th of the weight of water, and were it subjected to any subsequent purification, this proportion would probably be reduced to 1/20th, which is nearly double the quantity obtained at Newcastle, by solar evaporation, from sea water, where from 30 to 40 tons of water produced but one of salt, and is on the other hand, considerably less than the saturated solution of rock-salt and sea-water, from which salt is obtained in the proportion of 23 per cent."

Historically, the kings of Manipur assigned the Loi communities to manufacture salt. According to McCulloch (quoted in Hudson 1997: 30), "the Loee population is exceedingly useful. Amongst them are the silk manufacturers, the smelters of iron, the distillers of spirits, the makers of earthen vessels for containing water or for cooking in, the cutters of pots, beams and canoes, manufacturers of salt, fishers, cutters of grass for the Raja's ponies, the payers of tribute in *Sel*, the coin of the country, etc". The Loi, from the historical perspective, were a group of people who paid tribute to the king or who were ostracized and exiled to Loi villages for violation of cultural conventions and consequently degraded to be the Lois. The contextual specific connotation of the term *Loi* is found to be different from its historical connotation. In its present context and meaning it embraces only the Lois who have been enlisted as Scheduled Castes. Thus, the term, in its current sense, does not cover many of the Lois who were regarded as Lois in the historical past (Singh 2004). These contextual changes are clearly visible among the villagers of the present study area where traditional salt is manufactured.

Ningel Village

Ningel is a small village situated at a distance of about thirty-one kilometres to the east from Imphal city. From Imphal, it is well connected by a pucca road upto Yairipok which is its nearest town and it comes under the administrative control of Thoubal district of Manipur. The village society is homogeneous, solely inhabited by 60 households of the Meitei community. Ningel is one of the important villages, known to have existed since the beginning of salt production in Manipur.

Dr. Brown (quoted in Hudson 1997: 31) recorded that "Nearly the whole of the salt consumed by the Mannipories is obtained from salt wells situated in the valley. A small quantity is occasionally imported in times of scarcity from Burmah:

The principal salt wells are situated at the foot of the hills to the north-east, about fourteen miles from the capital; they are four in numbers and are named ***Ningail, Chundrakhong, Seekhong*** (*Chi*=salt, *Khong*=well), and ***Waikong***; they all lie close together and are surrounded by villages wherein reside those engaged in the salt manufacture. Wells have been opened in other parts of the valley but the supply has not been remunerative."

All the above villages are located near one another and the salt wells still exist. However, preparation of traditional salt is now only practised in the Ningel village. Ningel is reported to be the only surviving village where the production of local salt-cake is still in practice to meet the domestic, religious and ceremonial needs of the people of Manipur. According to Dr. Brown (quoted in Hudson 1997: 35), "Ningail is the oldest of all the wells, and has always given the greatest yield. The amount of salt manufactured varies according to the season, the most being made in the cold weather, when the water is at its strongest. About 150 maunds a month was the average last year (1867-68), of which more than half was furnished by Ningail alone." Dr. Brown also recorded that "the effect of the earthquake of January, 1869, has been to increase the yield of salt water in the well enormously; the water in the Ningail well after the earthquake rose six feet, and this rise has continued up to the present time undiminished. The effect of the earthquake has been observed before, but not to such an extent or remaining for such a long time."

The people of Ningel village have now shifted their occupation to agricultural work as their primary occupation. Only eight families are found manufacturing salt as their secondary occupation.

The village has three salt-wells; two of which are cemented and the remaining oldest one is a wooden structure. The villagers mainly used the oldest well as it carried a larger volume of salt water that remained filled all the time. There is a shrine of the guardian deity *Nongpok Ningthou* and *Panthoibi* in the northern extremity of the village which is very near the site of the salt well. Ningel river flows westward at the southern boundary of the village and it is the main water source of the village. The village has now received the connection of water and electricity from the government. Inter-village kuccha roads linking one village to another are muddy but motorable.

Meitei Salt

The general term for common salt in the Meitei dialect is *thum* and it is also called *chi.* Locally produced traditional salt in the form of a cake is called *Meitei thumpak.* Cakes of salt have been used as money in Ethiopia and elsewhere in Africa, and in Tibet. In the Roman army an allowance of salt was made to officers and men; in imperial times, this *salarium* (from which the English word "salary" is derived) was converted into an allowance of money for salt (*Encyclopedia Britannica* 1977: 193). In Manipur, indigenous salt in the olden days was considered as an item of reward, given by the Maharaja to the brave persons for their heroic deeds. According to an ancient text *Loiyam Shinyam* (the 12th Century Constitution) the rules of reward given by the Maharaja as a trophy for catching the tiger, mentions that," when ten persons catch the tiger, only three of them will be selected for the trophy: (1) To the first one will be rewarded one *Pari* of paddy field, *Thum namma* (equivalent to one hundred plates of common salt); (2) *Phimakhai phi* (cloth) and *Thum Nama* will be given to the next; (3) the third one will be given a share in the *Thum Nama* and clothes."

The word *thum* in itself is powerful to indicate the name of place, area, status of a person, economy, etc. when it is prefixed or suffixed to other words. It has been divinely placed to reckon the name of the presiding goddess of the salt well or site called *Thum Lairembi.* The Meitei term for 'coin' is referred to as *sel,* whereas the meaning of economy is incomplete without the suffix of *thum,* i.e. *Sel-thum.* Likewise, the word for valuables or wealth is also indicated with the suffix of *thum,* i.e. *Lan-thum. Thumrungba* represents the person appointed by the Maharaja to look after the salt wells. The combination of *thum* (salt) and *khong* (well) indicates the place of the salt well. Thus, the word *thum* has been a cultural element that projects the socio-religious and economic strength of the the people of Manipur.

Thum Khong (Salt Reservoir)

Salt waters in the Ningel foothill are reserved and stored in the well constructed by piercing a giant hollow wood of length about *Lam mapanga makhai shangba,* i.e. 54½ ft. in length. It is said that the wooden well (see illustration on p. 65) was installed during the reign of Maharaj Chingthangkhomba, popularly known as Rajshree Bhagyachandra in the 18th century A.D. The site is believed to have been guarded by the goddess *Thumkhong Lairembi* who is venerated and given reverence by the villagers and the common people while visiting the site.

Thum-Shung-Shang (Salt-Preparing Shed)

The shed where salt is manufactured is known as *Thum shung sang*. It is a structure with three walls, raised out of bamboo mats or splits duly supported with bamboo or wooden poles. The roof of the shed is two sided and thatched with local grasses. The shed looks simple but is very effective in receiving maximum amount of wind. (see illustration on p. 65)

Thum Leirang (Salt-Preparing Hearth/Kiln)

Salt is prepared in a typical form of longitudinal hearth called *thum leirang* (see illustration on p. 65). It is a raised structure made out of clay with two openings, one in front end and other in the rear end. The front opening or the mouth is called *Chamang*. It measures about 1½ ft in width and 1 ft in height. Fire wood is placed and set fire from this opening. The hearth comprises circular holes of two different sizes called *Kamit*. These holes serve as an oven upon which pan and trays are mounted. The larger holes in front of the hearth are mainly used for boiling the salt water, whereas the succeeding smaller holes are used for giving the shape to the salt. The length of hearth varies from one to another depending on the ability of the manufacturer that how much quantity of salt making he can afford. Normally, the breath and height of each hearth seem almost the same. The mouth of the hearth normally faces such a direction, where it can receive the maximum flow of wind for proper burning of fire. There are open spaces on two sides of the central hearth known as *Phambal* (space for the salt makers). *Kharung* (earthen vessels for storing fresh salt water), *La* (plaintain leaves) and other tools are kept in this open space.

The rear opening of the hearth is called *Chaning*. The ashes of the burnt fuels are collected from this end which are stuffed and stored in a basket called *Khari Polang*. It is kept on a raised platform at the extreme corner of the two walls. It is used for obtaining *Khari ichum* (liquid ashes) to prepare *Khari* (edible soda). Another wooden and bamboo platform built behind the hearth in close proximity of the rear wall is called *Lap yai*, which is mainly for stacking firewood to be used as a fuel for making salt.

Salt-Making Tools

1. *Ishaiphu*: It is a vessel used at the time of collecting fresh salt water from the well.
2. *Thum Kagok*: It is a form of iron pan, locally prepared from the sheet of coal drums. In the olden days earthen pans were reported to have been used as Thum Kagok.
3. *Tei (see p. 66)*: It is a flat and circular tray, made of iron used for shaping the salt in the form of a cake.
4. *Koret (see p. 66)*: A large sized spoon made of dry gourd used for pouring and stirring salt water.
5. *Meiphei*: A wooden device used for maintaining the temperature of heat that is surcharged by the burning of firewood inside the hearth. This spade like tool, hafted with a long wooden shaft is held by a lady, who regulates the temperature by inserting it inside the hearth and drawing the hot charcoals to desired holes of the hearth as demanded by the salt makers.
6. *Chilel (see p. 66)*: An important tool made of brass plate hafted with a wooden handle is used mainly to shape

the salt in the form of a cake. Chilel is reported to have been manufactured by a single family of metal workers in Yairipok town. The metal worker, namely Sanahongba in Yairipok was entrusted for making chilel. After the death of Sanahongba, his son continued the art and tradition of making chilel for the salt makers of Manipur.

7. *Chilenkhum*: It is an earthen vessel where plain waters are stored. It is used by the salt makers who dip and cool their chilels when it gets heated by continuous use for shaping the salt.
8. *Kambi*: It is an earthen plate used for collecting precipitate salt obtained after evaporation.
9. *Chegai*: It is potsherd or a piece of pot used for scraping the rim of salt cake to give a finishing touch.
10. *Shapa*: When precipitate salts are transformed into the form of salt cakes, it is marked with a wooden stamp on the surface of the salt. This wooden stamp is called shapa and the process of marking is called shapa namba. The shape of these wooden markers varies from one shed to another and it is marked to identify the place of manufacture.

Method of Preparation

Commercial salt is manufactured from rock salt, and from seawater and other natural and artificial brines. Most of the artificial brines are obtained by pumping water into underground salt beds. A considerable amount of brine itself is used directly in industrial countries (*Encyclopedia Britannica*, Vol. 16, 1977: 194)

Artificial evaporation method is used by boiling the salt water in an open oven. Womenfolk are generally found to be engaged in the whole process of making salt in the Ningel village. However, no social taboos exist whereby males are prohibited to participate in the making of salt. It is said that male folk engage mainly in the collection of firewood and *Lanou* (plaintain leaves). Making of salt in a shed requires at least six members such as:

1. Eeshing Kabi (those who fetch salt water from the well)
2. Mei thabi (those who control firing of the hearth)
3. Thum shabi (those who make salt)

Fresh salt water collected from the well is brought to the shed and stored in a large earthen pitcher. This process is called *Eeshing Kaba.* Fetching of salt water from the well is generally done by the female members (see illustration on p. 65) but it is taboo among those women and girls who are in the menstruation state. The site of salt-spring where the well is constructed is regarded highly sacred by the villagers. It is believed to be the abode of a goddess called *Thumkhong lairembi* or the goddess of salt.

The entire work of firing of the hearth, the maintenance of its temperature is solely under the care of *Mei thabi* who control the rise and fall of heat inside the hearth. Heat inside the oven is controlled by using a tool called *Meiphei.* The required quantities of fresh salt waters are uniformly poured over the pans that are placed on the larger holes in successive rows. It is allowed to boil till a preliminary concentration of the salt water is noticed. The concentrated waters are then transferred from one pan to another with the help of Koret (dry gourd spoon), where maximum heat is available. This process is called *Khang Yenthokpa*. The precipitate form of salt with larger concentration produces white bubbles arising inside the pan. It shows that the boiling of salt water at an appropriate temperature has been attained. These crystalline forms of concentrated salts are collected in an earthen plate called *kambi* and transferred to the salt makers who are sitting at Phambal for giving shape to the salt cake. Salt is given shape on the circular iron trays called *Tei* that are placed upon the smaller holes of the hearth. By placing plantain leaves on the surface of the tray salts are given shape at a low temperature. *Chilels* are used for shaping and transforming the salts in the form of a cake which are further stamped with a wooden mark for identification. To get a complete form of round structure it is finally given a finishing touch by rubbing the edges with the help of *Chegai* or the potsherds.

Types and Uses of Salt

The locally manufactured salt cakes found in Manipur are circular in form and almost look like the shape of a plate. It is produced in five different sizes, depending upon the nature of its use.

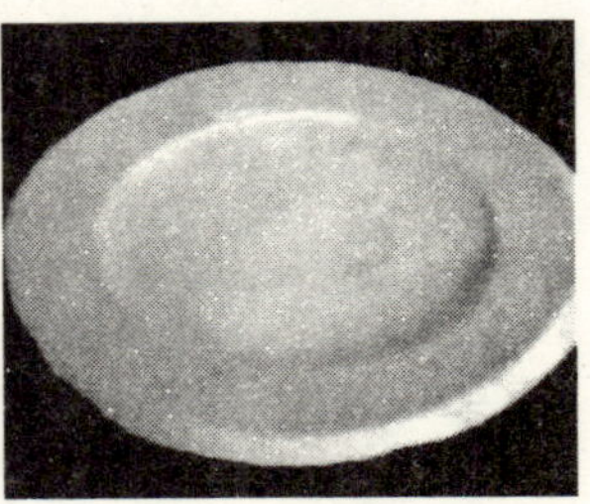

1. **Thumjao:** It is the biggest size of salt cake ever produced in Manipur. No bigger than this size of salt cake is available. It is a plate shaped structure with an undulated upper surface. An inner rim formed by circular pit at the centre is also larger in dimension. It has broad margin and the edge of the salt is smooth that gently tapers towards the bottom. The radius of the inner ring is also larger. It is used as an item of offering during ancestral worship and at the time of a marriage ceremony.

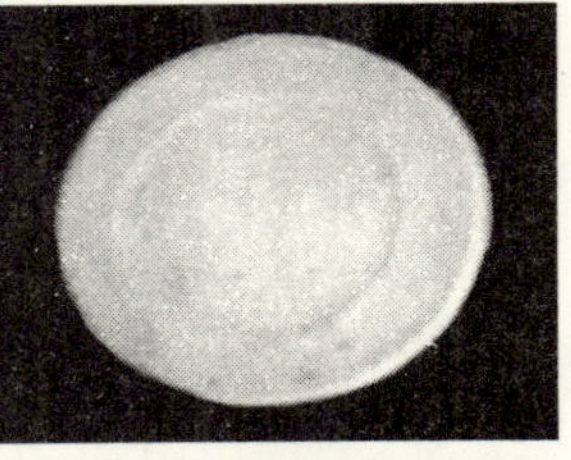

2. **Thum Talak:** It is slightly smaller than the *Thumjao*. A depression made at the central surface of the Talak is also small. It is mainly used for the purpose of consumption.

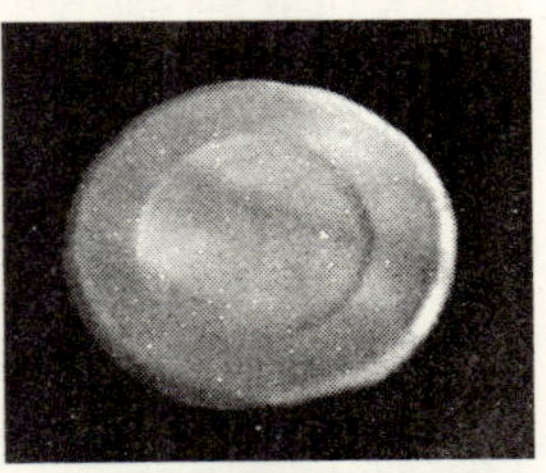

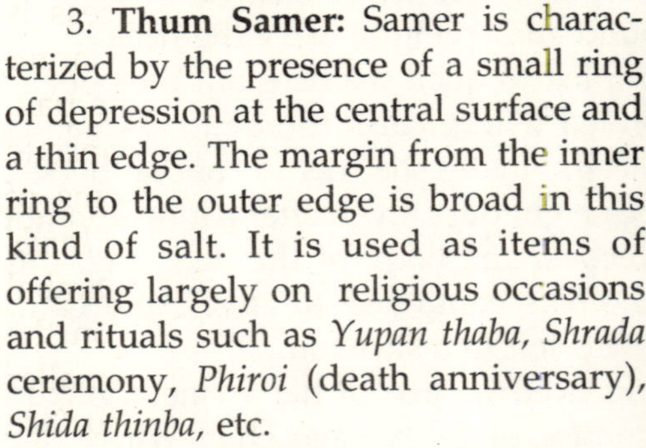

3. **Thum Samer:** Samer is characterized by the presence of a small ring of depression at the central surface and a thin edge. The margin from the inner ring to the outer edge is broad in this kind of salt. It is used as items of offering largely on religious occasions and rituals such as *Yupan thaba, Shrada* ceremony, *Phiroi* (death anniversary), *Shida thinba,* etc.

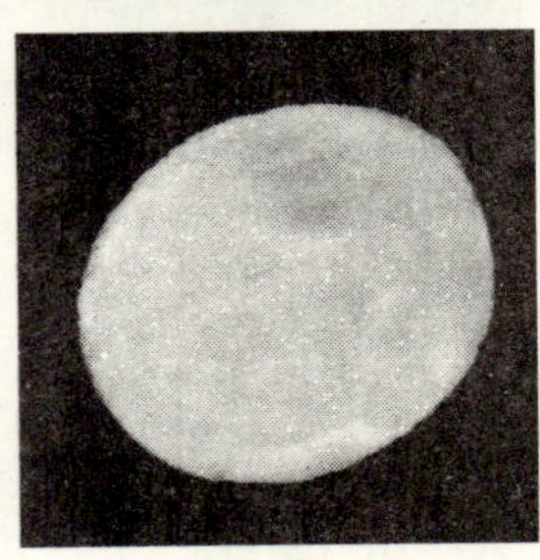

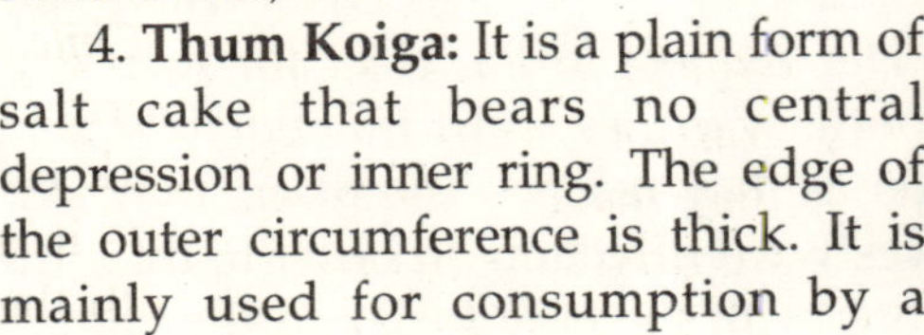

4. **Thum Koiga:** It is a plain form of salt cake that bears no central depression or inner ring. The edge of the outer circumference is thick. It is mainly used for consumption by a

common household. The fine qualities of Koiga are generally used in preparing food or curry during the pollution period for the lady after the delivery of her child.

5. **Thum Macha:** It is the smallest form of salt cakes produced by the Meitei salt makers. Thum macha is identified in its size of smallness which is about 7 inches in the surface diameter. The salt cakes though small do possess a depth of central depression forming an inner circle on the surface. It is used on auspicious occasions, feasts and festivals such as *Shajibu Cheiraoba* (Meitei New Year), *Lamtai thangja,* etc. and during the rituals involving ancestral worship.

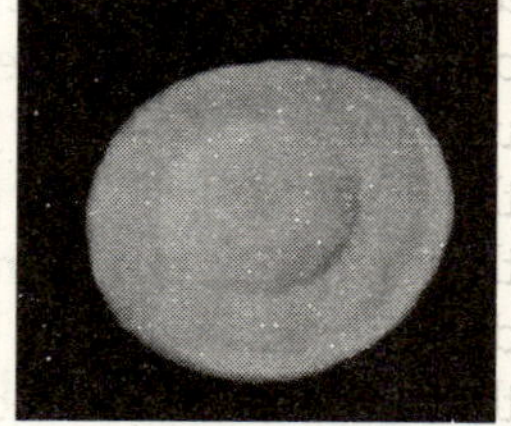

Myth of Salt

The village has a story that alludes to an ancient event of how the site of salt-spring was discovered. Shri. S. Jatishor Singh, a native of the village narrates that, "…long ago, there lived a widow in a Tangkhul village called *Lairam Khullen*[2]. She had a young pig which was nourished under her care. One day she found her beloved pig lying dead in the pig sty owing to the attack of a swarm of dreadful bees called *Khoiren*. These bees were humming all around and trying to carry the flesh of the pig in pieces. She attempted to quell the bees but they began to attack her. She defended with great fortitude to rescue her swine but did not succeed. Finally she had to conceal herself and seek the help of her neighbours. Even after a long attempt of the neighbours to recover the body of the dead pig, this ferocious swarm of Khoirens continued to attack and carry the flesh till the swine was left to a skeleton.

Pent up and wailing over the loss of her swine, the lady finally rushed to the house of the village chief where she narrated the incident. Her request to the chief for help was accepted and three young warriors were immediately sent along with her. As soon as they reached the place, they saw the bees flying in the westward direction. In order to trace the new hives, the boys along with the lady followed the path of the Khoirens. They carried some food with them to eat on the way. The whole day's toil to search for the *Khoirens* remained unsuccessful and surprisingly they had almost crossed the *Laimaton* hill ranges and lost their way to the western foothill. It was growing dark and the boys decided to make some arrangement for the night in that foothill. Disappointed the boys again resolved to continue their expedition with undaunted courage. The boys asked the lady to stay there till their return and to prepare a meal for them. Ensuring that they would be returning in a short while, they left in different directions in search of the *Khoirens*. To prepare the meal for them the lady fetched water from the small stream which was running nearby. To her surprise the meal took a long time to be completely cooked.

After some time one of the boys returned very exhausted and asked the lady to give him water to drink. The lady served him water in a fresh bamboo container. The taste of the water was very different and unusual. He shouted, "Why have you served me such defiled water which one cannot even relish? What have you added to this?" The lady was surprised at such a shameful and strange question. During this annoying situation, all the boys returned and assembled there with a dreary story of their unsuccessful expedition. They felt very disappointed to notice the rising hot tempers aroused between the two. There was no other option for the lady to prove her innocence. She tasted the water in front of all the boys and found that it was indeed very salty. With a quest to know the truth, all the boys began to taste the water. Finally, taking the matter seriously all of them rushed to the nearby stream. The taste of water murmuring into the small stream of the foothill was found salty and they felt sorry about their hot temper. To identify the spot they decided to plant a sapling of *Tarung* and finally resolved to inform the then Maharaja Bhagyachandra. The Maharaja and his councils immediately visited the site. The Maharaja was very much pleased with the discovery of the salt site in his kingdom. He ordered the people to dig a big canal to trace the exact location of the stream. Experts were called upon to suggest a plausible plan for making a reservoir. It was suggested to install a reservoir by attaching a giant hollow wooden log to the bottom of the soil. The Maharaja deployed some people to locate such a tree. A *Ching Yengsin* tree was traced that could be appropriately used for making a wooden reservoir. This tree was found growing near the confluence point of the *Thoubal* river and a rivulet running from the *Sagol lou*. The tree was felled on an auspicious day. Three elephants were engaged on the occasion of the pulling ceremony. The elephants could not move the log for even a short distance. In order to know the reason a ceremony was observed under the divinations conducted by famous priests and priestesses. The divination revealed the presence of a spirit as the presiding deity. The divine message revealed by the priestess suggested that the log could easily be pulled out by a single elephant when Pena (a kind of folk string instrument) played behind the elephant and necessary rituals were observed. The pulling of the log was commemorated with a grand merry making ceremony. An infuriated elephant was brought for the ceremony and it was accompanied by a famous *Pena*[3] singer, priest and priestess. The Pena player (fiddle player) played his instrument behind the elephant and made incantations related to the propitiation of the divine tree (Uron shakpa). With this grand ceremony and ritual observance the huge wooden log was lifted and pulled up to the Nigel area where it was hollowed and installed at the present site.

It was Maharaja Bhagyachandra (1850-86), who announced with gratification to the Ningel villagers to reserve a place of honour for the widow in the annual *Lai Haraoba* festival of the village. The tradition of *Lei langba* (offering of flowers) by collecting flowers from the Lairam Naga village in the annual merry making ceremony continued to exist after the death of the lady, to mark the honour and pride of her presence in the village festival.

Religious Importance

The habitual use of salt is intimately connected with the advance from nomadic to agricultural life, a step in civilization that influenced the rituals and cults of almost all ancient nations. The gods were worshipped as the giver of the kindly fruits of the earth, and salt was usually included in offerings consisting wholly or partly of cereal elements. Such offerings were prevalent among the Greeks and Romans and among a number of Semitic people (*Encyclopedia Britannica* 1997: 192). *Meitei Thumpak* is also an important item of ritual among the Meiteis. The locally produced *Thumpak* (salt cakes) are not only meant for consumption but also an item of offering at various ceremonies and ancestral worship. Among the Ningel villagers, the salt produced by them is required to exchange with flowers from the neighbouring tribal communites during their annual *Lai haraoba* (merry making festival) of the village.

A shrine of the guardian deity *Nongpok Ningthou* and *Panthoibi* situated at the northern extremity of the village is collectively worshipped by the villagers every year marked with a grand merry making ceremony called *Lai Haraoba*. It generally falls in the month of April-May. *Lai Haraoba* is an age-old religious festival of the Meiteis celebrated in annual appeasement of the ancestral gods and goddesses in the entire valley of Manipur.

During *Ningel Lai Haraoba* it is obligatory for the villagers to perform a ceremony called *Lei langba* (offering of flowers from a tribal village). The activity of *Lei langba* is regulated by a practice whereby male members of the village in three, five or seven go in a ritual procession. They have to visit *Lairam Khullen* village for collecting flowers to be offered to the deity. The rules and customs in collecting the flowers with a ritual procession are strictly observed. It is believed that the flowers that are brought from the *Lairam Khullen* village possess the divine spirit of the Naga lady.

Those who are entrusted with the ritual procession have to carry salt cakes in an appropriate quantity, which is known as *Thumpot ama*[4]. This is carried for distribution among the Naga villages to mark the ongoing ritual procession. On the way, out of these *thumpot*, some amount of salt *Thum namma*[5] will be distributed to the *Erong* village. Distribution of salt to the villagers is an indication for the commencement of the *Lei langba* ritual. The ultimate destination of their journey will be the house of the *Khullakpa* (village chief), where the remaining cakes of salt have to be handed over. These salts will be distributed to every household and the chief will make a formal announcement for the collection of flowers to be offered. With this announcement, the unmarried boys and girls of the village prepare themselves and engage in collecting flowers. A special basket will be prepared by the chief where the flowers will be filled and decorated. Finally, with a prayer of good fortune and blessings, the chief will bid farewell by offering the basketful of flowers to the flower collectors. These flowers are offered during the merry making festival of the village deity at Ningel village. They have a strong belief that one should not cross the path when the ritual procession goes on and especially at the time of their return journey from the *Lairam Khullen* village after collecting flowers, because the basket of flowers carried by them is possessed by an ancestral soul of a tribal lady who is to participate in the merry making festival. This ancestral soul has been regarded as the one who first identified the *thum iphut* (salt spring). In order to avoid the evil effect of the soul, the villagers strictly follow the rule and never try to cross their path during the procession.

Salt cake is one of the important items of offering in various rituals and ceremonies. Salt is indispensably used in the birth ritual of a new born baby. Sanajaoba (1991) describes that "...on the sixth day, there is a ritual *Ipan Thaba* following the divine tradition of the birth of *Konchin Tukthaba*, son of *Salailel* by *Leimalel*. On this day, the ritual of sanctification with *Tairel Pungfai* leaves by the priest takes place. *Naheirol*, the sanctification hymn is given by the *maiba* (priest). The entire premises of the child's parents is thus sanctified. This is called *Yum Sengba* ritual of the Meiteis. The cultic requirements are (a) a pot of water full to the brim (Ishaifu), (b) two round discs of salt, (c) a basketful of paddy, (d) a garland of flowers having the colour of the particular *salai* (clan), (e) a garland of dry fish, (f) coins, (g) a piece of gold and (h) fruit and betel nut offerings. With these cultic arrangements, the primal deities of fire, water, air, earth and the heaven and also the sun are worshipped as the primal manifestations of the Supreme ultimate being. The offerings are usually made to him for the long life and prosperity of the child."

Medicinal Use

An old man of the village narrates that "Meitei thum bears medicinal value as it is obtained after burning completely on the fire and the question of the presence *Timu-laimu* (pathogens and evil agents) does not arise. It is helpful in curing gastric troubles, indigestion and loss of appetite etc. By packing the *Yengshin akuppi* (a kind of herb) in plantain leaves, it has to be buried inside the burning ashes for a few minutes. After some time, by squashing these *Yenshin*, juice has to be collected in a bowl. Then, with a pinch of salt about a finger tip, it has to be burnt in the fire till it is red-hot. When dropping this red-hot salt inside the bowl there will be smoke coming out of it leaving behind a very useful drink which can cure all the above troubles." The old man added that one should regularly use the best quality of *thumpak* for cleaning teeth which is a good practice for oral hygiene. It will strengthen the teeth and help to get rid of the problem of the foul smell coming from the mouth.

Government Initiatives

Government and private organizations are drawing their attention towards the exploration of the site for the last two or three years. Realizing the need towards the preservation of this age-old tradition, steps were taken by the Indira Gandhi Rashtriya Manav Sangrahalaya, Bhopal, an autonomous organization under the Department of Culture, Government of India. It was in the year 2004, when this organization with generous support from the Department of Art & Culture, Government of Manipur, initiated a plan to develop the entire paraphernalia of the salt making site at its open air exhibition premises. Raw materials like thatching grasses, wood and bamboo poles including a replicated life size large wooden reservoir were transported from Manipur to Bhopal. Skilled people from the Ningel village were invited to develop an exhibition. In the succeeding year, the museum undertook a field documentation programme, emphasizing the need for audio-visual recordings of the methods and techniques of salt-making in Manipur. Towards the end of February, 2006, this museum hosted a two-day workshop-cum-demonstration programme on the traditional salt-making technique of Manipur in its exhibition campus. Six expert salt-makers from Ningel village were invited to the museum for the demonstration workshop. Natural salt water of about 25 litres was also brought from the village. Although the demonstration workshop had a favourable response but there were certain problems that the salt makers encountered. The complete change in the context of executing the work of salt making from their own environment led them to make a greater effort in producing the salt in a desirable shape and quantity. The new buds of plantain leaves brought for the demonstration workshop were spoiled due to the climatic changes and there was no option of replacing them by any other kind of leaves collected locally, because the use of leaves as a base of salt cakes was necessary to them and believed to be associated with their concept of sanctity and purity. All unwanted activities that could affect their belief system were totally avoided.

Conclusion

Before the advent of branded and imported salt in Manipur region this valuable item of food ingredients was either obtained from distant places through exchange of goods from the traders or imported by the then rulers. Finding of salt deposits in these hilly terrains was indeed a treasure of any kingdom in this region to feel pride in its assets and bountiful resources. This may perhaps be one of the reasons that salt sites in Manipur were given royal patronage. Traditional salt in Manipur is considered to be the item of socio-economic and religious importance and every *Thumkhong* (site of salt deposition) is believed to have been guarded by the *Thum Lairembi* (goddess of salt). At all religious ceremonies, festivals and many other important occasions of Meitei social life, traditional salt is indispensably used as an important item of offering. Women who deliver a new baby and undergo the pollution period are fed with this salt. It is also used in the rituals associated with naming ceremony, marriage and death. In community festivals like *Cheiraoba* (New Year), *Lamtai Thaangja* (an annual event observed to drive out the evil spirits on the community level) and *Lai Haraoba* (annual merry making ceremony of the ancestral and guardian deities) traditional salts are used.

Traditional salt is important in every sphere of Meitei socio-religious and economic life. The meaning of the terms like 'economy' and 'valuables' sounds incomplete without the suffix and prefix of the word *Thum or Chi.*

Traditional salt is not only a commodity of human needs among the Meiteis of Manipur but also an important cultural element that bridges the age-old social and cultural relationship with the neigbouring tribal people. An annual *Lai Haraoba* of the Ningel festival is incomplete without giving their salts to the neigbouring Tangkhul tribes and without accepting the flowers offered by this tribal population. The myths and legends prevalent among the villagers together with their religious practices are relevant to understand social relations. In the present era of conflicting claims, arising out of ethnocentrism in the name of ethnic and social identity, it is important to explore the implicit concept of intangible culture in binding human relations. The above findings show that the traditional salt in Manipur is a symbol of prosperity, peaceful culture and social solidarity.

Acknowledgements

Heartfelt acknowledgement and thanks to the informants Shri S. Jatishor Singh, Shri L. Ibomcha Meitei and to the salt makers of the Ningel village who rendered immense support during the course of our field investigation.

Notes

1. *Meeyang Kalichas/ Pangal Maar* are a sect of western immigrants. According to Sharma (1991: 62), they came into first contact

with the Khuman King Adon Tingkholhanba in the year 930 A.D., who raided their villages and brought some of them as war captives and made their settlement in the Meeyang Yumpham (presently known as Mayang Imphal).

2. Lairam Khullen is a Tangkhul village situated at the eastern Laimaton hill ranges in the adjoining Ukhrul and Thoubal districts of Manipur. The village is homogeneously inhabited by the Tangkhul tribe.
3. Pena is one of the ancient and popular string instruments used by the Meiteis in Manipur. Pena is mainly used as an accompaniment in *Lai Haraoba* (merry making festival of the ancestral deities), Pena folk songs and many other folk festivals of Manipur. An expert, who sings and plays the instrument, is called *Pena Shakpa*.
4. Thumpot Ama is a unit consisting of 20 plates of salt.
5. Thum Namma is also a unit consisting of 10 plates of salt.

References

Encyclopedia Britannica 1977. Vol. 16, Chicago: Encyclopedia Britannica, Inc.

Hudson, T.C. 1908. *The Meitheis* (Reprint 1997) Delhi: Low Price Publications.

Kabui, Gangumei 1991. *History of Manipur, Pre-colonial Period,* Vol. I, New Delhi: National Publishing House.

Sharma, B. K. 1991. *Meitrabakki Khunthok Khundarol (Migration and Settlement of Manipur from Prehistoric Age to Historical Medieval Period),* Imphal, Manipur: Tama Publications.

Sanajaoba, N. (ed.) 1993. *Manipur Treaties and Documents (1110-1971).* Vol. I. New Delhi: Mittal Publications.

Sanajaoba, N. (ed.) 1991. *Manipur: Past and Present.* Vol. 2, New Delhi: Mittal Publications.

Singh, Nabakumar W. 2004. "Continuty and Change: A Village of Manipur". *The Eastern Anthropologist* 57: 202-203.

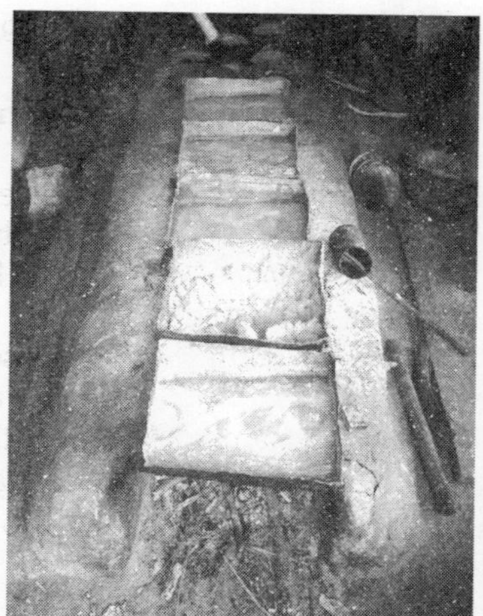

Thum Leirang: Longitudinal form of an earthen hearth used for manufacturing salt

Thum Khong: Wooden reservoir for storing salt water at Ningel village

Ladies in the salt-making process

Thum-Shung-Shang: A view of the salt site at Ningel village

Some of The Salt-Making Tools

Chilel- brass made ladle with wooden handle used for shaping the salt

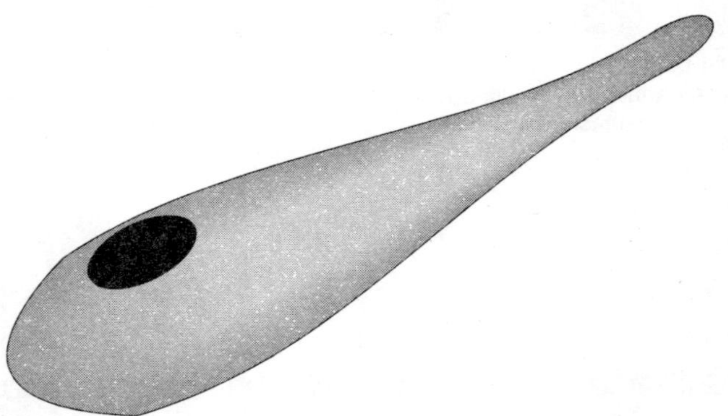

Koret- dry gourd spoon used for pouring salt water

Tei- iron tray used for making salt disc

हल्वा जनजाति के लोक विश्वास में धनकुल गीत

अशोक शर्मा

बस्तर अंचल में हल्वा, भतरा, राजा मुरिया, अबुझमाड़िया, दण्डामी माडिया, घोटुल-मुरिया, झोरिया-मुरिया, परजां, धुरवा, दोरला, जनजाति तथा सुण्डी, माहरा, मिरगन, चण्डार घासिया आदि अनेक पिछड़ी जातियों के लोग विभिन्न स्थानों में निवासरत हैं। इन जनजातियों एवं जातियों के मध्य विभिन्न प्रकार की लोक बोलियां, गीत, धुन, नृत्य प्रचलित हैं। ये सभी इनकी सांस्कृतिक, सामाजिक और आार्थिक आवश्यकताओं की पूर्ति करने में सहायक सिद्ध होते रहते हैं। लोक गीत व लोक संगीत देव गुड़ियों के अनुष्ठान में निहित आस्था की अभिव्यक्ति का एक सशक्त माध्यम सिद्ध होते आ रहे हैं और पूरे बस्तर अंचल में हल्बी भतरी एव कोयतूर लोक भाषायें ब्यवहार में प्रचलित हैं। हल्बी भाषा परिवेश में प्रमुख रूप से लेजा गीत, चूड़ामन गीत, चइतपरब गीत, छेरता गीत, देरता गीत, और खेल गीतों का प्रचलन है ही, साथ ही धनकुल गीत के अंतर्गत तीना जगार, लक्ष्मी जगार, आठे जगार, बाली जगार जैसे लोक महाकाव्य भी प्रचलित हैं। इन लोक गाथाओं को एक धुन (संगीत) के साथ प्रस्तुत किया जाता है जिसे धनकुल धुन कहते हैं। इसी धुन के आधार पर गीत गाये जाते हैं जिसे धनकुल गीत कहते हैं। ये गीत पूर्णतः वाचिक परम्परा के सहारे पीढ़ी दर-पीढ़ी मुखान्तरित होते आ रहे लोक महाकाव्य हैं। धनकुल लोक बाद्य का प्रचलन हल्बी भतरी परिवेश के अतिरिक्त ओडिया तथा छत्तीसगढ़ी परिवेश में भी देखने में आया है। किंतु गोड़ी धुखा, परजा दोरला परिवेश में नहीं। धनकुल नामक इस तत वाद्य का वादन प्रायः दो जगार गायिकाँ करती हैं। इन्होंने लोक संस्कृति के इस महत्वपूर्ण उपादान को निष्ठा एवं यत्नपूर्वक अब तक अक्षुण्ण बनाये रखा है। धनकुल गीत वस्तुतः देवाराधना और उत्सवधर्मों के गीत होते हैं। तीजा जगार महादेब और पारबती, आठे जगार किरिस्ना (भगवान श्रीकृष्ण), लक्ष्मी जगार (धान्य देवी महालक्ष्मी) और बाली जगार (वर्षा के देवता बाली) और भिमादेव की आराधना के निमित्त हैं।

तीजा जगार न्यूनतम 7 एवं अधिकतम 30 दिनों के लिये, आठे जगार का आयोजन 2 दिनों के लिए तथा लक्ष्मी जगार न्यूतम 5 और अधिकतम 11 दिन एवं बाली जगार 93 दिनों के लिये होता है। इन सभी दिनों में गीत गाये जाते हैं। धनकुल गीतों के गायन के समय प्रमुख गायिका एवं कई बार उसकी सहायिकाओं पर भी पुरखों की आत्मा अथवा देवी-देवताओं का प्रभाव होने लगता है, जिनका वे आह्वान कर रही होती हैं। जगार-गायन की अवधि में कुछ महिलायें ऐसे प्रभाव में दिखाई पड़ती है किंतु आयोजन के अंतिम दिन तो यह प्रभाव विभिन्न आयु वर्ग की बहुत सी महिलाओं और बालिकाओं पर दिखलायी पड़ता है। धनकुल गीतों को प्रमुख एवं गौण दो श्रेणियों में विभक्त किया जा सकता है। प्रमुख श्रेणी के अंतर्गत जगार गीव्र आते हैं, और इनकी प्रकृति लोक महाकाव्य की है जबकि गौण श्रेणी के अंतर्गत विभिन्न जगारों के अवसर पर गाये जाने वाले चाख्रना गीत आते हैं और इसकी प्रकृति कथात्मक और अकथात्मक भी होती है। कुमारी बाई समरथ गुरूमांय द्वारा गये जाने वाले तीजा जगार में लगभग 24, 350 गीत पक्तियां होती हैं। इसी तरह अन्य गुरूमांयों द्वारा गाये जाने वाले ''जगार'' भी हजारों गीत पंक्तियों वाले हैं ये सभी जगार इन गुरूमांयों को आश्यर्यजनक ढंग से कण्ठस्थ हैं।

वाद्य की उत्पत्ति

हल्बी भाषा के वरिष्ठ कवि श्री सोनसिंह पुजारी के अनुसार इस वाद्य की उत्पत्ति बस्तर में हुई है। मध्य प्रांत के तत्कालीन पोलिटिकल एजेन्ट ई.ए.ड. ब्रेट, आई.सी.एस. द्वारा 1906 में प्रकाशित सेन्ट्रल प्रॉविन्सेज़ गज़ेटियर (छत्तीसगढ़ फयूडेटरी स्टेट्स) नामक किताब के हवाले से उनका कहना है कि आज के ओड़िसा प्रांत का नवरंगपुर व छत्तीसगढ़ के धमतरी, सिहरवा एवं नगरी वर्षों पूर्व तत्कालीन बस्तर रियासत के भाग रहे हैं और इन्हीं में से किसी भाग में इस वाद्य की उत्पति हुई है।

साहित्यकार श्री लाला जगदलपुरी की पुस्तक 'बस्तर इतिहास एवं संस्कृति' के अनुसार धनकुल वाद्य रचना का आविष्कार धनुर्धर हल्वा समाज ने किया है। इस लोक वाद्य की उत्पत्ति भी घर-गृहस्थी की वस्तुओं से ही हुई है। यहां पर सूप धान या चावल साफ़ करने के काम आता है, हण्डी में पानी भरा जाता है, बांस की सींक से दोना व पत्तल को सील किया जाता है और धनुष इनका अस्त्र है इससे हिंस्त्र पशुओं से आत्मरक्षा की जाती है, साथ ही वन्य जीवों का शिकार भी किया जाता है। धनकुल गीत में संगीत का आधार धनुष ही है। विश्व में कई देशों में बो म्यूजिक (धनुसंगीत) का प्रचलन है। नृतत्वशास्त्री एच. बाल्फ़र ने 1899 की अपनी पुस्तक 'द नेचुरल हिस्ट्री ऑफ़ द म्यूज़िकल बो' के अध्याय द डेवलपमेंटल हिस्ट्री ऑफ़

इन्सट्रुमेंट्स ऑफ़ म्यूज़िक में इस वाद्य का सचित्र वर्णन किया है। इसके अलावा 'ए सर्वे ऑफ़ म्यूज़िकल इन्सट्रुमेन्ट्स' के लेखक एस. मारकस के अनुसार अफ़्रीका में धनुष संगीत के विकास की तथा वादन की अद्‌भुत शैली देखने को मिलती है। तिब्बत तथा मंगोलिया में लिबेद और अल्टेंक समुदाय के बीच भी धनुष जादुई संगीत का एक उपकरण है। इसी तरह भारत में उत्तरप्रदेश राज्य के मिर्ज़ापुर की पहाड़ियों में रहने वाली मुंइयार जनजाति के मध्य इसका स्वरूप बस्तर जिले में प्रचलित धनकुल की तरह ही है पर यहां इसका उपयोग सूपा पर नहीं होता। इनके धनुर्संगीत में पिनाक और दरकुन प्रकार के धनुष होते हैं। स्टूअर्ट एच. ब्लैकबर्न (1988) ने अपनी पुस्तक 'सिंगिंग ऑफ़ बर्थ एंड डैथ टैकस्ट्स इन पर्फ़ोमेंस' में तमिलनाडु राज्य के कन्याकुमारी ज़िले में लोक प्रचलित गीत ''विल्लु पट्ठु'' का विस्तार से वर्णन किया है। यहां विल्लु मतलब धनुष तथा पट्ठु का अर्थ गीत होता है। इसी प्रकार गोंडी में धनुष को 'बिल' तथा गीत को 'पाटा' कहते हैं। विल्लु पट्ठु में बजाये जाने वाले इस वाद्य का स्वरूप बस्तर के धनकुल वाद्य से थोड़ा अलग होता है। विल्लु पट्ठु में धनुष की डोरी में छोटे छोटे घुंघरू बंधे होते हैं, बस्तर में नहीं होते। यहां धनुष का एक सिरा तिरछी रखी गयी हाण्डी के मुंह पर ढके सूपा के उपर टिका होता है। तमिलनाडु में सूपा का उपयोग नहीं होता, यहां धनुष का सिरा औंधे मुंह रखी गयी हण्डी को दूसरा वादक ताल वाद्य की तरह बजाता है। विल्लु पट्ठु गायन शैली का विकास 15वीं सदी के आस पास हुआ था। बस्तर में धनकुल शैली के प्रादुर्भाव और विकास के काल का निर्धारण नहीं किया जा सका है पर आसपास के राज्य में इसके प्रचलन से यह साबित होता है कि इसकी उत्पत्ति बस्तर के तटीय क्षेत्र जो ओड़िसा राज्य से लगे हैं वहां पर रहने वाले हल्वा जनजातियों के मध्य हुआ होगा। वर्तमान में ओड़िसा के कई क्षेत्रों में भी यह शैली प्रचलित है। नवरंगपूर (ओड़िसा) में प्रचलित वाद्य में जहां बस्तर की तरह 'धिनरी बाड़ी' होती है वहीं गंजाम व बरगढ़ (ओड़िसा) क्षेत्रों में इस वाद्य में धिरनी बाड़ी की जगह एक पतले बांस की कमची के सिरे पर छोटे-छोटे घुंघरू बंधे होते हैं। वाद्य के इस उपकरण को घुमा या घुमराए कुला धनु या देणु या ढण तथा सरबरी कहा जाता है। ऐसा माना जा सकता है कि बस्तर में इस वाद्य के उपकरण हण्डी को घुमरा हंडी या धुमरा कहा जाने लगा। इस तरह ढेणु भी धनु का ही बिगड़ा रूप है और कोइला शब्द भी कुला का ही विकृत स्वरूप है। इस प्रकार धनुकुला धीरे-धीरे धनकुल बन गया और वर्तमान में बस्तर, ओड़िसा, छत्तीसगढ़ के कई क्षेत्रों में धनकुल के नाम से ही जाना जाता है। धमतरी ज़िले में धनकुल से सम्बधित उपकरणों की उत्पत्ति कमार जनजाति के यहां से हुई है, ऐसा साक्ष्य धनकुल गीत के प्रारंभ में प्रार्थना गीत से मिलता है।

वाद्य का संयोजन

धनुष, हण्डी, सूपा, और बांस की छिरनी काड़ी के संयोजन से धनकुल वाद्य बना होता है, हण्डी को धान के पुआल से बने गुड़री के उपर हल्का से तिरछा रखकर उसके मुंह पर सूपा को ढक दिया जाता है, और इसके उपर धनुष का एक छोर टिका होता है तथा दूसरा छोर ज़मीन पर होता है। धनुष के ऊपरी भाग को हल्का कांटेदार बनाया जाता है। धनुष की लम्बाई लगभग 2 मीटर होती है। इसके दाहिने भाग में लगभग 1.5 मीटर पर 08 इंच की लम्बाई के हल्के खांचे बने होते है।

गुरूमांयें धनुष के इसी दूसरे सिरे के पास एक लकड़ी की मचिया पर बैठती हैं और दाहिने हाथ में छिरनी काड़ी से धनुष डंडी के खांचे वाले भाग में घर्षण करती हैं तथा बाये हाथ से झिकन डोरी (प्रत्यंचा) को हल्के-हल्के खींचती हैं। घषर्ण से जहां छर-छर-छर-छर की ध्वनि वहीं डोरी को खींचने पर घुम्म घुम्म की ध्वनि 'घुमका हंडी' से निकलती है। इस तरह ताल वाद्य और तत वाद्य का सम्मिलित संगीत इस लोक वाद्य से निकलता है। दण्डकराण्य के पठार में प्रचलित यह वाद्य अपने आप में मौलिक एवं अनूठा है।

वाद्य यंत्र का प्रयोग

धनकुल वाद्य को प्राय: महिलाएं ही बजाती हैं। ओड़िसा राज्य के नवरंगपुर क्षेत्र में कुछ कुछ जगहों में पुरुषों को सहायक के रूप में वादन करते देखा गया है। इन महिलाओं में मुख्य गायिका एवं वादन करने वाली महिला को घाट गुरूमांय और उनके साथ देने वाली गायिका एव वादन करने वाली महिला को चेली गुरूमांय कहा जाता है। बस्तर में जो पुरुष धनकुल वाद्य बनाते हैं वे सरगोपाल के लुदरूराम कोर्राम, बस्तर के जयदेव और सुकदेव, बनियागांव के चैनसिंह कुरमी आदि हैं। इन लोक महाकाव्यों की गायिकाओं को गुरूमांय कहा जाता है भले ही गायक पुरुष ही क्यों न हो। बस्तर में एक बार जो वाद्य बनाए जाते हैं उनका उपयोग प्राय: प्रति वर्ष होता है। अनुष्ठानों के अवसर पर इस वाद्य की विधि-विधान से पूजा की जाती है, गीत गा कर इन वाद्य यंत्रों को क्रियाशील करके होम, आरती अर्पित करते हैं। ओड़िसा के कई स्थानों में प्रत्येक आयोजन के लिए नये वाद्य तथा नई मचिया बनाये जाते हैं और कार्यक्रम की समाप्ति के पश्चात जला देते हैं। मुंइयार जनजाति में बजाये जाने वाले पिनाक तथा दरकुन वाद्य को एक ही व्यक्ति बजाता है। तमिलनाडु में विल्लु पर एक और पट्ठु पर दूसरा व्यक्ति वादन करता है। यहां प्राय: पुरुष ही वादक एवं गायक होते हैं परन्तु कभी कभी महिलाएं भी गाती बजाती हैं।

धनकुल वाद्य का सुनने वाले पर प्रभाव

इस वाद्य के वादन तथा गायन के साथ ही वहां पर उपस्थित कई महिलाओं के ऊपर देवी-देवता का प्रभाव देखने को मिलता है, वे झूमने लगती हैं। इस स्थिति पर आने को 'मोचतो' कहा जाता है। प्राय: धनुर्संगीत का प्रभाव महिलाओं पर होता है। परन्तु कभी कभी यह पुरुषों पर दिखाई पड़ता है, जो अधिकतर सिरहा होते हैं। 'द केटेल्पा बो: ए स्टडी ऑफ़ शैमनिक प्रेक्टिसेज़ इन जापान' नामक पुस्तक में प्रसिद्ध मानवशास्त्री सी. ब्लैकर (1986) ने कहा है कि धनुष एक शस्त्र के साथ ही बहुत अच्छा वाद्य यंत्र भी है। यह एक डोरी वाला वाद्य यंत्र है, इसको बजाने पर निकलने वाला स्वर आत्माओं की दुनिया में जा पहुंचता है और महिलायें इसके प्रभाव में आकर आत्माओं से सम्पर्क स्थापित कर प्रभावशील हो जाती हैं। एक तान्त्रिक प्राचीन काल से वर्तमान काल तक धनुष संगीत के प्रभाव से आत्माओं को अपने निकट आने के लिए विवश कर देता है और आने पर अपनी इच्छानुसार कार्य करवाने का प्रयास करता है। जापान में धनुर्संगीत का उपयोग तांत्रिक लोग करते हैं जबकि बस्तर में इस संगीत का उपयोग गुरूमांयें करती हैं। धनकुल संगीत से अधिकतर महिलायें आत्माओं के प्रभाव में आ जाती हैं।

वादन एवं गायन

बस्तर में धनकुल वाद्य का वादन एवं गायन प्राय: गुरूमांयें व चेली गुरूमांय करती हैं। इनके अलावा जो सुनने आती हैं वे भी गायन में भाग लेती हैं और सुर में सुर मिलाकर गाती हैं। कुछ जगह पुरुष भी गायन व वादन करते हैं। गुरूमांय की आयु लगभग 35 साल से उपर ही होती है। ये अधिकतर अपने घर गृहस्थी के उत्तरदायित्व से लगभग निवृत्त सी होकर गायन एवं वादन सीखने का कार्य प्रारंभ करती हैं। बस्तर में धनकुल वाद्य का वादन एवं जगार गायन किसी जाति या समुदाय विशेष की विशेषज्ञता नहीं होती। इस कार्य को किसी भी जाति के लोग कर सकते है। बस्तर में प्राय: हल्वा, धाकड़ गांड़ा, मरार, केवट बैरागी, कलार, घड़वा, आदि जाति की गुरूमांय धनकुल वाद्य का वादन एवं जगार गायन करती हैं। इन गुरूमांयों को वादन, गायन के एवज़ में धनराशि न देकर सामर्थ्यानुसार ससम्मान भेंट दी जाती है।

तीजा जगार की कथा वस्तु

तीजा जगार के गायन के कई स्वरूप हैं। उनमें से एक में सुरडोंगर ग्राम के श्री बलराम गोर जी की पुत्रवधु की पहली तीजा के समय आयोजित तीजाजगार में श्रीमती कुमारी बाई समरथ ने लोक गाथा प्रस्तुत की, जिसमें नागलोक से पृथ्वीलोक

में आकर सलभल रैप्याराजा व रानी कोतादाईए के राज्य में नाग नागिन अपना जीवन यापन करते हैं और राजा रानी द्वारा संतान प्राप्ति के लिए विविध्न अनुष्ठान किये जाते हैं। इसमें तुलसी का पौधा रोपण, कुंआ, बावड़ी और जलाशय के निर्माण तथा धर्मशाला बनवाने के पश्चात नागिन के गर्भ से पुत्र का जन्म होता है। वह बड़ा होकर डाहांकरैया के नाम से प्रसिद्व होता है। इसका विवाह माहा पातरिन रानी की पुत्री जनादई से होता है। यह रानी भी संतान प्राप्ति के लिए तुलसी रोपती है, तीजा का उपवास रखती है और सरोवर तथा कुआं खुदवाती है, पेड़ पौधे लगवाती है। इस सब करने से उसे संतान सुख की प्राप्ति होती है। रानी अपने आपको सम्पूर्णता में देखती है, इस विविध क्रम में काफी दुख का सामना करते हुए अंत में सुख की प्राप्ति होती है। संतान प्राप्ति का सुख है क्योंकि संतान के बिना नारी अपूर्ण है। उसकी सबसे बड़ी और उत्कट अभिलाषा है संतान प्राप्ति, इसके अलावा उसे कुछ नहीं चाहिए।

तीजा जगार का उद्देश्य

इसका सीधा संबंध ग्रामीण जीवन से जुड़ता है क्योंकि हल्वा जनजातियों में कुँआरी कन्यायें तीजा का उपवास नहीं रखतीं और न ही कोई अनुष्ठान करती हैं। इन जनजातियों के घरों में प्रथम बार नववधु के आगमन के बाद पड़ने वाले कृष्ण जन्माष्टमी के दूसरे दिन नवमी तिथि की शाम से कलश स्थापना कर धनकुल गीत गा कर लोक रुचि एवं कथा महत्व वाला तीजा जगार प्रारंभ किया जाता है। यह जगार प्रत्येक वर्ष इस क्षेत्र में निवासरत जनजातियों– हल्वा धाकड़, पनारा के घरों में जब पुत्र के विवाह के बाद नववधु आती है तो उस नववधु की प्रथम तीजा (हरतालिका तीज) को ससुराल में ही मनाया जाता है और इस अवसर पर धनकुल वादन युक्त तीजा जगार का गायन होता है। इसमें नववधु एवं वर के लगन-मुउर (विवाह के समय सिर पर धारण करने वाले मुकुट एवं पगड़ी) को पूजा गृह में सुरक्षित रख देते हैं। हरतालिका तीज से लगभग एक माह पहले जगार का आयोजन करते हैं और यह तीजा की रात्रि को सम्पन्न हो जाता है। इस समय पूजा गृह से मुकुट (लगन मुउर) को पुत्र एव पुत्रवधु को पहनाकर पूजा स्थल पर बिठाते हैं, फिर इनके द्वारा देवी एव आत्माओं का आह्वान कर पूजा स्थल पर आंमत्रित कर स्थापित करते हैं। तत्पश्चात गुरमांयों द्वारा धनकुल वाद्य यंत्र की स्थापना की जाती है और पुनः आत्माओं का आह्वान कर धनकुल गीत का गायन प्रांरभ किया जाता है, जिसे वर वधु एवं उपस्थित समूह सुनते हैं। गायन एव वादन खत्म होने पर पूजा करके अनुष्ठान के स्थान से उठकर अपने दैनंदिनी कार्य में शामिल हो जाते हैं।

प्रत्येक दिन दोपहर 3 बजे से शाम 7 बजे तक गायन वादन का कार्य होता है। अगर यह आयोजन सामूहिक है तो यह शाम 7 बजे प्रारंभ होकर रात्रि 10 बजे तक चलता है। इस कार्यक्रम में श्रद्धा-भक्ति से प्रेरित होकर महिलाओं व बच्चों समेत सभी ग्रामवासी सम्मिलित होते हैं। अगर तीजा जगार का आयोजन व्यक्तिगत है या सामूहिक है और पुत्र घर पर नहीं है तो पुत्रवधु को बिठाकर उसे धनकुल गीत सुनवाते हैं। अगर पुत्र वधु मासिक धर्म से है तो घर की किसी दूसरी महिला को पूजास्थल पर बिठाते हैं। पुत्रवधु किसी दूसरे कमरे में बैठकर धनकुल गीत श्रवण करती है। इस प्रकार तीन दिन तक चले इस अनुष्ठान का समापन तीजा के दिन भेजली ठंडा करने पुत्र एवं पुत्रवधु तलाब या नदी जाते हैं, वहां से रेत या भेजली के टुकड़े लेकर घर वापस आते हैं। यह कार्य पुत्र एवं पुत्रवधु द्वारा ही किये जाते हैं, तत्पश्चात शाम के समय पूजा पाठ करके पूरी रात्रि धनकुल गीत श्रवण करते हैं। सुबह होने पर देवी तथा आत्माओं की पूजा अर्चना कर उनके लोक में उन्हें विदा करते हैं। क्षेत्रीय मान्यताओं, लोक विश्वास एवं रीति रिवाजों के परिपालन हेतु नववधु को भावी जीवन में आने वाली कठिनाइयों का सामना करते हुए देवी एवं आत्माओं के प्रति आस्था व विश्वास के साथ अनुष्ठान करते हुए जीवन निर्वाह करना धनकुल गीत सुनने का प्रमुख उद्देश्य होता है। नववधु विवाह के पश्चात पहली तीजा धनकुल गीत जगार सुनकर अपने ससुराल में तीजा मनाती है। तत्पश्चात सुबह मायके जाने आने के लिए वह स्वतंत्र हो जाती है।

आठे जगार

इस जगार में भगवान श्री कृष्ण की कथा के लोक रूप का गायन किया जाता है। इसका आयोजन जन्माष्टमी के प्रातः प्रारंभ होकर दूसरे दिन सुबह समाप्त होता है। इस जगार की अवधि पूरे 24 घंटे की होती है हल्बी भाषा में गायन करने वाली गुरमांय अब नहीं के बराबर हैं। वर्तमान में आठे जगार का आयोजन जगदलपुर तहसील के कुछ क्षेत्र में ही देखने को मिलता है, बाकी जगह लुप्त प्राय ही हो गया है।

लछमी जगार

लछमी जगार की कथा बस्तर में ही अलग अलग क्षेत्र में अलग-अलग है। इसका आयोजन कार्तिक महीने में नवाखानी के बाद आरम्भ हो जाता है। धान की फसल पकने के बाद लछमी जगार का आयोजन गांव-गांव में होने लगता है। यह हल्बी जनभाषा में गाया जाता है। अगहन का महिना इस जगार के लिए सर्वाधिक सही

मौसम होता है। अगहन महीने के अंतिम दिन जगार का कार्य अंतिम होता है। इस दिन को बड़ा जगार कहते हैं। वैसे तो बस्तर में लछमी जगार का कार्यक्रम माघ महिने तक चलता रहता है। लछमी जगार चाहे पांच दिन का हो या सात अथवा नौ या ग्यारह दिनों का परन्तु इसकी समाप्ति गुरुवार के दिन ही होती है। इस लोक महाकाव्य में सृष्टि की उत्पत्ति, धान की उत्पत्ति, वर्षा की उत्पत्ति की कहानी है। यहां जाति भेद का कोई स्थान नहीं है। यह उत्सव प्राय: सामूहिक रूप से आयोजित किया जाता है जिसे गांव जगार कहते है। मनौती मानने पर इस जगार का आयोजन व्यक्तिग भले ही होता है पर भागीदारी सभी गांव वाले करते हैं। इसका आयोजन स्थल प्राय: देवगुड़ी होता है। आयोजन स्थल को लीप पोतकर सुंदर ढंग से सजाकर दीवार पर भितिचित्र अंकित किया जाता है। इस चित्र में जगार की कथा संक्षेप में अंकित होती है। चित्रांकन का कार्य लोक चित्रकारों द्वारा किया जाता है। इसे गढ़ लिखना कहते हैं।

बाली जगार

जिले के भतरी बदुल क्षेत्रों में इस जगार का आयोजन ज्यादा है और इसका गायन भतरी जनभाषा में किया जाता है। इसका आयोजन 12 वर्षों में एक बार किया जाता है। लोक जीवन के विविध पक्षों को समेटे 03 महीने तक चलने वाले इस आयोजन में प्रात: एव सायं पूजा-अर्चना की जाती है। इस जगार में बालिकाओं एव युवतियों पर देवी की आत्मा आती है जिसे सवारी आना कहते हैं। इसमें वे अपना सुध-बुध खो बैठती हैं और झूमते हुए नृत्य करती हैं।

गायन की भाषा

धनकुल गीत प्राय: हल्बी लोक भाषा में गाये जाते हैं। यह लोकभाषा आर्य भाषा परिवार की पूर्वी हिन्दी की एक उपभाषा है। इसमें अवधी, बघेली एवं छत्तीसगढ़ी लोकभाषाओं के शब्द भी हैं। इस लोकभाषा को हल्बा जनजाति की बोली कहा गया है, किन्तु यह सम्भवत: सहज सुगम होने के कारण बस्तर अंचल की सभी जातियों द्वारा बोली जाती है। हल्बी की कई उपबोलियां जैसे मिरगानी, चंडारी, घसिया, पनारी आदि हैं। कतीय राजवंश के काल में यह बस्तर राज्य की राज-भाषा के रूप में प्रतिष्ठित थी। इस कारण आज भी सम्पर्क भाषा के रूप में यह पूरे बस्तर में बोली जाती है। कोडागांव एवं बीजपुर तहसील के क्षेत्रों में बोली जाने वाली हल्बी भाषा मानक हल्बी भाषा मानी जाती है।

धनकुल गीत की प्रकृति

धनकुल गीत के अंतर्गत गाये जाने वाले लोकमहाकाव्य (तीजा जगार, लछमी जगार, आठे जगार, बाली जगार) अलिखित हैं और पूरी तरह मौखिक परम्परा के सहारे विद्यमान हैं। इन गीतों में जगार गीत कथात्मक प्रकृति के होते हैं और जगार गीतों के समय बीच-बीच में गाये जाने वाले ''चाखना गीत'' अकथात्मक प्रकृति के होते हैं। चाखना गीत भी दो प्रकार के होते हैं, पहला समान्य तौर पर गाया जाने वाला चाखना गीत जिससे हास्य, श्रृंगार और निवेदन का समायोजन होता है इसे 'सादा चाखना' कहते हैं। यह मनोरंजन प्रधान होता है। नीति सम्बधी गीत भी इस चाखना में गाये जाते है। दूसरा चाखना गीत देव आराधना से सम्बंधित होता है। इसमें प्राय: देवी स्वयं ही गुरूमांय से आग्रह करती है और देवी की आत्मा किसी स्त्री के शरीर में आकर नृत्य करने लगती है और इस नृत्य में देवी कोई व्यवधान सहन नहीं कर सकती। व्यवधान हो तो अमंगल हो जाता है। इस गीत को 'देव चाखना' कहते हैं। इसमें देवी को दिखाने और उसकी आराधना में गाये जाने वाले गीत होते हैं।

धनकुल क्षेत्र

वर्तमान में धनकुल गीत अधिकतर जगदलपुर, कोड़ागांव केशकाल नारायणपुर, छोटे डोंगर, अंतागढ़, दंतेबाड़ा गोदम क्षेत्रों में प्रचलित हैं। कांकेर जिले के पूर्वी भाग और घमतटी जिले के पूर्वी भाग में भी इनका प्रचलन है। ऐसा देखा गया है कि जहां पर हल्बा जनजातियों की बहुलता हो और ओड़िया भाषा एवं संस्कृति के प्रभाव वाले क्षेत्रों में धनकुल गीत का प्रचलन स्पष्ट रूप से देखने को मिलता है।

उद्देश्य

धनकुल गीत के अंतर्गत गाये जाने वाले जगार का उद्देश्य ऊपरी तौर से मनोरंजन कार्यक्रम लगती है परन्तु गहराई से सोचने एवं समझने पर विभिन्न संस्कारों से आबद्ध अनुष्ठान नज़र आता है। तीजा जगार में दाम्पत्य-जीवन की सफलता एवं लक्ष्मी जगार देवताओं को निद्रा से जगाना और अन्न की उपज इनके मूलभूत उद्देश्य हैं। जगार में वर्षा न होने की चिन्ता से मुक्ति दिला कर इंद्र देवता को वर्षा करने के लिए बाध्य करने का प्रयास है एवं आठे जगार में श्रीकृष्ण चरित के माध्यम से अन्याय पर न्याय, बुराई पर अच्छाई की विजय गाथा का गायन किया जाता है। इन सभी महागाथाओं में लोकतत्व अपनी मौलिकता के साथ विद्यमान रहते हैं। बस्तर अंचल में निवासरत जनजातियां मातृ शक्ति की आराधना करती हैं। मातृ शक्ति की

रूप मां दंतेश्वरी, हिमलार्जन माई, सितलामाई, जलनी बूड़ी गंगादई, पेंडरावॅदिन माई, करना कोटिन, आदि की पूजा अर्चना विविध अवसरों पर होती है। जगार में नैतिक मूल्यों के उद्घोष के साथ-साथ कुछ विपरीत स्थितियां भी देखने में आती हैं। जाने अनजाने में की गई प्रतिज्ञा को पूरा करने या दिये हुए वचन को निभाने का नैतिक साहस इस धनकुल गीतों के पात्रों में दिखाई देता है। ये गीत लोक जीवन में नैतिक मूल्यों के प्रति गहरी आस्था को रेखांकित करते हैं। इन जगार गीतों में मुख्यतः नकारात्मक मूल्यों की स्थिति सही सांस्कारिक व अनुष्ठानिक कृत्यों के द्वारा सकारात्मक मूल्यों की स्थिति तक पहुंचती दिखलायी पड़ती है। ये सभी जगार बस्तर की महिलाओं के लिए पवित्र अनुष्ठान हैं। इस प्रकार के आयोजन के सभी संस्कारों में प्रायः महिलायें ही सहभागी होती हैं। पुरुष संगीतकार, पुजारी और केन्द्रीय भूमिका निभाने वाले पात्रों के रूप में सहभागी होते हैं। इनमें से अधिकतर संस्कार के समय देवी के प्रभाव में आते देखे जाते हैं। इस प्रकार के अनुष्ठानिक आयोजन में खर्च 1000 रुपए से 50,000 रुपए तक आता है।

वर्तमान स्थिति

धनकुल वादन एवं गायन पर भी अन्य लोक कला रूपों की तरह इलेक्ट्रॉनिक माध्यमों का प्रभाव अधिक दिखाई पड़ रहा है। पहले गांवों में आयोजित होने वाले विभिन्न जगारों में बालक, वृद्ध महिलायें, पुरुष सभी समान रूप से उपस्थित होकर सहभागिता करते थे पर वर्तमान में बहुत ही कम सहभागिता दिखाई पड़ती है। आयोजन स्थल पर प्रायः अब आयोजक परिवार के मुखिया और जगार गायिकाओं के अतिरिक्त कोई और दिखलाई नहीं पड़ता। पहले लोग अपने काम काज छोड़कर उत्सव में शामिल होते थे परन्तु वर्तमान में लोग इस प्रकार के उत्सव को त्याग कर अपने काम-काज में व्यस्त हो गये हैं। इससे सामाजिक विकास की दिशा बदल गई है। अगर इस पर वर्तमान में ध्यान नहीं दिया गया तो हमारी और उनकी मृत्यु के साथ ही हमारी यह समृद्ध परम्परा खत्म हो जायेगी। अतः नयी पीढ़ी के लिए इस परम्परा को जीवित रखने के लिए अनुष्ठानों एवं संस्कारों का प्रबलता से पालन आवश्यक है।

References

Balfour, H. 1899. *The Natural History of the Musical Bow.* Oxford: The Clarenden Press.

Blackburn, S.H. 1988. *Singing of Birth and Death: Texts in Performance.* Philadelphia: University of Pennsylvania Press.

Blacker, C. 1986. *The Catalpa Bow: A Study of Shamanistic Practices in Japan.* London: Unwin Hyman Ltd.

de Brett, E.A. 1906. *Central Provinces Gazetteer.* Vol. 10. (Chhattisgarh Feudatory States). Bombay: The Times Press.

Jagdalpuri, Lala. 2007. *Bastar Itihas Evam Sanskriti.* Bhopal: Madhya Pradesh Hindi Granth Akademi.

Marcuse, Sybil. 1975. *A Survey of Musical Instruments.* New York: Harper and Row.

Woods and Livelihoods

P. Sanakara Rao

The use of wood may be traced to the pre-historic period. It was used in different forms like making fire, fuel, boxes, tools, toys, domestic articles, building materials of the habitats, pillars, doors, gateways transportation, ritualistic symbols, marriage palanquins, musical instruments, oil expellers, etc. Since the ancient past to the contemporary period the wood and wooden craft have been in continuous promulgation in human society. For centuries Indian craftsmen have used wood as one of the important media of art expression from the very beginning, mainly because of its availability and also being an art-friendly medium. We still use age-old wooden objects and other items in our households because of their long life. They are traditional and have been in service for several generations standing for wisdom and wealth. A variety of these works of arts and crafts are one of the most important cultural heritages of mankind. The wooden material culture, knowledge and technology of our tribal and rural artisans and craftsmen have a rich heritage in this very old craft of wood carving that reflects the artistic skills on objects of design, function, utility, aesthetics, style and beautiful composition of wood and wooden art is highly appreciated in the present society. The wood craft is widely prevalent all over India, but variation and exception are noticed in different regions, provinces and locality.

The present paper is inspired by various wood and wooden material culture objects of Indira Gandhi Rashtriya Manav Sangrahalaya (IGRMS or National Museum of Mankind), Bhopal in Central India, Madhya Pradesh, which is one of the largest ethnographic museums in India. The museum is dedicated to represent, promote and preserve the material culture of different states across the country and also deals with large scale wooden objects for documentation, display in different exhibitions, research and reference. It focuses on the social, economic, cultural and environmental importance of wood. It also tries to project its sustenance and how some aspects of India's various regional cultures, which facilitate creativity, imagination and divergent thinking of

wooden arts and crafts, can effectively offer the learning process as a joyful experience.

The trees played an important part in the evolution of Indian culture; the history of forests is linked with the history of civilization. Modern science too recognizes that forests are mothers of the rivers and factories of soil manufacture. A tree is the most important renewable resource and its adoption contributes substantially to the social and economic development of the country. At the same time, trees provide the environment in which we live by moderating climate and improving air quality and sustainable livelihoods.

The concept of livelihood is increasingly used in development debates in which people's capabilities and social as well as material assets are important as a means of living (Kanji and Barrientos 2002: 2). According to Gow (1990: 161), livelihood refers to the basic survival sources that are accessible to an individual or group. It is defined as adequate stocks and flows of food and cash to meet basic needs. It also implies a kind of security, which refers to the secure ownership of, or access to resources and income generating activities. A livelihood comprises the capabilities, activities, assets and entitlements by which people make a living. In operational terms a livelihood should be sufficient to avoid poverty, and preferably, increase well-being for agricultural labourers and their dependents, it implies systems of how rural people make a living and whether their livelihoods are secure or vulnerable overtime. Livelihoods are also seen as the ways in which people satisfy their needs, or gain a living. Arts and crafts associated with wood have proved to be a continuous source of livelihood to rural and/or tribal people all over India. IGRMS collection of wood items is a living proof of this fact.

Conclusion

Trees and forests preceded man. They are the greatest purifiers in the world. Trees and forests are the sanctuaries of animals and birds. They are homes of many tribes and forest dwellers. They give us wood and food. Trees hold the soil tightly. Hence, they keep the land safe from soil erosion, floods and droughts.

By planting trees, we return to a more natural, less artificial environment. Living and working with wood in the lap of nature is a joyous and blissful experience.

References

Gow, D.G. 1990. Forestry for Sustainable Development. *UNASYLVA* No. 169.

Kanji, N. and S. Barrientos 2002. Trade Liberalization, Poverty and Livelihoods: Understanding the Linkages. Working Paper 159. Institute of Development Studies: Brighton (www.furure.agriculture.org/pdf accessed on 12.7.2011).

Between the Potter and the Elephant:
A Discourse on the Contemporariness of Tradition

Shampa Shah

Amulya Malakar, an artist from Assam was narrating the myth of the genesis of an aquatic plant called sola and the beginning of the subsequent sola-craft. He had been talking for more than an hour now, and he hadn't even as much as mentioned the word sola. I wondered if he had got the query right as he was talking about the myth of Manasa, the snake goddess instead. I must have mumbled something to that effect expressing the doubt because Amulya Malakar's surprised voice was heard saying, "Why, of course it is the myth of sola! Don't I have to begin at the beginning?" At this one of my colleagues blurted out. "What has sola got to do with the goddess Manasa?" Amulyakar Malakar seemed to resent this impatience on the part of his audience. Pointing towards a fellow potter making a clay elephant, he quipped, "what is the relation between clay and elephant, say?"

In the silence that followed, the crudeness of our propensity for simplifying and reducing everything into neat compartments echoed. How accustomed we are to disrobe a thing of its multifold, inalienable mysteries to fit our cause-effect frame. Perhaps to be able to comprehend his angry retort one will have to read carefully between the lines to gauge the curious relationship between the clay, the potter and the elephant.

In Banki Sendra, Kalipad Kumbhkar, a potter, over eighty-five years, is making the Bonga elephant, his own bit of creative addition to the terracotta tradition of Bankura for which he was recognized and awarded by the President of India.

"When was the first time he made a Bonga hathi?"

One day it so happened that some Santhals of his region traversing twenty miles on foot, came to him with a strange request. They wanted him to make an elephant for them. One that would please their Bonga Dev. The elephants that Kalipad usually made were all on display before the Santhals. Obviously they were searching for something else. The potter wanted to know what exactly it was. Could they perhaps tell him something about their Bonga Dev, what he looked like, where he lived, what he did and so on? This perplexed the Santhals.

"Whoever has seen Bonga Dev? And after all he is a God, no deed is beyond him, what can we say about such a one. Only when a jungle fire breaks out the elders say, there goes Bonga Dev."

Kalipad wanted some time. The Santhals were asked to return after a month's time for their elephants. Thereafter Kalipad spent restless days and nights worrying about the form of the elephant that would please the Bonga Dev. If Bonga Dev does not have a face, his elephant too cannot have a face. But then that was not all. Could there be an elephant without a trunk or those big ears? The elephant that did emerge out of this prolonged dialogue with the self was such as must have left the Master Creator wondering. The huge bulk of the elephant's body itself slides down the slope, over the space of a face to become a trunk. There are a trunk, two eyes, two ears and one standing tail on that Bonga hathi but they are all as if they are not. The detachable ears and tail are actually made so, keeping the transportation hassles in mind. When fitted with these the Bonga hathi immediately acquires the lightness of a feather. Obviously, the Santhals had not traversed twenty miles on foot for a mere clay elephant and of course they had sought the right person who recognized the responsibility he had been entrusted with. To the Santhals who had a vision of Bonga Dev in the spreading fire of the forest perhaps Kalipad's Bonga hathi seemed a fitting tribute. They were so happy, says Kalipad that they gave him twice the weight of the food grains as remuneration for the same.

The Bonga elephant

A similar account—a childhood event was told by Sahdev Rana of Bastar. Some men of the Bhatra tribe had come to his father from afar for a terracotta elephant that they needed to propitiate their God. There was no dearth of potters in their village or the ones around, but they had undertaken this arduous journey in the belief that the elephant that would please their deity, could only be made by this particular artist.

Two significant points emerge from these examples.

What is to be made, through which medium it has to be realized, and by whose hands it will be fashioned—all these variables have been decided. Yet the expectation from this trio is beyond realistic calculations. Its outlines are quite vague and it is in this sphere of indeterminacy that the whole possibility or potential is concealed. Somewhere a transcending of the limits is expected of both the artist and the medium while they engage in this dialogue with the self within the set confines.

Secondly, the popular assumption that there is no individual distinction in the realm of the traditional arts and crafts and that it is the prerogative of the modern artists is also refuted by these examples. In addition it brings to light that the discerning eye that recognizes the individual talents like Mahadev Rana or Kalipad Kumbhkar is also not a thing restricted to a set of people. Like Neelmani, the potter from Manipur remembers distinctly that even as a child making those pots, there was not only a distinct recognition of her pots among hundreds of other pots in the weekly bazaar, but also a willingness to pay a few rupees more for the same.

Forms in traditional arts are more or less determined by their utility. In other words, the use value of the thing is the primary concern. The so-called aesthetic value or the status value is quite secondary. Here the artist's relationship with the medium is the narrow lane through which the artist himself or his art acquires a unique character.

Kalipad Kumbhkar was called to make the shrine of Manasa devi - worshipped throughout Bengal for the Mythological Trail at the National Museum of Mankind Bhopal. I asked him to make all the various forms of the Manasa ghat that existed in his knowledge. At which he laughed, "Even if I worked all my life, the forms of Manasa ghat will not be exhausted. Will your Museum be willing to employ me for life?"

This reminded me of Sara Ibrahim, the potter from Kutch. During a workshop organized on the idea of traditional artists in dialogue with the modern artist, a British lady working with Sara Ibrahim, stressed that she would rather make her own designs as it was boring for her to repeat the same motifs. Sara ben was busy painting her plate while this was said by the British lady at her side. The comment had been made in English, a language that Sara ben does not know. So I was surprised when she looked up from her work and addressing me said,

"Shampa Ben, tell her to give me as many plates as she wants to paint and rest assured that no two designs will be the same."

The word tradition so glibly uttered is fast losing its real meaning. On the one hand there are the so-called upholders of tradition who swear by it. They straitjacket it into an eternal, unchangeable, perfect entity. While on the other hand there are the modernists for whom tradition has no room for creative innovation, individual expression and is thus deemed unfit for bearing any contemporary consciousness. Both come round to a similar reading, the only difference being that one sees virtue in it while the other rejects it precisely for the same reason. Is it not a matter of surprise that of all premier art institutions in India there is not a single one that cares to include any of the traditional techniques and styles as full courses in their curriculum? No one is taught to work in the tradition of Kalighat or Patna painting styles. Even the traditional form of the miniature is has not been extensively explored. The tacit assumption behind the mind set is clearly that there is no scope in these styles of yore for contemporary expression. I wonder if this is not a self-imposed taboo that asks for a serious review. In fact if one looks at the art from countries like Pakistan and Iran that choose to hold on to the traditional and manage to find a modern syntax working through the constraints speaks for the inexhaustible depths of a medium or a style. The fact is that a medium or a style is hardly ever redundant and has to be looked at as a formal aspect that lends itself to any number of renewals.

When it comes to taboo, the women potters of Manipur immediately come to mind. Across the various social groups in India one of the taboos that stands for women everywhere is one that bars them from sitting on the wheel. They were able to invent a novel technique from within the taboo, in which the pot remains still and the potter woman moves around it giving it the shape desired. It hardly needs adding that their forms can put to shame most of the wheel pottery in its roundness. Again without using the potter's wheel, Sara Ibrahim of Kutch makes plates of such huge dimensions as perhaps no one would dare to make on the wheel.

Thavli Balji of Jhabua began by using the ready-made pots as templates to mould her cooking pots from. Eventually she evolved the technique of coating the inner surface with some resinous liquid which made her pots non-porous and thus suitable for cooking. All these are examples of artists who worked their way through the taboos and arrived at something so unique that almost made the taboo petty and ridiculous.

A vast repertoire of myths, proverbs and songs are found among potters from various parts of the country that tell us about the nature, the capacity, the virtues and defects that pertain to the medium of earth. And at the same time, these songs and proverbs also invariably hint at the fact that the family of a potter is forever condemned to remain earth-bound and in dire poverty. On the other hand, they also carry the suggestion that the potter's craft is so unique and central to all existence that no important affair of life can be conducted without her or him. Even the gods after all found themselves helpless without pots and so they created this indispensable one—the potter. So this is told in many of the potters' myths. Another thing that emerges from this ubiquitous myth is that if the potter today lives in poverty, it is because he has chosen this life for himself by preferring a superior human value to that of worldly gains.

In ancient times, potters used to spend six months making their pots and the next six months baking them. Once it so happened that, as soon as a potter was about to light the fire, a group of eunuchs came running and hid themselves inside the big pots. The potter warned them but they refused to pay heed declaring that they would prefer death by fire than let the king's men get hold of them who were close on their heels. The fire was lit and the kiln started. The king's men came, searched in vain and returned, and the potter exhausted by the six months' unremitting labour, fell asleep. A holy voice talked to the potter in his dream,

"Wake up O potter and look, since your pots have turned to gold."

The potter did not get up. After a while the voice came again,

"Hurry up potter, for your pots have turned to silver."

The potter heard but did not pay attention. The voice was heard a third time now,

"O potter go and see, your pots are half-baked and half-unbaked."

At this the potter got up and rushed to his kiln and found

to his amazement that those pots in which the eunuchs had taken shelter had remained unbaked saving all those lives. Ever since the potter's kiln always came out half-baked and half-unbaked. This was the potter who did not care much for gold or silver but chose life, earth and poverty over these riches.

In the myths told by these craftsmen this wisdom, unique to their ancient art, comes out distilled through the sheer transparency of their day-to-day language.

In the Kutchi language, the word used for the kiln is 'niyani'. The same word is used by parents for their daughters, and by brothers for sisters. 'Niyani'—the dearest possession you have, which exacts the utmost care from you, on which depends the glory of the household. Even a slight carelessness in the setting of the kiln can put the weeks of labour of love in jeopardy. Likewise in the Manipuri language, the work for clay is 'leipak' which is also the word for 'people'. One can find a Manipuri remarking now and then, "Our 'leipak' has lost the former touch; it is only full of gravel and sand now."

In order to work in any material, the economic viability and local availability is of utmost importance. At the same time, one has to have a perfect knowledge of the nature of the material clay in our context and an intimate relationship with it. Where good clay is not available, potters are not there either. Similarly, where the clay has the right proportion of organic material as well as quartz, one is likely to find a plethora of forms. The potter with the knowledge of his ancestors, seeped into his consciousness, knows the subtleties of the clay only too well not to make a mistake about its composition. It is of vital importance to understand that if a potter's child is helping him in preparation of his clay or any other work he is not being subjected to premature labour. These are his first lessons. It is this that is his real school and the learning he receives now is going to be with him all his life. If he misses out on it now, he will never be able to make up for the loss.

Coming to the next stage one has to talk of firing material. To fire the things made of clay, different materials are used in different regions depending on the various factors. Around a potter's house in desert regions, one will come across pits where all sorts of waste, thorny bushes, excreta of animals are dumped. This gets converted into manure and is used as fuel for baking the pots. In Pachmura village of West Bengal, the government has planted eucalyptus in the name of social forestry. It was a discovery to find the village potters using its dry leaves as fuel for their kiln. To put it in Salinger's (1951: 4) words "it killed me". The potters has so devised the kiln that he is able to feed it non-stop with these leaves with the help of his specially designed shovel. In both the above examples, a temperature of around nine hundred degrees centigrade is achieved which is a miraculous achievement for our simple but innovative and resourceful people. Moreover this particular idea of using the eucalyptus leaves as fuel is certainly not old.

Levi-Strauss (1966: 16-17) made this comparison long ago between the tribal mind and the bricoleur, the handy man who is able to set things right by the use of a limited number of tools in his kit. The same seems to hold true here too. Like the specialist here, they do not need special implements for coping with special situations. Needless to say, it is this instinct for improvisation that is responsible for many important turns in traditional arts. But since, the primary purpose is not to create anything new or distinct, nor do they advertise their innovations, it is mistakenly assumed that nothing new happens here. Yes, it is true that in the clay horse of Sahdev Rana one can hear the canter of the horses made by his ancestors; yes, in the earthen drum of Rudraiya, one can hear the echo of ancient drums similarly made; and, of course the pot made by Neelmani does resemble the very first pot made on this planet earth. But please do not make the mistake of presuming that it is the same pot, the same horse, the same drum. For, whenever clay receives the intimate touch of the hands of a Neelmani or a Kalipad it is wholly transformed: albeit, it simultaneously manages to preserve something of the warmth, and the intimacy of all those earlier hands which had touched it.

References

Levi-Strauss, C. 1966. *The Savage Mind.* London: Weidenfeld and Nicolson.

Salinger, J.D. 1951. *The Catcher in the Rye.* New York: Little Brown & Co.

Ethnographic Notes

N. Shakamacha Singh

A—Saling: A Memorial of the Ancestral Past[1]

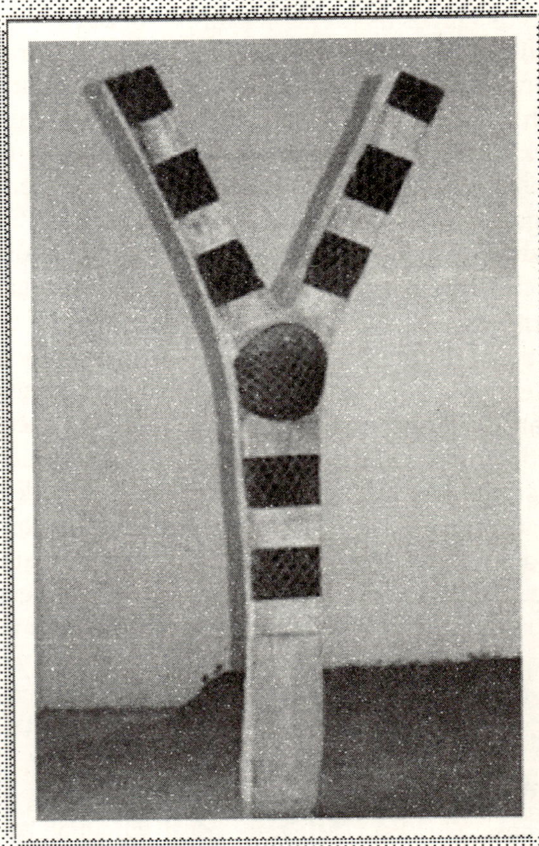

Y-shaped Memorial Pillar among the Kom Tribe of Manipur

Kom is an important tribal group among the 33 Scheduled Tribes of Manipur. This hill tribe inhabits Churachandpur, Chandel, Senapati and Bishnupur districts of Manipur. Most of their concentration is in the Churachandpur District. From the available oral tradition of the tribe, it can be said that they believe that their ancestors came to the present land from the *Khurpui* (a cave) by piercing a ferocious tiger that stood in their way. This is also reflected in their folk songs, myths and legends. The Kom tribe are fondly referred to as the turbaned people because they adorn their Lukom (traditional turban) symbolizing a prestigious head dress of each male of the tribe.

The tradition of erecting a memorial pillar as a symbol of status for a noble or rich person in a village was prevalent among the Kom tribe of Manipur in their ancient past. Such a memorial pillar, traditionally known as Saling represents a unique structure of 'Y'-shaped post with two equal branches rising upwards from a single pillar. This Y-Post has beautiful carvings laid with traditional motifs on one of its sides. Since the post appears like the Roman letter 'Y', people of this tribe fondly call it Wairo. The geometrical motifs carved on the two branches of the post symbolize their prestigious gown called *Pasaipon* signifying that the person had a number of Pasaipon in his possession. A projected circular motif on the body of the post is called Sumlaipong representing the Gong, which is also an item of pride possession. Below this motif another geometrical motif is carved called *Borhui*. This represents the strap for the carrying basket carried by women. The motif shows that the person was able to host a community feast and he was successful in arranging a number of festivals for the youth of his village when he was alive.

A rich man among the Kom tribe is known as a person who gets the richest harvest of crops in the village and he is the one who stores sufficient grains surplus to the annual consumption of his family. He is the person who can afford to host feasts for the villagers and the one who can arrange rice beers, meals and can also sacrifice Mithun for celebrations. According to the Kom tradition in villages when unmarried boys and girls wish to celebrate a festival of dance, joy and merriment, they have to visit the house of the richest person of the village by carrying a pot full of *Ju* (rice beer) and request him to host a feast for celebration. The person then has to seek the consent of the village chief and with his permission the formal announcement is made to commemorate the ceremonial rites. Then starts the process to locate the tree, carve and prepare it as a sacrificial post in the forest.

In an open space or a predetermined place of celebration, the Y post or Saling has to be erected for sacrificing Sithik (Mithun) and a grand feast is hosted by the rich man. The celebration is called Saling Phun (the festival of erecting Saling) which is celebrated by hosting day and night varieties of dance performances, songs, traditional games, etc.

In the olden days the Kom tribe used to perform Lukshun, a ritual ceremony associated with the dead. During this ceremony Saling (Y post) was erected in honour of the departed soul and in memory of his noble deeds. It was believed that unless this ritual was performed the soul of the dead would never get a place in the spiritual world of ancestors. The body of the dead after the burial was unearthed again after six months or a year to perform purification rites. The skull was separated from the body and sanctified with the application of pure *Ju* (rice beer) and *Lukom* (traditional turban) was wrapped around it. The skull was then kept under a pitcher and buried separately near the body and a Y-shaped memorial pillar was erected on it. The ritual ceremony of this kind was performed with the consent of the village priest.

Now, the Lukshun ceremony is no longer performed and practised after the adoption of Christainity among the Kom tribe. However, preparation of Sanka (a sacred platform), Saling(memorial Y-post), and Berphun (bird shooting ceremony) have become a symbol of festivity and cultural identity among this colourful tribe.

B—The Morans and Their Traditional House

The Morans are mostly found in Dibrugarh and Tinsukia Districts of Assam. The larger concentration of this population is in the eastern extremity of the Tinisukia district, and those inhabiting this region are traditionally known as Morans of the Samarpith. We often find that Moran-Matak as a single nomenclature is simultaneously used and sometimes they are also called the Mayamaria or Moamaria. This creates some confusion to the people who visit them. It seems sometimes that Moran and Matak are synonymous to one another. This juxtaposition, however, is confusing, but provides some interesting aspects of socio-cultural and historical blending of their ancestral past. Before 1251 A.D., the region between the Brahmaputra and the Burhi Dihing in Dibrugarh district, was called Matak country and was ruled by Bor Senapati (see Sen 1999:154). Matak is a politically organized, greater community formed by several groups of tribal and non-tribal communities who belong to a Mayamaria/Moamaria sect of the Vaishnav religion.

According to Dutta (1985: 20), Moran is a tribe, Moamaria or Mayamaria is a sect whose followers are called Maomarias or Mayamarias and Matak is a community which includes all the disciples of Mayamaria Satra belonging to different castes, tribes and professional groups. The Morans constitute one of the very old ethnic groups and on the basis of their racial and linguistic affinities, they are ascribed Bodo origin. The Morans of Samarpith area identify themselves as the people who devote their life to domestication of elephants. According to a native of Ubon village, Shri Dilip Moran, "the elephant is our cultural property and we have been living together since time immemorial. Our ancestors came to this land with elephants."

Well-trained in catching wild elephants, people of the region also refer to them as true friends of this beautiful animal. Several years of coexistence between the Morans and elephants have given rise to a situation whereby the elephants occupy an important place in the socio-cultural, religious and economic life of the Moran people. Morans are the elephant catchers, trainers and caretakers, and at the same time they cherish the tradition of keeping elephants, not merely as an animal but also as a family member and this practice makes the tribal group unique. The Morans live in close conjunction with the elephant territory. However, they respect its territorial habitat and they believe in harmonious coexistence. Their love and affection for the elephant is well reflected in their culture too. According to a Moran folk saying, elephants are complimented to be one of the dearest members of the family. It is said that, "*Atikoi Senehor nati, tatootkoi Senehor hati*" which means that 'a grandson is dear to the grandparents but elephants are the dearest'. The elephants are not merely a property of pride and honour among the the Morans but they become their cultural symbol and identity. Most of the folk sayings, idioms and riddles used in the social life of the Morans refer to the elephants. The Morans have a wealth of traditional wisdom which they apply in reading the mind of an elephant. They have good knowledge of elephant behaviour. In some instances, the Morans celebrate *Hati-Bihu* in honour of their elephants.

The Morans were expert in catching and training elephants; the Ahom elephantry was practically monopolized by them. Because they were brave warriors, they also contributed a major share to the man-power of the Ahom Army. Thus the service of the Morans was of great help in expansion and consolidation of the Ahom power in Assam (cf. Dutta 1985).

Traditional Moran houses are very few in existence. Even in the Samarpith belt, where larger concentration of the Moran tribe is found only three traditional houses exist. Among these houses, the one which is located at *Ritukothalguri* village is the oldest and it is about half a century old. Nowadays, Moran villages and their settlement patterns have undergone considerable change. It is difficult to distinguish them from other communities at a glance. Apart from these changes, they have retained and continued to use some of the basic structures like *Bhoral Ghar* (granary), *Randhoni Ghar* (the place of Randhon or cooking members of the house), *Sora Ghar* (a place of the household head). These traditional spaces more or less exist in an innovated form and the elements of continuity are visible in every household. Morans live in joint families. The father or elderly male member being the head of the house is obeyed by all the members of the family. No separate hearth can come up unless a new establishment of the married son is allowed to set up.

Moran settlements are found often in close proximity of the jungle and those located in the Samarpith area are surrounded by a thick natural forest cover that extends to the east towards Myanmar and Arunachal Pradesh. According to the Morans, this is the home to a large number of wild elephants. Fenced with uniformly woven bamboo, the Moran settlement at present gives a clear demarcation of family and individual landholdings. The Moran habitat has additional structures of Bhoral ghar, Guhali ghar, Tantor hali and Hahor goral. Traditionally, a Moran house is constructed on a rectangular ground plan with an extension of kitchen as another segment of the house followed by rooms for the family members. The house is constructed with bamboo as wall structures and roofing frames, Jengu/Toko Pat as thatching leaves, *Komor Khuta, Pasor Khuta, Soti,* etc. as wooden pillars, post and beams. Huge wooden pillars and beams called Komor Khuta and Soti are used in the interior super-built-up structure to support the entire house. The appropriate use of Komor khuta (huge wooden pilllar) rested horizontally with Soti (wooden beams) presents a magnificent look of the house from the interior and these massive wooden structures symbolically represent the power and strength of an elephant and are believed to withstand any kind of untoward incidence of natural, human and spiritual forces. Their traditional house has a reserved space in the front verandah and is called Arula. This space is used especially for keeping the belongings of their elephants.

The Moran house has three rooms arrayed with bamboo wall partitions. The front hall called *Sora Ghar* is regarded as the most important part of the house. This common room has a fireplace called *Jui Hali,* and surrounding it is the meeting place. The space adjoining to the main *Khuta* (pillar), is the place for the household head. According to the Moran tradition, *Jui Hali* (fireplace) should remain lighted all the time throughout the year, be it winter, summer or the rainy season. It is the place where every important decision of the family is taken. Morans are very hospitable, and those who visit them are given a warm welcome. The guests have to take their seat in the Sora Ghar, where various items of food, tea and fresh *Tamul, pan,* etc. are offered to entertain them. Hanging platforms are used above the Jui Hali to preserve food items and also for stacking items of household use. *Dhenki* (husking lever) for pounding grains are generally installed or kept in this room.

The main entrance door of the house lies at left side of the front wall and this serves as a corridor which is unidirectional with another door passing to other rooms like the *Huwa ghar*. The side door called *Pet Duwar* lies at the left side wall. It is used by the family members especially the women when respectable people are present in the *Sora Ghar*. Adjoining the Sora Ghar is the *Huwa Ghar* (bedrooms) and sometimes extended with partitions depending on the number of married sons and family members.

Welcoming guests at the Sora Ghar

The last room of the extension is called *Randhoni Ghar* or *Pak Ghor* (Kitchen). Randhoni is a title associated with the female members of the family who are responsible for cooking. One who prepares the meal for the day becomes *Randhoni* of the day. *Randhoni* for the day holds the complete responsibility for managing, preparing, serving food for the family and any guests who visit it. She takes utmost care in satisfying all those, who take their seats to taste the meal prepared by the Randhoni. Meals are generally served at *Randhoni Ghar*. It is arranged in a fashion that members can easily take their seats in a descending order, depending on the age groups. Unless, all the members finish their meal, it is a tradition that one should bear in mind to avoid untimely lifting their hands from the dish/plate as a mark of respect. When all the members have taken their meal, the *Randhoni* sprinkles some water and rubs it on the floor making a circular pattern. This traditionally marks the completion of the meal.

The *Bhoral Ghar* (granary) that lies in the courtyard is apparently more interesting. The *Bhoral* structure is unique, and raised upon nine pieces of wooden logs that are arrayed in rows (see illustration above). These logs are called *Lotikai* that are sometimes huge ranging from 3 to 5 ft in diameter. Use of *Lotikais* in the Bhoral structure, is meant, not only to provide firm support to the entire structure, but also to present the underlying idea of their socio-cultural and economic relationship with their elephants. It is said that in the olden days, rich people among the Moran used to construct many Bhoral ghars, some of which they would construct in the name of their elephants. They do not consume grains from those granaries which are dedicated to their elephants. They would rather spend its grains for the care of their elephants. The Bhoral ghar has four side-walls covered with tightly woven bamboo-matted structure. This raised structure is constructed in a manner that it looks proportionate with the size of logs they use. The roof structure is two-sided and thatched with locally available leaves called *Tokou pat*/or *Jengu Pat*. It is generally believed that the grains should be stuffed inside the Bhoral ghar in such a way that it virtually represents a fully fed and pot-bellied elephant sitting in the yard. The side walls of the granary are used for keeping and hanging agricultural implements, fishing tools and sometimes large sizes ropes for elephants.

There are three other essential structures generally used in every Moran house. These are;

1. *Guhali Ghor* (cow shed)
2. *Tantorhali* (weaving shed)
3. *Hahor Ghoral* (duck enclosure)

The position of the *Guhali Ghor* is generally in the south direction to the Sora Ghor. It is a simple shed without any wall structures. *Guhali Ghor* is used as a cow shed for keeping domesticated cows and bulls. *Tantorhali* is a separate shed prepared at a convenient place to keep looms and other weaving materials. Female members of the family weave clothes in this shed. The position of the *Hahor Ghoral* is generally in the west direction to the *Sora Ghor*. *Hahor Goral* is a circular bamboo enclosure raised and shortened at the top. It is used for keeping ducks, geese etc.

Remembering the past, Shri Tarun Madhav Moran narrates, "two and a half decades ago from now, there were 15 to 20 elephants in every Moran village. The surroundings of Moran inhabiting areas were abundant with large vegetation and thick forests. Those days every family of the Moran was capable of constructing the unique traditional house of this kind. But with the passage of time, the Morans gradually became unable to support their elephants as the forests and grassland were reduced with the intervention of human activities of felling trees and destroying the jungles. Ironically, middle class families among the Morans used to engage their elephants for transporting these very logs from one place to another and earn handsome money and could afford to feed their elephants".[3]

It seems that the traditional design and structure of Moran houses are not only determined by the environmental conditions alone but also reflect a great influence of culturally defined elements that provides a clear picture of their age-old coexistence and harmonious relationship with the elephants. A team of IGRMS conducted extensive field visits to the Moran villages in Tinisukia district of Assam.

During the field visit an attempt was made to collect and transport the material cutural items of the tribe together with traditional housing materials from the villages to IGRMS, which has been successful in adding a traditional Moran house to its open air complex. It was in the month of April and May 2010, a team of Moran people from the villages of the Tinsukia district of Assam were invited by the museum. They had constructed their house and exhibited many items of their cultural belongings. The Moran house as an exhibit is ready and open for the visitors.

C—Tui-Changshu: A Water-Operated Pounding Lever

Among the Kuki tribe, a water-operated husking lever is called Tui-Changshu or Tui-shum. In the past decades husking levers of this kind were extensively used by the tribal villages in many of the hill districts of Manipur.

This unique form of husking lever is still found operational in Haipi village. The village is situated in the foothill of the Sadar Hills about 6 kms west from Kangpokpi Sub-Division in Senapati District of Manipur. The most fascinating aspect of the village is that almost every household possesses Tui-Changsu as one of their important household assets. Water from the fast flowing streams of the hills is diverted to the centre of the village and from there to pass every settlement area for use of this kind of lever by every household and

Haipai village houses with Tui-shum

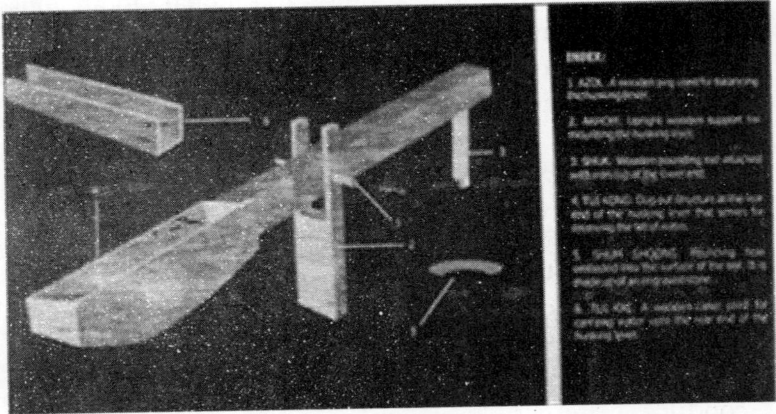

Tui-shum parts

further the lever allows the water to pass their paddy field for irrigation through a small canal.

Tui Shum is about a 12 feet long heavy wooden lever dug out at one end like a Ladle/spoon (see illustration above). The ladle or spoon-shaped structure serves the purpose of receiving water to tread up and down. The other end has a pestle. On the bank of the stream, this wooden lever is mounted on an iron axle supported by two upright posts about 1 to 2 ft above the ground to sustain the level of balance required for the structure. For installing the lever, a small shed is constructed in a way that the spoon-shaped portion of the lever is extended horizontally from the rear wall and left to a level where this spoon shaped structure could receive the fall of water from above and simultaneously can drop it down to a pit with considerable depth lying downwards. A mortar with a cavity engraved in a block of stone is embedded on the floor inside the shed to an exact distance where the jerk of the pestle attached with the lever could be harnessed. From a certain height of about 3-4 ft the water of the running stream is allowed to fall on the dug-out spoon-shaped structure of the lever. When it receives full volume of water, it immediately falls down and drops the water into the pit and again rises quickly in an upward action through a weight loaded at the front end of the lever. This continuous process of treading the lever up and down by the flow of water enables it to function as a unique husking implement. In the morning hours before the family members leave their home for agricultural work, they put some desired quantity of paddy into the cavity of mortar and leave it for pounding till they return. In the evening, it is removed and winnowed to store for their day-to-day consumption. Tui-shum has become one of the items of pride possession among all households of the village. Tui-shum displays not only their ability to use a sustainable technology but also an attempt to live in harmony with nature. It was in 2007 that the Indira Gandhi Rashtriya Manav Sangrahalaya (the National Museum of Mankind), Bhopal, conducted a week long fieldwork in the Haipi village and collected this unique pounding lever from a resident of the village Shri Tongleng Kipgen. Shri Tonglen headed a team of three members. The team was invited to the museum in March 2008 for installation of Tui-shum as an important exhibit that represented the State of Manipur in the Traditional Technology Park—an open air exhibition in the National Museum premises.

D—An Appraisal of the Tribal Museum and Research Centre, Imphal

Tribal Museum and Research Centre (TMRC), Imphal, Manipur, a private museum established in 1987 brought out a very popular programme entitled "Know Your Manipur" in 1997. "Know Your Manipur" as a programme of study tour, adventure, self-discovery began with a three-day tour to Willong Khullen village (see below for its distant view) inhabited by one of the important tribal groups of Manipur called Maram. Thirty-three members from different academic disciplines participated in the tour. The team carried out visual and textual documentation on ethno-cultural aspects of the tribe and soon after one month, the museum conducted another tour to Lunghar village inhabited by the Tangkhul tribe of Manipur under the second phase of the programme. The visual and textual materials collected during the tour were systematically compiled and the findings were published and a book was released in September 1997. The book titled *Know*

Distant view of Willong Khullen village
Senapati District, Manipur (2007)

View of a Rahangki (Boys Dormitory)

Megalithic structures in Willong Khullen village

Your Manipur edited by Salam Rajesh as part of the Museum Publications was indeed a remarkable achievement of the museum not only in disseminating the knowledge of indigenous tribal culture but also gave impetus to the museum movement. Community involvement in the museum programmes gained a new lease of life through the two tours. At the same time, the museum came out with a documentary based on the visual collections. This short film provides important visual information into the colourful culture and tradition of the Maram and Tangkhul tribes. One can view the life and habitat of these tribal populations during the past decade and earlier.

The programme was instrumental in bridging the cultural relations between different ethnic communities. Venturing into the activities of this kind one can definitely feel the sense of communal harmony and respect for other cultures. This I could realize after watching the visuals and reading the book *Know Your Manipur*. I had the opportunity to watch the film *Know Your Manipur* at TMRC, Imphal when I visited the museum on my official tour in 2005.

After watching the film, I became curious to visit Willong Khullen village and after one year our team visited the village with Shri Y. Gyaneshwar, Director, TMRC in 2007. This time I observed a great change in the village as compared to the visuals taken a decade before. I specially visited the village to see the most enchanting view of the hundreds of megalithic monuments erected at the western fringe of the village and also the bedstead installed inside the Rahangki (boy's dormitory) that could accommodate more than 30 persons to sleep on it. Construction work for the *pakka* road was in progress those days and I could see one or two megaliths unearthed and lying on the roadside. We were told that the megalith was removed in order to construct the road. It was indeed a shocking moment for me to see the cultural remains of the past being removed from their original site without care and proper reason. I got deeply hurt again when I saw the damaged condition of a majestic bedstead that was lying inside the Rahangki into two pieces (see illustration on p. 104).

Inside view of Rahangki with bedstead lying in two pieces

I was told that it was cut down at the time of renovating the Rahangki. One of the natives said, "the soil was eroding and the condition was bad and we had to reduce the size of Rahangki. In order to move the rear wall about three or four feet inside we had to cut a piece of our bedstead." Then I came to realize that community consciousness and *in situ* conservation and preservation of material heritage are necessary. We need to conserve their material heritage in a museum. Developing a sense of respect towards the cultural antiquities with historical value is as much required in the tribal and rural villages as in the cases of protected monuments, sites of archaeological importance, cultural institutions, etc. There are still many of the tribal and rural villages where remnants of their ancient past are lying around. It is not possible that all these items are collected and preserved in a museum. There are many items which are sentimentally attached to the life and culture of the individual, family, clan, village or community. In such cases the people will not be motivated to hand them over to a museum. In such cases *in situ* conservation plays an important role that applies not only to the material conservation but also to the community awareness programme that could generate a sense of love and respect for material culture of their the past. Proper documentation with better exposition of the intangible value of the object under the curatorship of the people concerned would be an effective medium of preserving the cultures of the past. This would indirectly benefit the community concerned to develop the village into a living heritage and these resources of their ancient past would undoubtedly become an important source of their earnings. Compared to earlier times now people are anxious to visit the places and to spend the money when they can experience something different.

It is the right time for the museums to organize the programmes of cultural expedition that could give the visitors a warm feeling of cultural experiences and work as an interface between the visitors and the cultural communities.

E—Rushem: A Traditional Wind Instrument[2]

Rushem (see illustration below) being an important accompaniment of song and dance is played on every festive and ceremonial occasion among the Kom people and other Kuki-Chin tribal groups of Manipur. It is a wind instrument prepared by master craftsmen in a local fashion by using locally available materials like bamboo, dry gourd, bee-wax, powder of conch-shells and feathers of a cock.

November and December are the right months to collect fine props of bamboo to be used as wind pipes of different sizes to be passed inside the body of a gourd from six different holes to produce different tunes of a defined note and scale. The interesting part of Rushem is the appropriate use of a bitter-gourd/bottle gourd shell (*Langenaria siceraria*) (See illustration at right) as resonator.

The bitter gourd either wild or planted in the surrounding field or homestead land is given appropriate care and protection from any kind of unwanted damage or loss till it is collected. It is harvested when the lower part of the body

Rushem: A traditional wind instrument

turns brown in colour. The upper layer (skin) of the gourd selected for the preparation of Rushem is scraped with a sharp knife and it is exposed to the sun for a few days. For further seasoning, it is kept above the hanging platform of the fireplace (hearth) to get constantly fumigated. This traditional method of preservation is applied to prevent the instrument from unwanted attack of insects and termites. Similarly, small bamboo props/reeds are also seasoned to be used while preparing Rushem.

Bitter gourd ready to harvest for preparing the Rushem shell

Rushem consists of a resonating body prepared from the shell of the bottle gourd. It is six reeds of bamboo with buzzers (*Rushem Jang*) made from a thin plate of brass fixed uniformly in each of the wind pipes by inserting into the holes as arrayed in the figure illustrated below. The upper holes contain three large size *Kache* (bamboo reeds/wind pipe) while the other three are fitted in a specified order just below the upper holes. While fitting these wind pipes bee-wax is used to conceal the holes tightly. Each of these *Kache* bears holes called Khor and is used to play different tunes and notes. A bellow (*Atumna*), made of bamboo pipe is inserted from the mouth of the gourd. This bellow contains a notch near the bottom called *Athi Supna* for

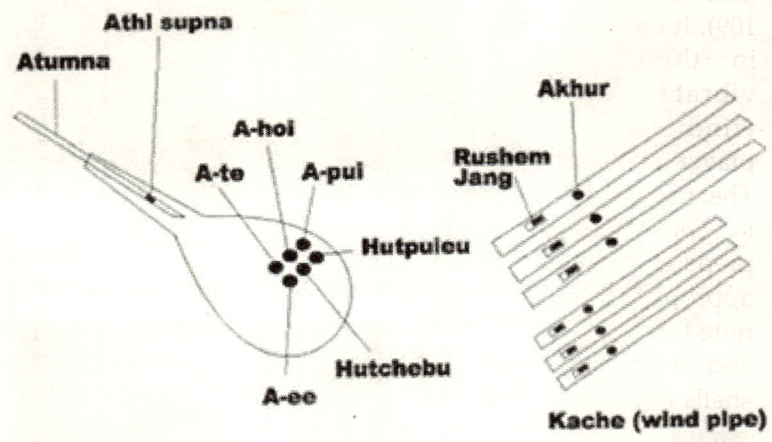

Parts of Rushem

supplying wind uniformly into the shell to resonate from the vibrating sound of the buzzer. The buzzer, being the most important part of the Rushem, creates desirable sounds and notes. It is meaningfully represented by the name *Rushem Jung* which literally means the root/genital of Rushem. According to a folk belief, 'Rushem Jung is the divine representation of the father, the creator while the womb-shaped body represents the divine mother. The divine union creates the most enchanting and beautiful sound of Rushem'.

Rushem Jung as an important textile motif (see illustration on p. 109) are also found in the woven designs of prestigious tribal gowns and ceremonial shawls, which are especially worn by the chieftain and noble family during special social events.

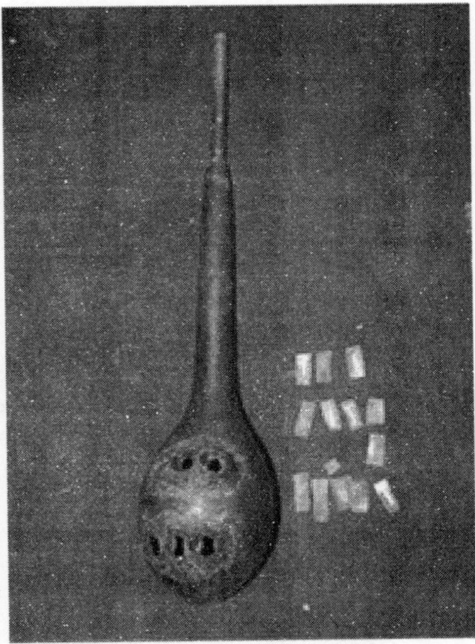
Bottle-gourd showing six holes and metal buzzers

Rushem Jung's buzzer is prepared from a thin plate of rectangular brass (see illustration on p. 109). It contains a trigger in the middle that vibrates through the wind blown by the player from the bellow. The trigger of the plate is sharpened and prepared very fine till the appropriate sound is attained. When the desirable sound and note from the buzzer is attained, it is fitted into the wind pipe and sealed with paste prepared from the powder of conch shells obtained by rubbing on stone. According to traditional

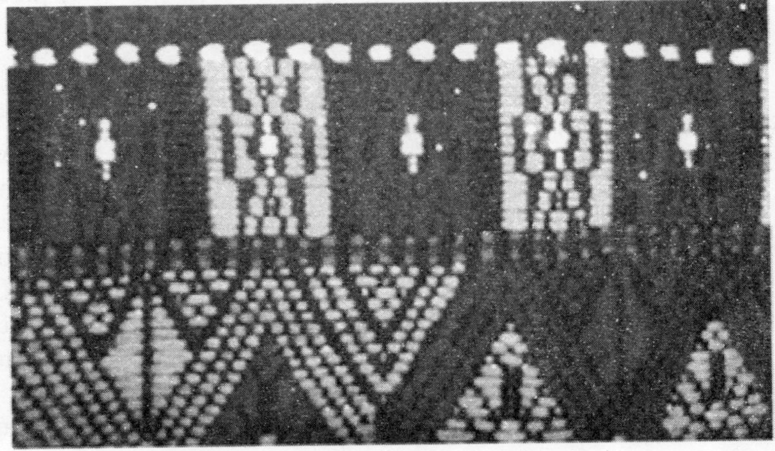
Textile motif showing *Rushem Jung* (in colour)

Kom belief, 'preparation of Rushem must undergo the ceremonial conduct.' The Rushem-maker has to perform sanctification rites with the help of a priest before it is prepared.

Nowadays, only a few elderly people from Kom villages know this age-old craft of making Rushem. This traditional folk instrument having accumulated native cultural elements provides valuable insights into the socio-cultural and religious life of the Kom tribe.

NOTES

1. Based on the information collected by the author during field work and documentation on the Heritage of Kom tribe organised at Khoirentak Khuman village, Churachandpur District, Manipur.
2. Based on the field documentation held at Khoirentak Khuman, Kom Village, Manipur.

References

Dutta, S. 1985. *The Mataks and Their Kingdom; Castes and Tribes of Assam.* Allahabad: Chugh publications.

Sen, Sipra (1999). *Tribes and Castes of Assam; Anthropology and Sociology.* Delhi: Gyan Publishing House.

PART TWO:
INTERVIEWS

Preface to the Interviews

IGRMS has the reputation of being the biggest open air museum in Asia. The sheer expanse occupied by it and the siting of museum objects within it make it a distinctive cultural display in the country. IGRMS grew far beyond the imagination of its founders. The annals of the institution show how it was initially conceived as a repository of India's diverse culture. The initial correspondence between the social anthropologist M.N. Srinivas and Mrs. Indira Gandhi, then Prime Minister of India, bears testimony to their vision of this Museum of Mankind as a show-case of Indian culture to the world at large. The sheer expanse of the space eventually made available to the IGRMS, however, fired the imagination of its early curators/directors to raise something on a grand scale. The story of the gradual building of this Museum of Mankind is told in so many words by the curators interviewed by me in the following pages. Also, they all, in one way or another, underscore the live culture aspect of this museum. Let me try and explain in a nutshell the emergence and shaping of this live cultural repository, and I do so by simply focusing on the development of what are known as Tribal Habitats (TH) in IGRMS. Without fail, the growth of IGRMS and personal encounters of the various curators narrate the story of TH.

Tribal Habitat as a genre idea belongs to the entirely legitimate and valued aspect of Indian culture, namely, its dynamism displayed in architecture, story, dance, art, music, styles of living, ritual—in other words, all the performative aspects of human life. Once space, in terms of the sheer expanse of land, became available to IGRMS it became possible to conceive implanting of the diverse cultural heritage of India—in all its performative richness—in the space provided. It was a propitious bounty for IGRMS to have been provided a site with ancient rock shelters, a gently unadulating land and its location, beautifully, on the edge of Bhopal lake. All these elements, as we shall see, have been incorporated and deployed in the scheme of the Tribal Habitat. Let me here itself reiterate, as I pointed out earlier, that TH is, in the context of IGRMS, a 'genre idea'. By this one means that though there is a prefix 'tribal' to habitat, in fact all the variety of tribal and rural habitation and its performative culture is sought to be

A Naga house in IGRMS

represented at IGRMS *in situ*. Thus, whereas there are replicas of genuine tribal houses from different parts of India, there is also the recreation of the rich rural coastal culture of Kerala and *haveli* type of residential structures from Rajasthan. Further, the genre idea has meant constant interaction, from the time of transportation of men and materials imported from these distant areas, with communities that actually lead the lives represented here, in their natural habitats. Thus troupes of communities from Manipur, Kerala, Odisha, and Madhya Pradesh are invited to perform in the open air spaces though encompassing especially the spaces occupied their TH. The genre idea has been successfully implemented as particular regional festivals with their own dance-drama, music, ritual, and cuisine, are presented in the open campus that is IGRMS. It is noteworthy that regional cultural performances take place also in remote tribal and rural areas by troupes of collectors and performing artistes who go there in search of objects and ideas for IGRMS. These outreach programmes generate reciprocal interest between groups of performing artistes from different regions. And, as narrated in the testimonies of my interviewees, the linkages are of an enduring nature so much so, that artistes from the Kerala region when they visit IGRMS in Bhopal, speak of these journeys as visits to their own distant villages in another part of India!

In its own way, the genre idea of IGRMS has given rise to discovering, restoring, and in some areas, even initiating, indigenous museum movements and practices in different parts of the country. Sample, for instance, the Majuli river island Vaishnavite centre in Assam and the recovery and celebration of rich Vaishnavite heritage in West Bengal. Since IGRMS curators often themselves hail from different regions of India, they bring to bear in their collection and interpretation the genuine colouring of the culture areas they come from. Two more features of the initial and in-house training of these curators add a special flavour to their endeavour. Firstly, a majority of them are graduates of socio-cultural anthropology and a remarkably increasing number of them have either qualified for PhD degrees in the subject or weave in, effortlessly, their field data being gathered for higher degrees, in their display and interpretation of museum collections.

I invite the readers of the following interviews to savour all the features listed above. Let me add, finally, that the transcribed interview texts have been edited very lightly. I have deliberately tried to preserve the flavour of oral narration, even at the risk of ignoring sometimes grammatical infelicities or variations in pronunciation (e.g. Halwa or Halba). My interviewees were self-conscious about their lack of facility in textual articulation of their ideas and experiences. In what follows I have tried not to mow down with a heavy editorial hand something that is distinctive of face-to-face oral narration in our interaction.

So that the spirit of these interviews is preserved, let me say that we had consensus on some of the ways in which these conversations were conducted. It was made amply clear that the interviewees were the real 'heroes' of the project and that their personal views were being solicited. If the latter were of a critical nature, that tone will have to be preserved in the transcripts. The criticisms conveyed in their own words are meant to be taken in a positive spirit. In that sense, even though IGRMS emerges as a unique and commendable institution, like any other institution, it has gaps that need to be filled in order to improve its present condition.

संग्रहालय में मैं आदिवासी

अरुण कीरो

अरुण कीरो, मैं आपसे जानना चाहूंगा कि शुरु में आपकी शिक्षा कहां हुई? आप कब से मानव संग्रहालय में आए? इसके पहले कहां थे?

मेरी शिक्षा रांची में हुई। वहां नृविज्ञान में बी ए (ऑनर्स) करने के बाद रांची विश्वविद्यालय में ही नृविज्ञान में सामाजिक और सांस्कृतिक specilisation को लेकर एम.ए. किया। पास होने के बाद लगभग आठ महीने तक मैंने विश्वविद्यालय में ही अनुसंधान किया था। इस दौरान मेरे गुरु विद्यार्थी साहब (Prof. L. P. Vidyarthi) का निधन हो गया, उसके बाद जो मुझे support मिलना था वह नहीं मिल पाया फिर लगभग आठ या दस महीने तक बेकार रहने के साथ competition के लिए तैयारी की। उसके बाद यहां job के लिये apply किया। यहां साक्षात्कायर के लिए आया और नियुक्ति मिलने पर यहां join किया। उस वक्त आर. एस. नेगी निदेशक थे। मैंने 1987 में 8 जून को यहां join किया। नृविज्ञान का विद्यार्थी होने के नाते मेरे मन में म्यूज़ियम के बारे में अवधारणा यही थी कि चारों तरफ़ दीवारें होंगी और सब सामान वहां सुरक्षित रखा होगा। यहां आने के बाद उसी दिन मुझे प्रशासनिक अधिकारी श्रीवास्तव जी और एक अधिकारी सुरजीत सोम मानव संग्रहालय ले आए। उस समय यहां बड़ी मुश्किल से जीप घुस पाई। वे दोनों बोले, तुम्हारी ड्यूटी कल से है। दो तीन दिन होटल में रहने के बाद मैंने किराये का मकान देखा। फिर वहां से सुबह आता था। यहां तो कुछ नहीं था। एक कप चाय पीने के लिये भी पहाड़ी से उतर कर नीचे जाना पड़ता था।

आपको उन्होंने क्या बतलाया, कि आपकी ड्यूटी क्या होगी?

मुझे मज़दूरों को मैनेज करना था। उस वक्त यहां निर्माण कार्य हो रहा था। एक बहुत बड़ा सहारा यह मिला कि उस वक्त निदेशक नेगी साहब ने यहां आने की अपनी दिनचर्या बना ली। कार्यालय उस समय यहां से करीब दस किलोमीटर दूर हुआ करता था। मैं यहां संग्रहालय की साइट पर अकेला था। हमेशा शाम को

कार्यालय बंद होने के बाद नेगी साहब यहां आते थे, मुझे बिठाकर बातें करते थे कि यहां ऐसी योजना है, कैसे करना है फिर धीरे-धीरे मजदूरों के साथ मैं काम में लग गया? कभी देर हो गई तो रात में रुक कर संग्रहालय में काम की जगह ही मजदूरों के साथ खाना खाकर सो जाता था? मैंने एक बार अपने बड़े भाई को फ़ोन किया। वे बोकारो स्टील नगर में व्यक्तिगत अधिकारी थे। उन्होंने पूछा कि नौकरी कैसी चल रही है? जब मैंने बताया कि मज़दूरों को manage करता हूं तो वे बोले कि तुम श्रम निरीक्षक बन गये हो परंतु तुम तो एक मानव विज्ञानी की हैसियत से संग्रहालय में गए थे? मैंने बताया कि मेरी ग़लतफ़हमी थी कि भोपाल में मानव संग्रहालय है। अभी तो यहां ओपन एयर संग्रहालय की अवधारणा मात्र है इसीलिए ऐसी स्थिति है। प्रोफेसर सचिन रॉय संग्रहालय के संस्थापक के रूप में जाने जाते हैं। उन्होंने बैंगलौर में मानवविज्ञान कांग्रेस में ओपन एअर संग्रहालय की अवधारणा को रखा था। यह 1975 या 1976 की बात है। आज मैं गर्व से कह सकता हूं कि यही ओपन एअर संग्रहालय का मूल था? आदिवासी habitat को बनाने में मेरा भी महत्वहपूर्ण योगदान है।

आपने सबसे पहले कौन सा habitat बनवाया?

पहले Agariya बना था। लेकिन उसको दूसरी जगह बनवाना पड़ा क्योंकि पहली जगह नियोजन की कुछ परेशानियां हुईं। इस वजह से वह लगभग टूट सा गया था? उसका माप लेकर उसको अलग जगह shift करवाया था। यह बन जाने के बाद स्वतंत्र रूप से बिहार में संथाल जनजाति पर एक प्रोजेक्ट था। मैं अपने कालेज के समय में भी विद्यार्थी साहब के साथ डुमका गया था? वहां मिटटी के घर इतने खूबसूरत थे कि उन्होंने मेरे मन को मोह लिया था। यहां आने के बाद मैंने यह सोचा कि उनका घर यहां क्यों नहीं हो सकता? फिर उसको एक प्रोजेक्ट का आकार दिया और उस समय के निदेशक चक्रवर्ती साहब को सबमिट किया। मैंने उनको आश्वासित किया। एक बार क्षेत्र के काम पर गया तो कुछ तस्वीरें लेकर आया। तब वह बोले 'कोशिश करिए'।

तब फिर कैसे बन पाया? आपने क्या किया?

डुमका एक बहुत पारंपरिक जगह है जहां आदिवासियों का एक कार्यालय है। वहां संपर्क किया। उन्होंने कहा कि अगर आपको परम्परा देखनी है तो गांव में जाना और लगभग चार दिन गांव में रुकना भी। वहां हर दृष्टि से मुझे एक घर बहुत पसंद आया। मैंने उसकी पूरी तस्वीर का प्रलेखन किया, स्केच किया, सब कुछ माप किया। माल क्या क्या लगेगा और फिर सारा काम परियोजना की शक्ल में बदल

करके उसका यहां दिया और निदेशक ने उसका अनुमोदन किया। उसके बाद मैं डुमका गया। वहां के लोगों से बातें कीं। उसी गांव के सरपंच बोले कि मैं आपको सब अभी दे सकता हूं फिर वे दस लोगों को लेकर आए। उसमें चार महिलाएं थीं और छह पुरुष थे। उस छह में दो बढ़ई थे और दो mason थे।

एक बार गये, दो बार गये तो आप टीम में जाते थे या अकेले जाते थे?

अकेले। जैसे मैं फोटोग्राफ़ी भी खुद ही कर रहा था। उस समय छोटा हैंडी कैमरा हुआ करता था। जिस में बड़ा रोल लगता था। दो तीन रोल यहीं से ले जाता था व क्लिक करता रहता था। तब निश्चित रूप से समझ में आया कि जैसे मैं कुछ नया काम कर रहा हूं। क्योंकि मैं खुद एक जनजातीय समुदाय का हूं तो मुझे गांव में जाने व रहने में कभी कोई परेशानी नहीं हुई। बल्कि मुझे काफ़ी आसानी हुई। परंपरा और प्रकृति के साथ जुड़े हुए समुदाय की सोच सभी जनजातियों में लगभग बराबर है। मुझे कुछ चीज़ों को समझने में बहुत आसानी होती थी। या अगर कुछ दिक्कतें हुईं तो मैं वहां के लोगों से पूछ लेता था इसलिए कि वे तो सब कुछ जानते ही थे।

A Tribal Shrine

यहां habitats बनाने के अलावा आपने क्या कुछ objects भी collect किये थे?

जी हाँ। मैं वहां से उनके कृषि और मछली पकड़ने के व शिकार के implements

लाया। एक resource व्यक्ति ढूंढ कर उसके माध्यम से मैं collection के लिये जाता हूं। ऐसा नहीं होता है कि हमेशा आपका resource person सही व्यक्ति हो। कभी कभी वह एक बिचौलिया की भूमिका निभाता है। मैं एक सच्ची घटना बताता हूं।

1990 में मैं टाटा नगर से थोड़ा सा आगे खड़गपुर गया था। वहां पहाड़ी खारिया रहते हैं। असल में एक खारिया होते हुए भी मैंने पहाड़ी खारिया को कभी नहीं देखा था, तो मन में interest हो गया था। खंड विकास अधिकारी से बात की तो उन्होंने location बताई। उसने कहा कि हमारे यहां एक इंस्पैक्टर है उनको आपके साथ में भेज दूंगा। कोई दिक्कत नहीं होगी। मैंने कहा यह तो अच्छी बात है। वह बोले जिस दिन हाट है आप हाट attend करिए तो कुछ चीज़ें भी आपको मिल जाएंगी और सभी तरह के लोग देखने को मिलेंगें। हाट के दिन मैं वहां गया बहुत सारी चीज़ें देखीं। कुछ अच्छी चीज़ें मैंने खरीद भी लीं। जो मेरे साथ इंस्पैक्टर था उसको पीने की आदत थी। यह मैं नहीं जानता था। उसने जनजाति के साथ यह बिठा लिया था कि मुझे दारु पिलाओ नहीं तो मैं आपको चीज़े नहीं बेचने दूंगा। बात यह है कि एक object की कीमत निर्धारित करने में देखा जाता है कि object बनाने में कितने दिन लगे होंगे। एक दिन जंगल जाकर आदिवासी material लाया होगा। दो दिन object को बनाने में लगा होगा। तो local कीमत के हिसाब से कम से कम तीन दिन की मजदूरी तो आदिवासी को मिलनी चाहिए। बाजार में उन्हीं के भाई लोग खरीदेंगे तो पांच रुपये कम करके देंगे। क्योंकि मैं सोचता हूं कि ये उनका अधिकार है कि उनको पांच रुपये अधिक मिलें। इसलिए ज़्यादा लोग मुझे सामान देने को तैयार हो गये। वहां की स्थानीय भाषा में इंस्पैक्टर ने उनसे कहा कि मुझे दारु पिलाओ नहीं तो मैं सामान बेचने नहीं दूंगा। उन्होंने उसको पिला दिया और वह control के बाहर हो गया। फिर वहां लड़ाई हो गई व लड़ाई होने के बाद वे लोग मुझे मारने को उतरे। मैं रात में आठ किलोमीटर पैदल भागा। कंधे पर एक musical drum था क्योंकि उसका पैसा मैं pay कर चुका था और अपना एक बैग जिसमें कुछ ज़रूरी कागज़ थे, उनको लेकर भागा और भागने के बाद वहां भी नहीं रुका। घाटशीला आया। मन में अभी भी भय हो रहा था। अतः मैं वहां से जमशेदपुर भाग गया।

दरअसल चीज़ें बहुत सारी हैं। जैसे मैंने बचपन में देखा था कि उस समय घड़ी नहीं हुआ करती थी। मिट्टी के बर्तन में पानी भरकर टांग देते थे। एक तरफ़ उसमें छेद कर देते थे। पानी खत्म हुआ तो एक घंटा खत्म हुआ। लेकिन जब तक इन चीज़ों के बारे में कुछ करने के लिये अपने पास मंच होता है उसमें कुछ दूसरी

अड़चनें आ जाती हैं। उदाहरणत: मेरे पैतृक गांव में जहां अभी भी खेती है, एक बारिश होने के बाद वहां ढिंढोरा होता है। ढिंढोरा मतलब इस रविवार को रोपा होगा। रोपा मतलब वो अलग अलग मौसम में सबके पास अपने घर में जो भी फल के बीज मिले हैं वे हैं। बारिश हुई तो ढिंढोरा हो गया। सब झोले में बीज लेकर जंगल निकल गए। लकड़ी के बीच कहीं यहां दो बीज डाल दिया, वहां चार डाल दिया। पूरे गांव के इस पार उस पार बीज डाल देते हैं। स्वदेशी प्रणाली है। अभी उन्हीं लोगों को जंगल के अंदर जाने से मना कर दिया गया है। जिन लोगों ने उनको रोपा जिन्होंने उसको बढ़ाया उनको वहां जाने से रोक दिया गया है। यह अजीब बात है।

यहां संग्रहालय में हमें धीरे-धीरे यह अनुभव होने लगा कि हम tribal habitat की देखभाल के लिये हमेशा वहां के लोगों को नहीं बुला सकते हैं। तो हमने दैनिक देखभाल के लिये दो तीन किशोर श्रमिकों को ट्राइबल एरिया से आये हुए लोगों के साथ रख दिया ताकि वे उनसे दैनिक देखभाल सीख लें और फिर साल में एक बार जो प्रमुख देखभाल है उसके लिये ट्राइबल एरिया के लोगों को बुलाते हैं। एक बार उड़ीसा से जनजातीय अनुसंधान संस्थान की एक टीम आई थी। यहां की देखभाल के बारे में उनकी राय जानकर मुझे संतुष्टि ही हुई। मैं अन्य अधिकारियों के बारे में नहीं कहूँगा। पर उड़ीसा के अधिकारियों की बातों से मुझे लगा कि मेरा प्रयास कुछ हद तक सफल हुआ। उनमें से दो लोगों ने कहा कि हम यहां पर Gadaba tribe का model (परिपत्र) मकान देखने आये है, आज उड़ीसा में ऐसे घर नहीं मिलते।

अच्छा यह देखने के लिये वे लोग यहां आये?

हमने यहां Gadaba का जो पारंपरिक घर बनाया है, वह बिल्कुल परंपरागत घर का वास्तविक पतिदर्श (model) है जिसकी conical छत है। लेकिन आज वहां आयत आकार और चारों ओर छत ढलान में बदल दी गई है। हमारे प्रकार का model आज उड़ीसा में देखने को नहीं मिलता। यहां पर preserve करके रखा गया है व अच्छी तरह से बनाकर रखा है।

अपनी जनजाति के आप सदस्य है और वहां के लोगों का आप पर पूरा विश्वास है, परंतु अन्य आदिवासियों के साथ आपका कुछ प्रतिरोध तो नहीं होता है?

होता है। मैं एक बार Homunda जनजाति में गया था। यह उड़ीसा झारखंड और पश्चिम बंगाल की सीमा पर रहती है। वहां उन्होंने सब कुछ दिखाया व अपना संगीत सुनाया और बताया कि ये ड्रम है, ये बांसुरी है, ये क्लिपर है। फिर उन्होंने एक सवाल उठाया कि आप Homunda जनजाति को अपने संग्रहालय के माध्यम

से प्रसिद्ध करेंगे। उससे हमको क्या मिलेगा? मैंने कहा कि देखिए मैं कुछ भी नहीं दे सकता लेकिन एक एक खंड पर हम काम करके आपकी पहचान बनाने की कोशिश कर रहे हैं। उन्होंने कहा कि श्रीमान उस पहचान से हमारा पेट नहीं भरेगा। तो कहीं न कहीं मेरे मन में उनका प्रश्न बना रहा था। उसके बाद सन् 1996 या 1997 में जब चर्चा चली कि एक आदिवासी त्यौहार जैसा अवसर मनाया जाये जहां आगंतुकों के लिये शिल्प वस्तुएं उपलब्ध हों। मुझे लगा कि अगर हम उनके शिल्प को खरीद कर यहां आगंतुकों के लिये उपलब्ध करें तो कुछ हद तक उनकी रोज़ी रोटी में एक मदद होगी। इसी चीज को ध्यान में रखकर संग्रहालय में दुकान बनाई गई। बाज़ार के मेलों की तुलना में यहां कम कीमत में सामान मिलता है। क्योंकि हम कोई लाभ उठाने की कोशिश नहीं करते हैं। एक आदिवासी अगर हमें कोई वस्तु बीस रुपए में बेचे तो उसमें केवल बीस प्रतिशत ही बढ़ा कर हम बेचते हैं। इस बीस प्रतिशत में से दुकान में नियुक्त आदमी का वेतन जाता है क्योंकि उसकी एक नियमित रूप से लगाई हुई पोस्ट है। बीच में कोई बिचौलिया नहीं है। आदिवासी स्वयं आता है, यहां सामान देता है तथा दाम लेकर चला जाता है।

उत्तर पूर्व में मैंने असम से काम शुरु किया। वहां गुवाहाटी में मेरे ताऊ जी रहा करते थे। वे एक compounder थे। वास्तव में असम की मदर टेरेसा के रूप में उन्हें जाना जाता था। वे अपनी साइकिल के रैक पर छोटे मोटे आपरेशन थिएटर का सामान लेकर घूमते थे। बहुत बार उपचार के लिए उनकी kidnapping भी हुई थी। अपने पक्ष के लिए मैंने उनके नाम का बहुत उपयोग किया। हाल ही में एक घटना हुई थी। असम में Bharbita नामक एक झील है। मुझे पता चला कि वहां एक पेड़ है जिसका पीतल का आधार बहुत सजावटी है। उस पीतल की खली में काफ़ी कुछ बना हुआ है, कहीं तितली बनी हुई हैं, कहीं कुछ और है। उनके मिथक में कहीं यह भी है कि जब एक बच्चे का जन्म होता है उसी समय खली बनाई जाती है और उस में बच्चे की प्रतीकात्मक जन्म कुंडली बनती है।

अच्छा प्रतीकात्मक जन्म कुंडली बनाई जाती है?

जी। गुवाहाटी में भी लोगों से मैंने इस बारे में जानने की बहुत कोशिश की। उन्होंने कहा कि उन्होंने ऐसा कहीं नहीं पढ़ा। मैंने पूछा कि क्या आपकी कहानियों में कुछ ऐसा है। मुझे एक गांव के बुजुर्ग ने ही यह बताया था। जब मैं वहां गया तो वहां एक आइ. ए. एस. अधिकारी पुरुषोतम दास नाम के सांस्कृतिक सचिव थे। मैंने उन्हें बताया कहा कि मैं वहां जा रहा हूं। तो उन्होंने कहा कि मैं तुम्हें वहाँ जाने की अनुमति नहीं देता। आप नलबाड़ी पार करके जाओगे जो आतंकवाद का मुख्यालय माना जाता है। मैं आपको वहां जाने के लिये कभी सुझाव नहीं दूंगा, मैंने

उनसे कहा कि मैं तो जाउंगा ही। उन्होंने कहा कि आप अपने जोखिम पर जा रहे हैं। शाम को उनके घर पर जो आदिवासी आते थे उनसे बात करके उन्होंने उस गांव का पता किया जहां पीतल धातु शिल्प करने वाला आदमी रहता था। उसका पता लेकर उन्होंने एक आदमी को मेरे साथ कर दिया कि आप इनके साथ चले जाइए। यह तय हुआ कि सवेरे जो ड्राइवर मैंने hire किया था वह उस आदमी को लेकर सर्किट हाउस आएगा। फिर सर्किट हाउस से मैं चलूंगा। सवेरे मैं आया तो ड्राइवर के साथ एक दूसरा आदमी आया जिसने कहा कि उस आदमी की तबियत कुछ ठीक नहीं थी तो उसने अपने चचेरे भाई को भेज दिया था। नलबाड़ी enter करने के पहले military का एक बहुत बड़ा check post है। मेरे साथ वाले आदमी ने ड्राइवर से असमी में कुछ बात की और फिर check post की तरफ़ गया। ड्राइवर चल पड़ा तो मैंने पूछा कि भाई साहब क्या हुआ। ड्राइवर बोला कि वह आदमी आगे मिलेगा। आगे जाकर शहर पार करने के बाद, बाहरी चैक-पोस्ट से निकलने के बाद वह आदमी हमें उधर मिला। तब भी मुझे कुछ नहीं लगा कि ऐसा क्यों हुआ। गांव जाकर जब सामान देखा तो मैंने owner से कहा कि देखिए मेरी एक समस्या है कि मैं इस object का नौ हजार नौ सौ निन्यानवे से अधिक नहीं दे सकता। दस हजार होने से हमको सरपंच बुलाकर कमिटी करनी होगी। इसमें समय लगेगा। तभी लागत प्रमाणित होगी। तो owner बार बार घर के अंदर गया व कुछ बात करके आया। उसने कहा कि पंद्रह हजार के बिना वह object को नहीं दे सकता है। मैंने कहा कि मुझे क्षमा करें। अगर आप मुझे सरपंच उपलब्ध करा सकते हैं तब मैं उतना भी देने को तैयार हूं। फिर बाद में owner ने कहा कि सब बुला रहे हैं। मैंने पूछा कौन सब? उसने कहा कि उधर हैं। अंदर तीन लोग बैठे थे जो मेरे साथ आदमी आया था वह उनके साथ बैठा था। उसने अपनी पहचान देने के लिए बार-बार revolver का head मुझे दिखाया। तब मुझे strike किया कि यह मामला गड़बड़ है। अंदर-अंदर तो भय बहुत हो गया। तो फिर मैंने अपने ताऊजी का reference दिया। तो वे बोले, "क्या आप उनको जानते हैं?" उन लोगों ने कहा कि उनकी तबियत खराब हो गयी तथा वे तो मर गये। हम लोग उनके burial पर गये थे। हमको बहुत दुख लगा था। फिर कहा कि ठीक है आप पैसे दे दो। मैंने कहा देखिए मेरे पास सिर्फ पांच हजार रुपये हैं अत:अभी कीमत इतनी ही होगी। उन्होंने कहा कि ठीक है तो आप owner को उस object की कीमत चार हजार नौ सौ रुपए दिलवाइए। आप से सर्किट हाउस में सुबह आठ बजे कोई आकर पैसा ले लेगा। मैंने पूछा कि मुझे कैसे मालूम किसको पैसा देना है। उन्होंने कहा कि owner ने आपको नौ हजार नौ सौ की रसीद दे दी है। पैसे तो हमें आपसे मिल ही

जाएंगे। मेरी वापसी के समय मेरे साथ वाला आदमी फिर बाहरी check post के पहले चला गया और फिर check post की entry की दूसरी तरफ़ मिला। साफ़ था कि वहां के गांवों में आतंकवादियों की सलाह के बिना गांव वाले कुछ भी नहीं कर सकते हैं।

अच्छी वस्तुओं का संग्रहालय में प्रदर्शन है। और उनके साथ जुड़ी कहानियां हैं, क्या संग्रहालय में आने वाले आगंतुकों को आप इनके बारे में बतलाते हैं?

जब व्यक्ति विशेष या किसी समूह को गाइड करने के लिये अवसर होता है। विशेषकर समूह को गाइड करने का। उस समय अगर मैं गाइड कर रहा हूँ तो मैं अपने विशिष्टव अनुभवों के आधार पर उनको ज़्यादा विवरण दे सकता हूं। Video की सहायता से भंडारण या collections के बारे में visitors को जानकारी देने के लिये हमलोगों ने कोशिश की है। और काम चल रहा है। प्रोफेसर बास्सा जब director थे उस समय उन्होंने मुझे बताया कि यूनेस्को में आजकल ऐसा काम चल रहा है। क्या हम भी कुछ ऐसा कर सकते हैं? मैंने सोचा यह तो बहुत अच्छी बात है। संग्रहालय की दुकान पर भी भीड़ कुछ कम हो जाएगी। इस दुकान में स्थान सीमित है। उन्होंने पूछा कैसे करोगे। फिर मैंने कुछ योजना बनाई और उनको दिखाई जो उनको पसंद आई। उन्होंने बताया कि दस नंबर गैलरी में नेत्रहीन के लिए 17 कार्यात्मक श्रेणियां बनाई गईं हैं और household से काम शुरु किया जाना है। पहले हमनें terracotta की वस्तुओं को रखा। फिर लकड़ी पर आये। फिर धातु पर आये। इसी तरह संगीत को अलग-अलग किया। ध्वनि के अनुसार वाद्य में एकल membrane, डबल membrane, tambourine, फिर स्ट्रिंग में विभिन्न प्रकार के वायलिन व सितार। फिर हवा के माध्यम से बजाने वाले वाद्य में बांसुरी और कुछ हाथ से घुमाकर बजाने वाला वाद्य रखे। इस तरह से अलग अलग करके 17 श्रेणियां बनाई हैं। दस नंबर गैलरी का नाम दृश्य भंडारण ही है। उसमें साढ़े चार हजार सामान रखे हुए हैं। यह काम सभी को काफ़ी पसंद आया था।

मेरी यात्राएं और अनुभव

एस. के. रावत

आप यहां कब आए और इसके पहले कहां थे?

1981 में मैं संग्रहालय में आया। इसके पहले 1977 में मैंने Assam University से M.Sc. किया। उसके बाद मैं सीधे 1981 में यहाँ आया। संग्रहालय के बारे पहले तो मैं नहीं जानता था। फिर यहाँ आने के बाद सारी चीज़ों की जानकारी मिली कि मानव संग्रहालय क्या है। जब मैं field पर गया, मुझे अधिक मालूम हुआ।

आपने field trip के बारे में लिखा है?

जी, जब यहाँ एक हिंदी प्रतियोगिता हुई थी तभी मैंने यात्रा संस्मरण लिखा था। संग्रहालय में थोड़े से experience के बाद मेरा पहला टूर हुआ। उस समय आने जाने के इतने साधन नहीं हुआ करते थे। मध्य प्रदेश में बैगा एक tribe है। जो मांडला, डिंडोरी में अधिक पाई जाती है (आजकल तो डिंडोरी जिला बन गया है। पहले यह तहसील हुआ करता था।) आज से लगभग तीस साल पहले 1981 में बैगा तक पहुँचना बहुत मुश्किल था। वहाँ तक पहुंचने का अपना अनुभव मैंने उस यात्रा संस्मरण में लिखा था। उसके बाद 1984 में मैं भोंदुप tribe में गया। यह tribe उड़ीसा में है। मैं और सोम साहब हम दोनों वहां गये थे। यह भी अन्य जगहों से अलग-थलग कटी हुई एक जगह है। उस समय वहां जाने के लिए commissioner से permission लेनी पड़ती थी। वह जगह दुर्गम थी। उस समय राज्य सरकार की Bhondup Development Agency (BDA) हुआ करती थी, जिसने भोंदुप के लिए थोड़ा काम चालू किया था। भोंदुप के नीचे BDA का एक आश्रम था। वहाँ तक हम दोनों किसी तरह बड़ी मुश्किल से पहुँच गये। मैं और सुरजीत सोम साहब। हम दोनों वहाँ तक पहुंचे। वहाँ BDA का एक दो कमरे का मकान था। उसको वे लोग guest house की तरह इस्तेमाल करते थे। जब भी कोई आते थे, कोई agency के development officer या कोई और आते तो वहाँ

रुकते थे। हम वहाँ रूके हुए थे। सुबह सोम साहब कुछ पता करने के लिए भोंदुप लोगों के बीच गये। सामने पहाड़ था। उसके ऊपर दुसरे साइड पर बताया गया कि भोंदुप लोगों का गांव है। थोड़ी देर में हम क्या देखते हैं कि पहाड़ के ऊपर काले काले कुछ लोग आये। ठण्ड का मौसम था और पूरी पहाड़ी पर सरसों लगी हुई थी। बहुत खूबसूरत नज़ारा था। पीली-पीली पूरी पहाड़ी। उस पीले पहाड़ के बीच में हमने देखा कि कुछ हिल रहा है। उस वक्त हम वरांडे में बैठे थे। थोड़ी देर में हमने देखा कि काले काले से आदमी दिख रहे थे। तकरीबन सौ दो सौ फुट की दूरी थी। हमने देखा कि चुपके से आदमी आगे बढ़ रहे थे। थोड़ी देर में हमने देखा कि कोई आदमी नहीं आये, एक तीर आया। वो सामने एक पिलर में आकर टकराया। तब हमें लगा कि कुछ गड़बड़ है। हम उठकर अंदर की ओर चले।

वो आदमी कौन थे?

वो भोंदुप के आदमी थे। हमने देखा कि चार-पांच लोग तीर इस तरफ निशाना लगाकर खड़े थे। उसके बाद हमने धीरे से कमरे के अंदर जाकर दरवाज़ा बंद कर दिया। सोम साहब एक mediator को जानते थे जो उन लोगों की भाषा बोलता था। जब हमने और निकट जाकर देखा तो पाया कि वे लोग वहाँ से वापस चले गये थे। जो mediator आना था, वह नहीं आया। वह गाँव में कहीं गया हुआ था। जब वह आया और हमने उसको सब बताया। तो उसने कहा कि जब भी बाहरी लोगों को देखते हैं, या डरते हैं, तो ये लोग हमला करने की कोशिश करते हैं।

यह तो आपका बड़ा रोमांचक अनुभव है।

जी हाँ। फिर उसके बाद हम तीनों, मतलब, सोम साहब, मैं और mediator उनके पास गए। mediator उनकी भाषा में बातें करने लगा। (वो तो हिंदी नहीं बोल पाते थे, या कुछ और जो हमारी समझ में आये।) mediator के माध्यम से उनलोगों की भाषा में कुछ चर्चा हुई। वे लोग चारों तरफ इकट्ठा हुए। उन्होंने हम लोगों को अपने काफी collection भी दिये। हमनें ऐसे ही तीन चार गाँवों में और भी collection किया। तीन चार दिन के बाद, मैं एक गाँव में गया, सोम साहब दूसरे गाँव में गए। क्योंकि समय कम था, जल्दी लौटना था, उन्होंने कहा कि मैं एक गाँव में कर लेता हूं और तुम दूसरे गांव में collection कर लो। हमने भोंदुप में काफी photographs खींचीं थी। उस समय digital camera नहीं हुआ करता था। केवल colour film हुआ करती थी और 35mm का कैमरा हुआ करता था। उससे हमने उनकी काफ़ी तस्वीरें खींचीं। यहाँ संग्रहालय में एक building में एक छोटा सा काम्प्लेक्स बनाया गया है, उसमें सारी तस्वीरें लगाई हुई हैं।

IGRMS Vithi Sankul (Indoor Museum)

अच्छा, कौन सी gallery में हैं?

दो नंबर gallery में उसका पूरा एक छोटा सा enclosure बनाया है। उसमें भोंदुप महिला का एक छोटा सा मॉडल भी बनाया है। उनके ornaments और बहुत सारी अन्य चीज़ें भी हैं। उस टूर में मैंने और सोम साहब ने एक सौ अठारह चीज़ें collect की थीं। उन दिनों की एक बात है, हम एक गाँव में गए थे (गाँव का नाम याद नहीं है)। उस गाँव में हम उनके household की और उनकी बहुत सारी चीज़ों की, kitchen, garden की photography कर रहे थे, mediator भी साथ में था। जो थोड़ी बहुत उनकी भाषा बोलता था। उसने कुछ पूछा और चर्चा की तो और फ़ोटो खींची गईं। तभी तीन चार भोंदुप युवा आये जो बहुत ही कम कपड़े पहने थे। (वहां महिलाएँ भी कम कपड़े पहनती थीं, अब काफ़ी बदलाव हो गया है।) वे तीन चार युवक पीये हुए थे। यह तो आदिवासियों का आम features होता है। हम लोगों को भी कोई दिक्कत नहीं होती, आसानी से बात कर सकते थे यदि हमें उनकी भाषा आती होती। जब हम photos खीच रहे थे, तो सिर्फ लंगोट पहने हुए तीन चार लड़के आये और उनकी बग़ल में इतना सा एक औज़ार था जिसमें वे चाकू लगाये हुए थे और कंधे पर बाण लटकाये थे। चारों पीये हुए थे और चारों ही नाचने लगे। हमें कुछ अजीब नहीं लगा। हमें और भी तस्वीरें खींचनी थी और वो चारों तो हटें ही नहीं, चक्कर लगाते रहे। बाद में mediator ने हमें बताया कि चारों

कह रहे हैं कि जो फ़ोटो तुमने खींची हैं, वह फोटो हमें दे दो। हमने बताया कि फ़ोटो हम अभी नहीं दे सकते। जब हम दुल्हेलरी वापस जायेंगे, वहाँ print बनायेंगे, तब उन्हें फ़ोटो भेज देंगे। वे लोग बोले कि फ़ोटो हमें अभी चाहिए, वे काफी पीये हुए थे। हमने कहा कि यह तो संभव नहीं है, इनको समझाओ कि अभी तो फ़ोटो नहीं दे सकते। चारों बोले कि अभी नहीं देते तो फ़ोटो कभी नहीं दोगे। हमने कहा ऐसा नहीं है, हम ज़रुर भेज़ेंगे। चारों काफ़ी देर तक घूमते और चक्कर लगाते रहे। तो हमने पूछा, इसके अलावा क्या चाहिए? वे बोले हमें डब्बू दो (डब्बू मतलब पैसा)। हमने कहा 'पैसों से क्या करेंगे?'। वे बोले कि जाकर और भी दारू खरीदेंगे और दारू पीयेंगे। सुबह से वे लोग चालू हो जाते हैं। हम लोगों ने उनको दस, बीस रुपये दिए। उस पैसे से वे इतना खुश हो गए कि जब हम दूसरी चीज़ों की तस्वीर खींचने लगे, तो वे हमको और बहुत सारी चीज़ें दिखाने लगे। एक दम cooperation। इतने पीने के बावजूद भी इतना cooperation। उन लोगों का जीवन बहुत सरल और सहज होता है। उन्होंने हमें सब चीज़ें दे भी दीं।

संग्रहालय के उपादानों का एकत्रीकरण

श्रीकांत गुप्ता

मेरे साथ श्रीकांतजी बैठे है। अपने बारे में बता रहे हैं।

दिल्ली विश्वविद्यालय के Anthropology department में D.K. Bhattacharya के साथ मेरा पहला experience था, उन्होंने मुझे फ़ोन किया। उनका एक project था उस समय मैं University में ही था। उसको मैंने accept किया। उसमें मुझे 1800 रुपये मिलते थे। दिल्ली में 1800 में रहना possible नहीं था, पर मैंने उसको accept किया। यह 1994 की बात है। तभी मैंने M.Sc. किया था। उस समय दिल्ली विश्वविद्यालय के Anthropology Department में Professor R.S. Negi थे। उन्होंने मुझे बुलाया व मैंने उन्हें बताया कि मैं D.K. Bhattacharya वाला प्रोजेक्ट ले रहा हूँ। प्रोजेक्ट में मैंने देखा कि नैनीताल तराई के tribal लोगों की economy केवल agriculture पर निर्भर है। और स्थिति यह है कि पूरी सिख community उस पर हावी हो चुकी है। क्योंकि वहाँ पर local wine production है, तराई के tribal लोग wine पीते हैं और सिखों ने wine के through उनको अपने अधीन बनाया। थारु अनपढ़ लोग हैं ही, उनसे जितना हो सके उतना land लिखवा लिया। अभी स्थिति यह है कि मेरे ख्याल से 70 प्रतिशत सिख होंगे 30 प्रतिशत थारु होंगे जिनके पास ज़मीन है। बाकी सब ऐसे ही हैं। मज़दूरी कर रहे हैं।

यह कौन सी locality है?

खटीमा एक जगह है, जो नैनीताल foot hills में है। उस में पूरा field work किया। खटीमा से जुड़े जितने भी गांव थे, maximum around 39 villages, सब मैंने cover किये और उस पर आधारित किताब अभी Anthropology Survey of India ने publish भी की। Anthropology Survey of India के through ही थारु पर मेरा वह project था, हिंदी में है। और इसके बाद 2000

में इंदिरा गाँधी राष्ट्रीय मानव संग्रहालय में मैंने join किया था। उस समय चक्रवर्ती साहब डिरेक्टर थे और मेरा पहला field work बिहार में बिरहोर community पर था। उसके बाद, उतराखंड में भोटिया पर था। उसके बाद धीरे-धीरे जहां जहां पर यहां के उंचे अधिकारी proposal देते रहे, मैं field work करता रहा। इसमें कुछ advantage है कि अपने area में आदमी काम करता है। एक तो language का advantage मिलता है हर चीज़ में, वहाँ के अपने area के लोग है तो उनके बीच में एक relationship बनता है कि यह अपने area का है। तो इसको बताने में कोई hesitation नहीं होना चाहिए। यह सोचकर वे बताते हैं। किसी अनजानी जगह में जाते हैं तो हम को एक interpreter लेना पड़ता है। जब वे लोग अपना भाषा में बोलते हैं, तो वह translate करता है। मैं नेपाली जानता हूँ तो उतराखंड में कुछ problem नहीं हुई। फिर भी कुछ ऐसी languages हैं, उनमें कुछ ऐसे words आते हैं, जो हम समझ नहीं पाते हैं।

जो objects आप वहाँ से लाते है, उनको लाने में क्या कठिनाइयाँ हुईं?

Object collections में problems होती ही हैं। main problem तो यह है कि आप किसी भी area में जाकर एक दम से किसी को बोलेंगे कि ये लोटा मुझे दें दीजिए। तो उस व्यक्ति को शक होगा कि एक दम से आये और बोले कि लोटा दे दीजिए, museum के लिए चाहिए। ऐसे होता है कि पहले उनके बीच में बैठिये चाय पानी पीजिए, पहले उनकी बातों को सुनिये, उसके बाद उनके बीच में कुछ ऐसी बात को रखिये कि हम इस area के लिए कुछ करने के लिए आये हैं। कुछ चीज़ हमको बदलनी पड़ती है कि Government की कुछ ऐसी policy है, इत्याादि। कुछ ऐसे artefacts हैं जो उनके system से जुड़े हैं, जिन्हें वे देते नहीं। जैसे अस्सम में, मणिपुर में इस तरह के artefacts बहुत हैं। उन artefacts से उनका एक attachment है। वे सोचते हैं कि आप कभी न कभी museum से चले जायेंगे तो उसके बाद इनका क्या होगा। आज यह museum में चला जाएगा, अभी इसकी कीमत जो भी है बाद में तो बढ़ जाएगी। मान लीजिए, तीस साल पहले हज़ार रूपये थी। आज cost ज्यादा हो गई, bronze और brass या copper का rate ज़्यादा हो गया व market की value बढ़ती है। इसके पीछे जो history है सर, उसके according हम क़ीमत तय करते हैं। फिर वहाँ के कुछ local government servant हैं, उनसे पता करते है कि वाकई में यह इतने साल पुराने objects हैं। एक ऐसी committee हम लोग organise करते हैं, फिर हम evaluate करते हैं कि actually यह rate है कि नहीं। हम बोले सौ रुपये, वो बोले पाँच सौ की है या छे सौ की है, तब बड़ी मुश्किल होती है। वहाँ की local public को भी involve करना बहुत ज़रूरी है सर। ताकि एक genuine rate पर artefacts का purchase कर सकें।

असम और मणिपुर के बारे में आप कुछ बातें interesting बतला रहे थे।

Northeast में काम बहुत ही problematic है। अभी, recently 2010 में एक team में हम लोग (मैं, Mr. Shakamacha Singh और हमारे video section से सेनापति) collection के लिए गए थे, हम को वहाँ के house patterns का collections करना था। उनके चार पाँच houses और कुछ artefacts, असम में एक district है जो ULFA का hub है।। उसमें Murang एक community है। हम लोग field work कर रहे थे। चार पाँच दिन हो गये थे, field work करते करते कुछ ऐसे लोग वहाँ involved थे जो रात को इधर उधर घूमते रहते थे, पूछते थे कि यह कौन है क्या है। हमने उनको नहीं बताया कि हम लोग Government Servants हैं क्योंकि वे लोग Government Servants को ही target करते थे। हम लोगों ने वहीं के tribal लोगों के साथ वहाँ पर एक cultural program perform करवाया था, उन लोगों से बताया था कि जब हम उनके area में जायें तो आप लोग किसी भी तरह से हम लोगों का introduction मत कराइयेगा। Cultural program नवम्बर, दिसम्बर के आस पास 2009 में हुआ था। कुछ समय उस area से Cultural program के लिए artist लोगों को यहाँ बुलाया था व तभी हमारा उनसे interaction हुआ कि हम लोग उनके area में आयेंगे और आपकी community से related house patterns बनाना चाहेंगे। उसी प्रकार के houses यहाँ बनायेंगे। उसमें क्या क्या materials लगेगा वे हम लोग बतायेंगे। जब हम लोग वहाँ आयेंगे वे लोग cooperate करेंगे। जब हम लोग गए तो वादे के अनुसार उन लोगों ने cooperate किया। हम लोगों ने जाकर पूरा survey किया कि कितना material लगेगा, वे चीज़ें हमने पूरी purchase भी कीं। उनको एक truck में यहाँ transport किया। फिर उन artist लोगों को बुलाया, जिस community का मकान यहाँ बनाना था, उनको ही बुलाया और उन्होंने आकर यहाँ पूरा मकान complete किया।

इसमें कितना वक्त लगा मतलब, explore करने के बाद यहाँ आकर बनाने में कितना वक्त लगा?

सर, मुझे याद है, इस field work में यहाँ से 11th January को हम लोगों ने proceed किया था, और 5th April को वापस आये। हमारा तीन चार महीने का tour रहा। 7th या 8th April से यहाँ पर मैंने काम शुरू किया। पांचों मकान, चार

असम के और एक मणिपुर का एक महीने में complete हुए थे। Mr Shakamacha Singh को उस field work में बड़ी problem हुई थी, vehicle बहुत use करनी पड़ी क्योंकि हमारा काम ऐसा था कि रात को तीन बजे तक हम लोग visit कर रहे थे और गाडी़ के अंदर ही laptop पर काम कर रहे थे कि कितना सामान किससे लिया, इस information को note नहीं करते तो भूल जाते। इस तरह रास्ते में tour का पूरा काम हम गाड़ी के अंदर ज़्यादा और होटल में कम करते थे।

आप लोग ठरहते कहाँ थे?

कोशिश करते थे कि जो tribal गांव हैं, उनके बीच में रहें और हुआ ऐसा कि हम लोग मुरांडपुर meeting में आठ दस दिन तक उनके गांव में रहे। बाद में जब हमको स्थिति मालूम हुई कि ULFA वहाँ पर हैं, तो हम गांव छोड़कर होटल में रहे। चार पांच दिन आसपास के town के होटल में रहे, यदि कोई guest house होता तो वहाँ रुक जाते थे। इसके पहले 2003 में जब मैं मधुबनी गया था, तब वहां केवल एक ही होटल (समंता) हुआ करता था। आज वहाँ बढ़िया-बढ़िया होटल हो गए हैं। बात यह है कि अगर आप उस village में रहेंगे तो आपको काफ़ी information मिलेगी। एक तो गाँव वाले आपको समझेंगे कि ये दूसरी तरह के आदमी नहीं है और ये research work कर रहे हैं, museum के लिए काम कर रहे हैं। हमारी community से related काम कर रहे हैं तो उनको अपने area के बारे में बताने में कोई हानि नहीं।

उन लोगों का motivation क्या है कि किस वजह से अपने house types, artefacts वगैरा देते हैं, और यहाँ आते हैं, व काम करते हैं। मतलब, monetary gain तो marginal ही होगा, बहुत ज़्यादा नहीं?

सर, जो maximum लोग मिलते हैं उनको यह रहता है कि उनके artefacts को कोई ले लेगा, या टूट जाएंगे और इसकी कोई कीमत नहीं मिलेगी। अंततः केवल कबाड़ी वाले को देना पड़ेगा,तो उससे बेहतर है कि museum में जायेगा और लंबे समय के बाद भी हमारा नाम रहेगा। अगर वहां कोई रिश्तेदार भी गए तब उनको भी पता चलेगा कि हमने museum में अपनी चीज़ों को दिया, हमारा नाम भी आएगा। इस तरह से थोड़े monetary gain के अलावा साथ में उनको यश भी मिल जायेगा। हम यह भी बोलते है, कि अगर आपका कोई cultural program है जो आप traditional तरीक़े से करते हैं तो बताइये हम आपको invite करेंगे और आप वहाँ आकर perform कीजिये। तब ये लोग बताते हैं कि local इस तरह का festival करते हैं या इस तरह का डांस है, इस तरह का गाना है।

Madhubani Painting

मधुबनी वाले लोग आये हैं यहाँ?

एक workshop में मैंने मधुवनी के लोगों को यहाँ बुलाया था। जित्वारपुर गांव में painting के काम का origin हुआ था। वहाँ सीतादेवी करके एक artist हैं जो National awardee थीं। अभी तो वे expire हो चुकी हैं। यशोदादेवी ने उनसे कला सीखी थी। मैं यशोदादेवी को यहाँ संग्रहालय में लाया था। Gallery 5 में उनकी पूरी मधुबनी painting है। यशोदादेवी भी expire कर चुकीं पर उनकी painting अभी भी है। उस समय भट्ट साहब director थे, भट्ट साहब ने ही मुझे भेजा व कहा कि आप जाकर उनको लेकर आईये। तो मैं गया और उनके घर पर रहा। मैंने तो होटल समंता में book किया था। दोपहर में उन्होंने अपने लड़कों को भेजा और कहा कि सर को बुला लो, अपने घर पर रहेंगे। तो मैं उनके साथ ही रहा। सात आठ दिन उनके घर पर ही रहा। उनके साथ रहकर बहुत कुछ सीखने को मिला। मुझे उस गांव के बारे में भी बहुत information मिली। इस painting का origin कैसे हुआ, किस किस ने सीखा, उन सब चीज़ों की information मिली।

अच्छा मुझे एक बात बतलाइये, वहाँ जाकर आप लोग इतना effort करते हैं, और artist भी आते हैं यहाँ अपना काम बनाते हैं। इस सारी प्रक्रिया में, जिन लोगों को आप ये ज्ञान देना चाहते हैं, बाँटना चाहते हैं, जैसे school children हैं, adults हैं, और जो लोग यहाँ museum में visit करते हैं, उसमें success

का क्या proportion है, मतलब आप इस काम में कितना सफल हो पा रहे हैं? public का क्या participation है? कितना है, कितने लोग देखने आते हैं, क्या करते हैं?

इसमें अब ऐसा है कि indoor museum में एक छत के नीचे visitors इंडिया की पूरी different cultures को देखते हैं। और open air की exhibition में actual house pattern बनाये हैं। जैसे, नागालैंड का आप एक example ले लीजिए, जो मकान यहाँ है। आज उसके सामने से आप उसका एक photograph click करके ले आईए, कोई नहीं कहेगा कि यह इंदिरा गांधी राष्ट्रीय मानव संग्रहालय का है। यही कहेगा कि नागालैंड का है। क्योंकि वो naturally बनाया हुआ है कि लगता नहीं कि वह नागालैंड में न होकर भोपाल में है।।

पब्लिक को इन चीज़ों के बारे में explain करने के लिए काफ़ी लोग हैं या नहीं?

Indoor museum में हम लोगों ने text लगाए हैं, guide की कोई ज़रूरत नहीं है। जैसे कोई VIPs आते हैं, तो उनको हम उन्हें लेकर जाते हैं। कभी-कभी डिरेक्टर भी बीच बीच में आते हैं। indoor museum में information sufficient है। Open Air में एक guide है जो visit कराता है। अभी अपने यहाँ कुछ kiosks लगे हैं, ये text screen kiosks हैं। उसमें मैं और Mr Singh काम कर रहे थे। तीन चार और लोग भी काम कर रहे थे। बीच में कुछ ऐसी problems और ऐसे काम आ गये कि break करना पड़ा हमको। अभी कर रहे हैं। Suppose अगर कोई musical instrument है तो आप headphone के through सुन सकते हैं। तो इस तरह से हम लोग उसको बना रहे हैं। एक एक object का पूरा detail। क्योंकि कुछ पुराने objects ऐसे हैं जिनकी कोई detail ही नहीं हैं। उस चीज़ को हम डिरेक्टर साहब से पूछते हैं कि इसके बारे में क्या डाल सकते है। तो वो बताते हैं कि आप इसको डालिये या इसको ignore कीजिये।

इसके अलावा लोगों के समझने के लिए क्या audio visual aids हैं?

सर, अभी तो Indoor museum में हमने जितने exhibition develop किये हैं, उसमें हर exhibition के बारे में हमारे पास Braille में है कि इस exhibition में क्या चीज़ें हैं। भोपाल में आरुषी एक संस्था है, उसके बच्चे कई बार यहां आए हैं। They were very happy कि इस तरह की information first time हम लोग इस museum में पा रहे हैं। They were able to touch. हमारे museum में सब touch कर सकते हैं। अनेक लोगों को लगता है कि यह क्या चीज़ है व उसको touch करके देखें तो इन्हें पता चलता है कि यह क्या चीज़

है। हमारे museum में यह freedom है। कुछ area ऐसा भी है जिसमें चीज़ें showcase में रखी हुई हैं।

आपको यहाँ आए हुए कितने साल हुए हैं?

ग्यारह साल

ग्यारह साल में जो यहाँ की limitations हैं वे क्या लगीं, क्या कठिनाईयां हैं? या क्या होना चाहिए? आप अपने हिसाब से बोलिए।

कुछ government rules हैं उनको थोडा relax करना पड़ेगा, नहीं तो काम करने में बड़ी problem होती है। मान लीजिए, आप कुछ collections करके आते हैं। Government rules यह हैं कि पन्द्रह दिन में आपको submit करना पड़ेगा। मान लीजिए अगर आप 2000 या 200 collections लाते हैं, तो उसका पूरा data sheet भरना, A to Z information डालना, उसमें वक्त तो लगता है। 15 days में तो यह मुमकिन नहीं है। 15 objects का तो possible है, जिस तरह से जो collection हो उसके हिसाब से time period होना चाहिए। Time तो लगता ही है। कम समय में क्या होगा कि ग्लास क्या है इस शीर्षक में आप सिर्फ एक metal लिख देंगे बस, बाकी उसकी information क्या है, उसमें कुछ carving है, उसका base किस metal से बनाया है, proportion क्या है वो सब चीज़ें आप नहीं लिखेंगे। तो time period थोड़ा problem है सर।

अच्छा, उनसे related जो stories है क्या वह भी लिखते हैं?

जी वह भी लिखना पड़ता है सर। जैसे कोई कुछ artefacts हैं, जो उनके ancestors से पूरी तरह से जुड़े हुए हैं कि ये कब से आ रहा है, इसके पीछे history क्या है। हम लोग इनको सिर्फ festival में use करते हैं। कुछ marriage ceremony में ही use करते हैं। कुछ ऐसे artefacts हैं, जिसकी पूरी detail हम लोगों ने audio में record की होगी। तो हम लोग उसको audio video section में दे देते हैं। उस section में देने के बाद बस वहाँ store हो जाता है। उसके बाद उसका कुछ नहीं होता है।

उसकी delivery और उसके dissemination का क्या होता है?

जी, अभी हम लोगों ने एक प्लान बनाया है कि museum के ऊपर एक clipping बनायेंगे कि इस museum में क्या है। एक एक gallery को लेकर एक clipping बनाकर एक CD में convert करेंगे। काफी दिनों तक यह plan ही नहीं बना था। उस समय डिरेक्टर बासा साहब थे व traditional technology

का हम लोगों का प्रोग्राम चल रहा था। मैं उस समय रविवार को आता था और Mr Shakamacha Singh Tribal Habitat में रहते थे। Director ने मुझे बुलाया कि आप यहाँ आइये कुछ काम है। मैं गया। उस समय उनके पास laptop हुआ करता था। हम लोगों के पास नहीं था तो वे बोले कि इस में एक clipping डालकर हिंदी में कुछ narration करना था। अंग्रेजी में तो हो जायेगा, आप हिंदी में करो। मैंने कहा मेरी voice इतनी अच्छी नहीं कि मैं हिंदी में narration करूं। नहीं नहीं he said, you can try, देखते हैं कैसा होता है, करते हैं। मैंने किया। उसे CD में convert करके बासा साहब को दिखाया। आज वह CD मेरे ख्याल से विदेश में भी गयी है और डिरेक्टर साहब ने उसको दिल्ली में भी दिखाया था। वह चीज़ हम लोगों ने बनाई थी। इस तरह से अगर video section भी करे तो हर छोटा छोटा इस तरह record होना चाहिए ताकि visitors को यह मालूम चले कि यह चीज़ क्या है। एक Northeast के ऊपर हम लोगों ने CD बनायी थी, Glimpses of Northeast। यह पहली CD है जो हम लोगों ने बनायी है। इसमें narration भी रखा है, इसमें music और पूरा editing शकमाचा ने किया था, narration मैंने किया। हम लोगों ने अपना पूरा photographs collection कर के भी दिया था। Editing पूरी शकमाचा ने ही की थी।

क्या editing में उनकी कोई training है?

वह software कहीं कहीं से लाता था और मुझसे बोला कि श्रीकान्त सर इस में से कुछ कर सकते हैं। मैंने कहा कि कोशिश करते हैं। Try किया हम लोगों ने CD बनायी जो foundation day के समय पूरी public को दिखाया। और CD भी दस मिनट पंद्रह मिनट के ही बनाये हैं। अच्छा है। एक product हो जाता है। आप एक tour पर जा रहे हैं, उसी tour का ही आप एक clipping बनायें कि आपने वहाँ क्या क्या काम किया, कैसे किया। उससे related आप उसमें कुछ photos भी उसमें डालिये। फिर उसमें connector दे दीजिए। public को एक change भी मिलेगा। सिर्फ चीज़ों को देखने से public bore होती है कि यह क्या एक के बाद एक चीज़ हम देख रहे हैं। हर दो महिने या चार महिने में changes होने चाहिए। जो visitors पहली बार आ रहे हैं, वे objects वगैरा एक तरफ से देख रहे हैं तो थोड़ी dullness होती है। थोड़ा music होगा, थोड़ा visual होगा तो उसमें interest ज्यादा आयेगा। हमारी पहली CD देखकर बासा साहब ने फ़ोन करके बोला कि आप एक और CD बनाइये। फिर हम लोगों ने एक और सी डी बनाई। चक्रवर्ती साहब ने उसे बहुत appreciation भी किया और वे जब बाहर गये, लन्दन या कहीं गये तो वह CD वहाँ लेकर गये।

जैसे आप भोपाल के बाहर जाते हैं, तो यह utilise करते हैं dissemination के लिए, लोगों को दिखलाने के लिए?

एक film की तरह convert करके मैं कुछ ऐसे clipping को रखता हूँ। मैं अब यही कर रहा हूँ, जितने मैंने tour किये हैं, उन सबका एक एक clipping बनाकर इसी तरह से मैं अपने पास रखता हूँ। शकमाचा और हम दोनों ने तय किया कि कुछ वह बनायें और कुछ मैं बनाऊं।

उसके साथ-साथ भी visitors के लिए clippings वगैरा बनाने का equipment वगैरा क्या अपने यहाँ है?

है सर, video section में gallery से related पूरी clippings उनके पास available हैं। अपने संग्रहालय से related clippings भी हैं, संग्रहालय के programs की भी clippings हैं। संग्रहालय के operation में जितने भी programs होते हैं, या बाहर होते हैं, video section में उनकी पूरी recording है।

सवाल यह है कि इसका utilisation कितना है?

मेरा और शकमाचा का जो चार महिने का असम का tour रहा उसके ही हज़ार से ऊपर photographs हैं। हम लोग बोले कि सारे photographs को collect करके उनमें से अच्छे photographs का एक film में conversion करके हम उसकी CD बनाते हैं।

अब जैसे यह festivals और celebrations होते है, dances होते है, इसकी भी recording होना चाहिए। festivals और celebrations की recording के लिये यहां equipment है। Editing के लोग video section में है, वो लोग करते हैं। उन लोगों ने museum से related एक छोटी सी clipping बनाई व एक introductory CD भी बनाई है, जिसमें Narration के लिए कहीं बाहर से आदमी को hire किया था। मेरे ख्याल से उन लोगों ने पाँच सात CD प्रोग्राम बनाये हैं।

उसमें script वगैरा किसने बनाई?

उन लोगों को script तिवारी साहब ने दी। हम ने folder से ही matter निकाला था। उसमें से काटके और कुछ editing करके हम लोगों ने personal cd बनाया। बासा साहब ने देखा तो बोले उसको पूरा complete करो, पाँच मिनट का, या सात मिनट का या दस मिनट का बना लो। जब बना कर दिखाया तो उनको अच्छा लगा। बासा साहब बहुत ही enthusiastic आदमी हैं। उनमें बहुत ज़्यादा

urge है कि इस तरह का काम हो। यह सब करके उनको यही लगा हम लोग और भी कुछ कर सकते हैं। बोले कि यह काम और भी करना। हमने कहा कि सर हम कर देंगे, लेकिन थोड़ी freedom चाहिए हम को। freedom in the sense कि जब हम यह काम कर रहे हैं तो यह न हो कि दूसरा कोई हमको कुछ और काम दे यदि उसको भी करो, तो फिर यह काम disturbed हो जाता है। Clipping या narration का कुछ काम कर रहे हो तो उसी में लगना होता है। दूसरा कोई आये व बोले कि यह करो, यह मत करो तो फिर audio-visual recording का काम करना बड़ा मुश्किल हो जाता है सर। तो इस काम के लिए, हम Sunday को बैठते थे, किंतु Sunday को generally office पूरा बंद ही रहता था।

संग्रहालय कार्य और घुमक्कड़ी

राकेश न्याल

न्याल साहब आप कहाँ के रहने वाले हैं और कहां पढ़े हैं?

मैं गढ़वाल का हूं और वहीं पढ़ा हूँ।

आप कब से यहाँ हैं?

मैंने 1988 से यहीं काम शुरू किया और आज तक यहीं पर हूँ। उस वक्त यह संग्रहालय बहुत छोटा सा था। उस समय तो सारा पढ़ना लिखना छूट गया था। संग्रहालय से जुड़े रहने की वजह से बहुत बाद में मैंने Ph. D. किया।

1988 में आप यहाँ आये, उस समय कौन डिरेक्टर थे?

उस समय नेगी साहब डिरेक्टर थे। जब मैं आया उसके छ महीने बाद वे चले गए। उसके बाद फिर चक्रवर्ती साहब आये थे। इस तरह मैंने चार पांच डिरेक्टर के नीचे काम किया है सर।

आपका क्या क्या काम था जब आप यहाँ शुरू में आये?

जब मैं शुरू में आया, तब संग्रहालय बन ही रहा था। मैं हिमालय का रहनेवाला हूँ, इसलिए हिमालय में ज़्यादा काम करना शुरू किया। इस संग्रहालय में हिमालय के जितने भी collections हैं, वे सब मेरे लाये हुये हैं। यह सब मैंने कुछ लोगों के साथ मिल कर किया था। अत: दुर्भाग्य से मुझे उस में बहुत ज्यादा recognition नहीं मिला, हम लोग साल भर काम ही पूरा करते रहते थे। तीन चार साल तक हमने कोई छुट्टी भी नहीं ली। इतना करने पर आज लगता है कि हमने कुछ किया। मेरा उस वक्त ऐसे लोगों से संपर्क हुआ जो पहले से ही हिमाचल प्रदेश में थे। जैसे शिमला में डॉ शर्मा थे, जो पहले से उस area में काम कर चुके थे ही, उनके पास गये तो बहुत कठिनाइयाँ नहीं हुई, वरन् कुछ सीखने को ही मिला।

जब आप गांव में जाते थे, तो किस तरह के लोगों से संपर्क करते थे?

गांव में जाने के समय सबसे पहले प्रधान जी के पास जाता था, वहीं कुछ पढ़े-लिखे लोग भी मिल जाते थे। मैंने देखा कि हिमालय के लोग भले ही पढ़े लिखे कम हों पर उनकी जानकारी काफ़ी ज्यादा होती थी। मैंने एक घर collect किया, यहाँ पर चौखट वहीं के material से बनता है। बाहर का तो बनता नहीं। और इस material, मतलब, 50 feet long log को बाहर लाना है। अब वहाँ की सड़कें तो संकरी होती हैं, उसको कैसे लाएं? तब गाँववालों का knowledge मैंने देखा, वो बोले कि आप इसको देहरादून तक या कहीं जहाँ पर plane मिलता है वहाँ तक ले जाओ। मोटर गाड़ी तो जा नहीं सकती। तो क्या करें? वो बोले पहले आप छोटी लकड़ियों को लेकर जायें। और लगभग तीस चालीस बड़ी लकड़ियाँ जो हैं उनको उन्होंने रस्सियों से सीधा खिसकाया। तो वे नीचे आ गयीं। नीचे तो valley है और उसमें river है। तो उन लोगों ने इनको नदी में डाल दिया। तो कुछ लकड़ियों को हम ऐसे करके ले आये। और उस समय वर्षा का season नहीं था तो कुछ damage भी नहीं हुआ। यह गाँव वालों की knowledge का उदाहरण है। वो लोग बोले कि कैसे खोलेंगे आप, इसलिए इन लकड़ियों की numbering कर दो जैसे 1, 2, 3। First lot, second lot, हर एक का numbering करके। तो ज़्यादा दिक्कत नहीं हुई। वहाँ तक तो नदी से ले आये और उधर से तो बड़े बड़े ट्रक आते हैं। मैदान में ज़्यादा दिक्कत नहीं, पहाड़ों में ज़्यादा दिक्कत है। तो वो लकड़ियों को रस्सों से winding roads के through ही लाये।

बहुत सारा जो stone के utensils का collection है उनके बारे में घरों में रखे होने के बावजूद भी नये लोगों को पता नहीं होता है कि उनका क्या करते हैं, इसमें खाना बनाते थे या पानी गरम करते थे। जो गांव के बुड्ढे लोग हैं, वो बता देते कि इसमें क्या रखते थे और उसकी कहानी भी बता देते इसकी कहानी यह है करके। तो ऐसे बहुत सारी बातें हम लोग field में जाते तो उनको लिखते थे। उनको discuss करने का मौका कभी नहीं मिला।

क्या आप diary *रखते थे?*

diary तो है और बहुत सारा जो raw material होता है वो पड़ा भी है। ऐसा मौका नहीं मिला कि उसको थोड़ा लिख सकें।

आपके अनुभव में ऐसी कौन सी घटनाएं घटीं जिनको आप याद करते हैं।

एक घटना है। हम लोग मिज़ोरम गये थे, ऐज़वाल। वहाँ पर हम लोग field work कर रहे थे, एक seminar हुआ था, सोम साहब हमारे डिरेक्टर थे। तब आने जाने का साधन बड़ा कठिन था। वहाँ पर हमको ऐज़वाल से चलना था Guwahati

के लिए। शाम हो गई। शाम के टाइम एक bus आती थी, एक jeep जैसी। हम लोग चार पाँच बजे ऐज़वाल से बैठे और सिरिचार और ऐज़वाल के बीच में उन लोगों ने खाना खाके दारू पी ली। सब आगे बैठे, वहीं मेरा एक साथी भी बैठा था। उन लोगों ने बातें करनी शुरू की। 'ये है वो है' करके आपस में बातें कर रहे थे। बात करते करते गाड़ी को तेज़ चलाना शुरू किया। 90 में चलायी और गाड़ी पलटी। उसने कई पलटी मार दी। Rolling जैसा हो गया। अंधेरा उस समय हुआ। पूरा अंधेरा। हमारी ही गाड़ी थी। इतना सब होने के बाद भी मुझे कोई चोट नहीं आई। थोड़ी बहुत हल्की कहीं हुई। जो मेरा साथी था, ऐस के पांडे, उसको बड़ी चोट लगी। सब लोग गिरे पड़े थे। थोड़े समय के बाद मैंने देखा कि मैं ठीक हूँ और ढूंढ़ने लगा कि ऐस के पांडे कहाँ हैं। कोई आवाज़ नहीं आयी। सब लोग शायद बेहोश पड़े थे। गांव के कुछ आवारा लोग आये और सारा सामान लेकर चले गये। उस समय हम travellers cheque लेकर जाते थे, एक या डेढ़ लाख के। वो cheque भी लेकर चले गये। उस समय हमें किसी को पता नहीं था कि हमारा सामान चोरी हो गया। उस समय मैंने देखा कि jeep के नीचे पांडे का पैर फंसा हुआ है, उसका सर बाहर है और खून भी बह रहा है। Full bleeding हो रही है और ये बेहोश पड़ा हुआ। फिर मैंने उसको खींचा, रात में उस समय एक ट्रकवाला आया था। तो पांडे को हमने अपने कंधे पर रख कर ट्रक में रखा। ट्रकवाले को हम जानते भी नहीं थे। वो हिंदी भी थोड़ी बहुत बोलता था। पता नहीं उसके दिमाग में क्या था, उस आदमी ने हमारी ऐसे मदद की। उसने हमको एक अस्पताल में भर्ती करवाया, तीन दिन तक हमारे साथ था, हमें पानी देता था। हमको कुछ stitches भी लगीं तो हमको तीन चार दिन उधर रहना पड़ा। हमारे collections भी पता नहीं कहाँ गये।

कौन थे जिनको सबसे ज़्यादा चोट लगी?

जी, ऐस के पांडे को। ये तो काफ़ी दुखद घटना हुई। फिर मैं उनकी अस्पताल में देखभाल करता रहा इस बीच मैंने, वो भी किया, वो जो पैसे घुम हो गये थे हमारे। उनको ढूँढ़ा। उन लोगों के बीच अपना एक technique भी लगाया कहा कि भाई वो पैसे तो कुछ काम के नहीं, वो तो cheque है। यदि दिलवा दें तो कुछ पैसे दे देंगे। उन्होंने आपस में सुना होगा। तो वो बोले साहब हम देखते हैं, हमको आप बता दो कि उसमें क्या क्या था। मैंने उनको बोला कि यह सामान था। तीन दिन में वो लोग ढूँढ़ के ले आये। और मैंने उनको कुछ रुपया भी दिया। फिर हमलोग सिरिचार से Guwahati आये और flight से वहाँ से भोपाल आये।

तो आपने जब museum में काम शुरू किया, उसके बाद क्या आप अपने गांव भी जाते रहे?

गांव जाता था। ये समझिए कि साल में करीब तीन चार बार collection के लिए ही जाता था।

मतलब, अपने गांव या फिर कहीं भी जैसे मिज़ोरम?

दूसरे गांव में गया। अपने गांव आज तक नहीं गया field work के लिए। जैसे मैं अभी चमोली district में जो भोटिया tribe है वहाँ गया। हिमाचल प्रदेश में किन्नौर है, सिम्मोर है, चंपा वैली है। यह सब जगह visit किया है सर।

एक और बात है सर, एक बार हम लोग हिमाचल के उदयपुर होके वहाँ पर पांगी वैली गये, वहाँ collection अच्छा मिलता है पर वहाँ सड़क approachable नहीं है इसलिए अच्छा collection अभी भी है करके कई लोग बोले। हमने कहा चलो चलते हैं भले ही उधर की सड़क ठीक नहीं थी। हमने कहा जंगल की सड़क तो ऐसे ही होती है, ठीक है चलते हैं। हम वहाँ से चले, शिमला से उदयपुर चले। चलते रहे, चलते रहे। बड़ी खतरनाक सड़क। एक हमारा साथी था, उसने एक

On Collection Trail

सवाल किया कि सर हमको यहाँ जाना ज़रूरी है क्या? हमको तो ज़रूरी ही लगता है। यहाँ तो rare collections बता रहे हैं। हमारे संग्रहालय में उसको रखें तो अच्छा है। वहाँ पर सड़क ऐसी थी कि जैसे ही U-Turn होता था। तो हर turn पर jeep पीछे आती थी, हमको नीचे उतर कर धक्का मारना पड़ा। फिर थोड़ा आगे जाओ,

और फिर ऐसा करो। हर एक U-Turn पर ऐसा होता था। तो जब हम ऐसे जा रहे थे, तो एक खुला area आया, एक किनारे पर आये। मतलब दो चार जीपें चल रही हैं। वहाँ पर एक जीप Forest की थी, उस में एक DFO बैठे थे। अचानक वो जीप गायब हो गयी। हमने कहा वह जीप कहाँ गई। पता नहीं क्या हुआ, बहुत सारे लोग खड़े थे वहाँ। देखा तो वो जीप गिर गयी थी नीचे। नदी में चली गयी। हमको और भी डर हो गया। फिर किसी तरह से रात नौ बजे पहुंचे। एक Guest House का दरवाजा खटखटाया तो चौकीदार बोला कोई जगह नहीं है। जगह है या नहीं, तुम कहीं पर भी करो हम लोग government के आदमी हैं। फिर उसने किसी तरह कुछ किया। अगले दिन सुबह जब हमने वो रास्ता देखा जिससे हम आये रात को, हमें बहुत डर लगा।

अच्छा ये पांगी वैली जो है, यह शिमला से पास है?

नहीं यह मनाली से आगे जाकर एक रास्ता जाता है उदयपुर होकर पांगी वैली जाते हैं।

हिमालय area में आपको एक governent servant होने के कारण कोई परेशानी नहीं हुई?

परेशानी इतनी ज़्यादा नहीं हुई। North East में तो बहुत problem होती थी।

अभी आप हाल में कहां गये हैं?

मैं अभी बद्रीनाथ गया था, भोटिया tribe का house type बनाने के लिए।

तो भोटिया tribe *का* house type *नहीं है यहाँ?*

नहीं है सर, अभी भोटिया लोग आयेंगे बनाने के लिए सितम्बर में, हमने बात की है उनसे। वहां के मल्हारी गांव है के बारे में अभी न्यूज़ में भी आया कि एक सोने का मुकुट मिला वहाँ पर। वही जगह है। लोग उसी गांव से आएंगी। वो तीन चार महीने रहते हैं और खुद ही चले जाते हैं। वो भोटिया tribe के हैं। अब और लोग काफ़ी बहुत आगे बढ़ गये, पर भोटिया लोग वहीं पर है।

तो आपको क्या लगता है, जैसे यहाँ पर मानवसंग्रहालय में हैं आप, तो यहाँ display में जैसे आपने house types तरह तरह के बनाये हैं, जैसे आप north east से भी लाये हैं, भोटिया अभी बना रहे हैं। Desert trail भी है। ये सब है। जो लोग आते हैं, यहाँ देखने उन लोगों को क्या कोई समस्या है?

समस्या तो depend करता है visitors पर। हमारे यहाँ बहुत तरह के visitors आते हैं। Mostly ऐसे visitors आते है जो ऐसे ही हवा लेने आते हैं। उस तरह के

75 percent आते हैं। पच्चीस percent या 20 percent लोग आते हैं जिनको वास्तव में museum देखना है।

यह आपने अच्छी बात बतलाई की 75% जो हैं वो वैसे ही आते हैं।

जी, जैसे स्कूलवाले या ऐसे कोई भी ऐसे ही मस्ती के लिये चले आते हैं। पर बाकी 25% में से 20% बहुत serious होते हैं। कई चीज़ें जानना चाहते हैं, हम से मिलते भी हैं। Information जो हमसे लोग चाहते हैं, वह पक्ष हमारा थोड़ा weak है। जैसे suppose कि एक tribal habitat exhibition है तो लोगों के लिए हमारे display में एक दो page की information है। जैसे ये house types हैं, ये materials use करते हैं, लोगों के नाम क्या हैं। बस। अगर वो लोग ये जानना चाहें कि उन tribal लोगों के features कैसे होते हैं, उनके costumes क्या होते हैं, उनकी languages क्या हैं, उनके dances क्या हैं। उनकी कुछ कहानियां या कुछ painting का meaning क्या है। तब हमारे पास लिखित information कम है।

अच्छा जब आप लोग जाते हैं collect *करने, तो आप लोगों को तो ये* information *मिलती होगी। लेकिन लोगों को, जो 20% है जिनकी आप बात कर रहे हैं, उन लोगों को अगर पता करना हो तो उन लोगों को* accessibility *कितनी है? आप लोगों को इतनी फ़ुर्सत होती है कि उनको बतला पायें?*

फ़ुर्सत तो होती है। पर बात यह है कि अगर कोई visitor मुझसे interact करता है तो मैं उतनी ही information दे पाता हूँ जितनी मेरे पास है। जैसे मैं वर्ली की information दे पाता हूँ क्योंकि मैं वहाँ काम करता हूँ। मेरा कहना ये है कि हमारे पास जितनी भी जानकारी है यदि उसको एक ही जगह में collect करके रखें, जैसे CD में या किसी भी तरीक़े से जो 20% visitor को मिले। चाहे वो पैसे देकर लेकर जाएं, चाहे वो कुछ photographs हों, मतलब, अगर वो पूछें हमको चालीस फोटो चाहिए, मिल सकती हैं क्या? तो हम बोलें 'हाँ मिलेगा, आप एक application दे दीजिए और फ़ोटो मिल जाएगा। अभी तो एक लम्बा process हो जाता है। हम पहले उसको डिरेक्टर के पास देते हैं और वो फ़ॉरवर्ड करेंगे और वो फ़ोटो mark करेगा और उसके बाद print बनेगा। यह एक long procedure है। यदि हमारे पास एक एक CD या एक CD में चार पांच tribe की information हो। जो हमारे पास already हो, और उसमें कुछ text जो हमारे पास already लिखा हो, तो किसी को भी ज़्यादा समझाने की ज़रूरत नहीं। तो हम बोल सकते हैं कि यह list देखिये और बताइये आपको और क्या चाहिए।

Actually, हमें देखना चाहिए ये जो आपकी museum की shop है वो कैसी है, क्या है।

Shop है सर सिर्फ़ उसमें artifacts हैं। उसमें कुछ बहुत ज़्यादा information नहीं है। जो traditional artifacts हैं वही हैं। उसमें भी सर, अगर एक booklet बन जाए और किसी के बारे में, अगर कोई खरीदना चाहता है, जैसे कि एक foreigner है, वो ये booklet लिया कि ये सामान आपके यहाँ मिलता हैं। तो हम बाद में online भी उससे बातचीत कर सकते हैं।

हाँ कोई booklet हो, cassettes हों और भी कुछ illustrated publications हों।

मैं क्या बोलता हूँ कि हमारे पास सब कुछ है, पर सब कुछ raw पड़ा है। जैसे चावल है, पानी है अकेला। इसको एक तरफ़ एक हांडी में डालें और पका दें और खाया जाए तो अच्छा होगा।

आपने तो एक बहुत अच्छी बात कही। आपको 88 से आकर इधर चौबीस साल होने वाला है। आपका परिवार यहाँ ही है?

जी। मेरा परिवार यहाँ ही है। हमारी एक बच्ची B.Tech कर रही है, और दूसरी tenth में पढ़ रही है। यहीं पास में एक flat भी ले रखा है। हम राजपूत हैं। हमारे में थोड़े सा होन्यल, नोटयल ऐसे नाम होते हैं।

आपका क्या विचार है कि इस museum में और क्या होना चाहिए? क्या कोई समस्याएं हैं?

Museum के बारे में, जैसे ये Open Air Exhibition. हम सारे देश के बारे में Open Air Exhibition बनाना चाहते हैं। पर अब representation जितना भी है, उसका अच्छी तरह से documentation हो जैसे tribal habitat folder. मैं क़रीब तीन चार साल से काम कर रहा हूँ, कि tribal habitat का एक folder publish हो जाए। उसमें कई सारे चीज़ें हमने लिखी हैं। पहले के डिरेक्टर से कहा भी था कि इसमें ये भी होना चाहिए, वो भी होना चाहिए, पर वो कमी तो आज तक कमी ही रह गई।

अच्छा बच्चों के लिए क्या होना चाहिए?

बच्चों के लिए, बहुत पहले निकालते थे हम, बच्चों के लिए पर्चा। क्यूंकि इधर हिंदी ज़्यादा है तो हिंदी में निकालते थे, कुछ अंग्रेज़ी में भी निकालते थे। उस में कुछ sketch होता था। उसमें वारली का house types का sketch होता था,

दो पेज का। बच्चे आते थे, और ले जाते थे। और ऐसे हर tribe का करते थे। Full two pages का free होता था। अब लोग पैसे दे कर भी लेते हैं, उन लोगों को पैसे की problem नहीं है। पचास रुपये में एक book मिलती है। इसलिए हर exhibition पर एक दो CD, या एक book और एक CD दे दीजिए। ये होना चाहिए। जैसे हमारे storage में बीस हज़ार collections हैं। उसमें से अगर पांच हज़ार भी ऐसे ही हैं तो फिर भी पन्द्रह हज़ार बचते हैं। और उसमें से छे हज़ार display में हैं। अच्छा होगा कि यदि कुछ catalogue बनाये जायें, सक्माचार ने कुछ कोशिश भी की थी। थोड़ा उसका discussion हो जाए तो अच्छा होगा। क्यूंकि मुझे लगता है कि एक insititution होकर भी academically कोई काम नहीं हो तो कुछ value नहीं है। जी, यह इतनी बड़ी जगह है, स्कूल के बच्चे इतने हैं, इतनी हिंदी भाषी population है। फिर भी 75% लोग यहां केवल entertainment के लिए आते हैं। काम करनेवाले भी हैं, पर आगे आने के लिए कुछ माहौल होना चाहिए।

Thank you sir, अच्छा लगा आप से बात करके।

संग्रहालय और मानवशास्त्रीय अनुभव

अशोक शर्मा

अशोक, आप यहां कब से काम कर रहे हैं? आपकी initial appointment क्या थी?

सर। मैं यहां पर मार्च 1992 से एक daily wage worker के रूप में आया। उस समय मैं UPSC की तैयारी कर रहा था और मुझे कुछ पैसों की ज़रूरत थी। मैंने यहाँ भट्ट साहब से request किया। उन्होंने मुझे एक exhibition program में रख लिया। मैं उस काम को कर रहा था। ये ज़रूरत इसलिए पड़ी क्योंकि मेरे पिताजी expire हो गये। उस वक्त मुझे काम पाने की बहुत ज्यादा ज़रूरत थी। मैंने join किया। मैं काम करता रहा। उस समय ऐसा हुआ कि मैं UPSC clear नहीं कर पाया और उस समय मेरी उम्र twenty seven हो गयी थी। मुझको दुबारा UPSC में appear होने का chance नहीं था। मैंने request किया कि जब तक मुझको बाहर काम नहीं मिल जाता मैं कुछ दिनों के लिए यहाँ continue करता रहूँ। जो assignment उन्होंने मुझको दिया उसको मैंने fulfill किया और जब चक्रवर्ती साहब यहाँ पर Director बनकर आये, उन्होंने कहा कि आप छोडकर मत जाइये, मैं कुछ करता हूँ। उन्होंने confirmation दिया तो फिर मैं यहाँ काम करता रहा। मेरा actual में तब background M.Sc Botany का था और जब मैं UPSC की तैयारी कर रहा था, उस समय मैंने previous year Sociology में M.A. किया था। उस basis पर भट्ट साहब ने यहाँ पर exhibition program में काम करने के लिए अनुमति दी थी। मैंने काम किया। जब चक्रवर्ती साहब आये तो बोले कि आपकी education की कोई दिक्कत नहीं, जो आप काम करते हैं वो ज्यादा अच्छा है, आप उसको करते जाइये। उनके रहते रहते मैंने काम करना शुरू किया और यहाँ काम करते समय उनके समय मैंने M.A Archaeology में pass किया। Sociology भी मैंने यहाँ रहते समय clear किया क्योंकि चक्रवर्ती साहब हमेशा लोगों को पढ़ने के लिए कहते थे। तो पहले मैंने Sociology pass किया

और उसके बाद Archaeology में M.A. किया। उसके बाद मैंने Museology में Diploma भी किया। ये होने के बाद चक्रवर्ती साहब ने executive council में कुछ amendments करवाए और फिर उसके बाद March 2000 मेरा appointment regular हो गया, मेरे साथ मैडम शम्पा शाह और गरिमा शुक्ल। तीन लोगों को एक साथ पक्की नियुक्ति मिली। Amendments होने के बाद एक डेढ़, दो साल यहाँ काम किया। उसके बाद as Director डॉ. बासा साहब यहाँ पर आये। उस समय क्योंकि मैंने publication में दस साल काम किया और मेरा M.A. Anthropology भी 2006 में हो चुका था इसलिए सारे Anthropologist जब tour में जाते उनके साथ मैं field work पर भी जाता था।

आप कहाँ गये थे?

छत्तीसगढ़ मेरा पहला field work था। मेरा birth place रायपुर है। पूरे छत्तीसगढ़ और उड़ीसा और महाराष्ट्र में कोंकण के area, पुणे से लेकर शमाल्त्वादी और केरल में तिरुवनंतपुरम और क्लिोन के आस पास में, इन सब जगहों पर मैंने काम किया।

इन field works में क्या आपने museum के लिए collections किये हैं?

Museum के लिए collection के संदर्भ में objects की मात्रा कम रही। पर हमने house type का research work किया। बाद में जो लोग गये वे objects collect करके ले आये। हमने area की पूरी जानकारी collect करके लोगों को बताया कि इस region में क्या क्या है और वहाँ के लोगों को जोड़ा ताकि हमारे museum को अच्छे artist मिलें। जब जब हमने workshops कीं तो उसमें हम लोगों को museum के artists लिए मिले (देखें पृ. 149)। छत्तीसगढ़ बहुत ज्यादा naxalite affected area है और मैंने अपना सारा काम बस्तर पर किया है। मेरा Ph.D. का काम भी बस्तर के area में है। मैंने जब शुरुआत में काम किया तो यह जगह बहुत सुन्दर थी। Verrier Elwin साहब ने वहां काम किया था और anthropologists, sociologists और archaeologists ने बस्तर के अलग-अलग area पर काम किया है। दो तीन anthropologists ने जो काम किया, उसके आधार पर उन्होंने government को suggestions दिये पर government ने उनकी कोई बात नहीं मानी। आज जो नक्सलवाद की समस्या बड़े रूप में हुई है वह नहीं मानने की वजह से है। Anthropologists ने government को suggest किया कि बाकी कुछ ना करें एक छोटा सा काम कर दें। मैंने और भट्ट साहब ने भी कहा कि वहां के लोगों की जो parallel government या परगना माजी व्यवस्था

Artists at Work

थी, वो व्यवस्था आप मान्यता देकर लागू कर दें और उसको एक level पर जाकर तहसीलदार से जोड़ दें या जो भी आपकी administrative wing हो उससे जोड़ दें पर government ने उसको नहीं माना। वहां के लोगों का पूरा का पूरा जो system है वह belief system से जुड़ा हुआ है। belief system में माता का cult है। जो कुछ करेगी माँ करेगी। चाहे बहुत बड़ा प्रशासक ही क्यों न हो, कोई भी व्यक्ति कुछ हो, माँ सबसे supreme goddess है। उससे वो सब लोग linked हैं। यानी, पूरे बस्तर में यदि जो भी हो रहा है तो वह माँ ही कर रही हैं। चाहे कोई tribal हो या non-tribal, सबका माँ पर belief है। हमारी शिक्षा पद्धति मैकॉले के system से linked है और हमारा पूरा brain मैकॉले जैसा बन चुका है। जब हम मैकॉले वाली शिक्षा को बस्तर वालों की शिक्षा से correlate करते हैं तो naturally हमें ज़मीन आसमान का फ़र्क लगता है। हमने आज तक भारतीय शिक्षा को चालू नहीं किया। मैकॉले शिक्षा के तहत हम एकदम अंग्रेजी system में जाते है और छत्तीसगढ़ के लोग native Indian system में जाते हैं। क्योंकि हमारी शिक्षा अंग्रेज़ी में है, गांव में रहे, पर मैकॉले पद्धति से पढ़े हैं, अँगरेज़ बन चुके हैं अत: हम उनकी बातें समझ नहीं पाते हैं। जब हम स्थानीय लोगों से बात करते हैं तो पता लगता है कि वे इस system से भिन्न हैं। उनके आचार-विचार सब अलग हैं। और कहीं ना कहीं हम लोगों में और उनमें द्वंद्व आ जाता है। दूसरी बात यह है कि जब भारत में स्वतंत्रता संग्राम हुआ था, तो native Indians को स्वतंत्रता संग्राम में दर्जा दिया गया और इन्होंने अंग्रेज़ों के विरुद्ध लड़ाई की। अब क्या हुआ कि भारत में हम लोग जो प्रशासन में हैं उनके विरुद्ध हैं और हमारे प्रशासन की native Indians के विरुद्ध लड़ाई चल रही है। ये naxals की समस्या बहुत सारी इसी कारण हुई है।

आपकी analysis बहुत अच्छी है। मुझे आप अपने Ph.D के काम के बारे में बतलाइये।

मेरा Ph.D का काम बस्तर के एक सुर्दुंगा गांव में है। वहां पर हल्वा लोग रहते है। बस्तर के राजा की territory में धन्तीश्वरी थीं। धन्तीश्वरी की territory में तकरीबन nine tribes है। सारी गोंड tribes हैं। पर वे सब अलग-अलग groups में divided है, परजा हैं, मुरिया हैं, माडिया हैं, धोर्ला हैं, हलवा हैं और महरा हैं। सारी Scheduled Tribe Communities और महरा एक Scheduled Caste Community है। ऐसी सात आठ Communities वहां रहती हैं। गोंड की आराधना देवी धन्तीश्वरी हैं। धन्तीश्वरी basically इन tribes की ही देवी नहीं वरन राजा की देवी भी है। बस्तर के राजा अन्नम देव basically telengana से

बस्तर migrate किये थे। बस्तर में धन्तीश्वरी उनकी आराधित देवी थी। हलवा आदिवासियों के लोक विश्वास एवं अनुष्ठान पर मैं काम कर रहा हूँ। वहां पर सारे गांवों में वैसे बहुत सारी देवियाँ है और एक गांव में कम से कम दो या तीन देवी होती हैं। कभी-कभी पांच हो सकती हैं या सात हो सकती हैं। सारी देवियों का एक एक administrative काम होता हैं। administrative jobs उनके प्रभाव को फैलाते हैं, वे अपने administrative jobs बहुत अच्छी तरह से करती हैं। अब सुर्दुंगा गांव में हलवा tribes पर मैं काम कर रहा हूँ, वहाँ पर बंगाराम माई एक देवी है। बंगाराम माई मतलब बंगाराम और माई है अर्थात माँ और पिता दोनों साथ में है यानी अर्धनारीश्वर का रूप है और हल्वा आदिवासी लोग उसको बंगाराम माई कहते हैं। हल्वा आदिवासियों की वह supreme deity है व उसका field न्याय है। वह judge है।

मैंने हल्वा लोगों में देखा कि उनके यहां माता पिता का cult था और बंगाराम माई देवी को पूरी मान्यता मिल गयी। सब लोग उसकी पूजा करने लगे। आज हल्वा आदिवासी बहुत ज्यादा educated हैं, उस जगह में education अच्छी है। उनके कई लोग IAS Officers हैं, ministers हैं, administrative posts में भी अच्छी जगह में है, बहुत अच्छे teachers भी हैं। छत्तीसगढ़ में रायपुर से धंदारी के आसपास के area के लोग देवी देवताओं को कम मानते हैं वे हिन्दू cult को बहुत मानते हैं। ये कहते हैं कि इनकी उत्पति शिवजी और पार्वती जी से हुई है। शिव पार्वती को हिन्दू धर्म माना जाता है और धीरे धीरे ये हल्वा आदिवासी हिन्दू धर्म से रिश्ता बढ़ा कर स्वयं भी हिन्दू हो जाते हैं। अब इनके सारे देवी देवता हिन्दू हैं। उसी तरह प्रमुख रूप से उनके पुराने चार पांच देवी देवता धीरे धीरे upgrade हो रहे हैं। मैं आपको बता रहा था कि बंगाराम माई पुराने बस्तर में (अब बस्तर में पांच districts हो गये हैं। पहले बस्तर एक ही districts था और United Kingdom के बराबर था) एक ऐसी देवी थी जो supreme deity थी और वहां पर एक chief justice के रूप में थी। जैसा मैंने पहले बताया गांव की देवी की अपनी अपनी administrative jobs होती हैं और यदि कोई देवी उस administrative jobs को कहीं असफल कर दें या overlap कर दें, या अपने काम के अलावा दूसरे काम को करें तो उनकी न्याय प्रक्रिया में दंड का प्रावधान है। उस देवी से कोई गांववाला तो नहीं लड़ सकता, पर उस देवी के विरुद्ध परगना में appeal करते हैं तो परगना माजी कहता है अब इस देवी से और control नहीं हो रहा और उसके ऊपर state में बैठी supreme deity बंगाराम माई से उसकी complaint की जाती है और बंगाराम माई decide करती हैं कि उस देवी को गांव में रहना है या

नहीं रहना। देवी ने उस area में कुछ गलत काम किया व appeal बंगाराम माई के पास गयी। बंगाराम माई उसको सुन करके और यदि justified हो गया कि वह गलत है तो उसको उठा करके सीधा दंड दे दें, जेल में डाल दें, वहां एक जेल है, उसमें डाल दें, और नहीं तो उसको suspend करके उसकी power किसी दूसरे देवी को दें और दोषी देवी को तभी inactive कर दें।

ये system क्या आपने खुद study किया?

मैंने study करते हुए लोगों के बीच में रह कर इन चीज़ों को खुद देखा और समझा है। Actuallly 2007 July में मेरा Ph. D. में registration हो गया और चार साल लगातार मैं वहां जाता रहा। उनके साथ रहा और तीन चार बार जो उनके बड़े बड़े जात्रा होते हैं उसमें शामिल रहा। उनको मैंने महसूस किया। अब मैं उसको लिखने की शुरुआत कर रहा हूँ। मेरे पांच साल में चार साल खत्म हो गये और अब मेरा extension हो गया है। अब जाकर मैं लोगों को समझा हूं कि वहां लोग क्या करते हैं। जो मैंने बताया यह judiciary system के बारे में है। इस judiciary system से उनकी सारी culture जुड़ी हुई है। हर काम में उस देवी से पहले बात करते हैं, देवी response करती है हाँ ठीक है तो करते हैं। उनका सारा system उस विश्वास से जुड़ा हुआ हैं, पानी गिरना है तो इस विश्वास से जुडा़ हुआ, अकाल पड़ा तो इस विश्वास से जुडा़ हुआ, अचानक कोई मर गया, कुछ हो गया तो वह भी इस विश्वास से जुडा़ हुआ है। हालाकि वे दोनों तरह की चीज़ें करते हैं, क्योंकि वे educated हो गये हैं, health point of view से वे doctors को संपर्क करते हैं पर वे अपने system को भी revive करते हैं और कहते हैं कि हम दोनों system लगाते हैं व देखते हैं कि किससे हमको फ़ायदा होता है। क्योंकि हमारा traditional knowledge system बहुत पहले से चला आ रहा है, हम उसको खत्म नहीं करेंगे।

तो यह प्रक्रिया भी चल रही है और आपकी thesis कब तक complete हो जायेगी?

जी चल रही है। मैं कोशिश करूँगा, सर, इस नवम्बर तक पूरी हो जाए। मैं कुछ दिनों में अब छुट्टी लूँगा, मुझे छुट्टी नहीं मिली। बिना छुट्टी के काम नहीं कर सकते। ऐसा है कि मैंने जानकारी ले ली, सब कुछ हुआ। अभी जैसे अनुष्ठान में मैंने देखा कि वे पूजा करते हैं। वहां पर पूजा करने के लिए मैंने पहले देखा था कि अगरबती नहीं होती थी अब मैं देख रहा हूँ कि चार साल में अगरबती आ गयी। उसी तरह उनके यहाँ पूजा करने के लिए सिर्फ़ चावल महत्वपूर्ण था, अब उसमें colour आ

गया। पहले सिर्फ़ चावल में एक हल्दी का रंग होता था, अब चावल में लाल रंग की लाली का रंग आ गया है, गुलाल का रंग आ गया है। अब मार्केट में जो रंग मिल रहे हैं वो उसमें शामिल होते जा रहे है। उनकी संस्कृति में बाहर की संस्कृति involve हो रही है। यह भी एक recent परिवर्तन है। पहले ऐसा नहीं था। पर इधर सादा system था कि घर में चावल है और घर में खाना बनाते समय उसके लिए हल्दी (वही गाँव में हल्दी का पेड़ होता है) को मसलते है, उसको चावल में मिलाते हैं, और देवताओं को चढ़ाते हैं और प्रणाम करते हैं। ना उनके पास आरती के लिए कोई दिया है, ना अगरबती है। वे एक गोंद gum का इस्तेमाल करते हैं, जो साल वृक्ष का गम होता है। उसकी एक अजीब तरह की smell आती है और वे लोग मानते है कि उस smell से atmosphere में जो आत्माएं घूम रही हैं व जो देवी-देवता घूम रहे हैं, वो उसमें आते हैं। उनका माध्यम एक सीरा होता है, जिसके through वे बात करते हैं।

क्या ये चीज़ें आपने detail में लिखी हैं? आप जितनी ज्यादा अच्छी ethnography कर सकें कीजिये, इसमें आप details में जाईये, क्योंकि ऐसा काम केवल anthropologists करते रहे हैं, पर आज कल कम हो गया है।

कुछ कुछ लिखा है, अब मैं उसको final लिखूंगा। मैंने यह सब वास्तव में देखा है, अभी मेरे साथ जो समस्या आयी हुई है कि मैंने जिस प्रोफ़ेसर के नीचे Ph.D. का registration कराया है वो actually sociology professor हैं। उनका यह मानना है कि हर प्रोफेसर को साल में पांच Ph.D. कराने में फ़ायदा होता है। मेरी जब उन्होंने screening की थी, तो उन्होंने कहा कि आप ढाई साल तो लेंगे ही मुझको मालूम है। जब मैं काम कर रहा था तो मैं field में गया तो मेरी curiosity बढ़ गयी और मैं उस काम को पूरा करने की जगह और ज़्यादा सामग्री collect करने में लग गया। इस कारण से चार साल हो गये। अब मेरे ऊपर pressure आ रहा है कि जैसे भी Ph.D. को लिखकर जमा करूं बाद में research होती रहेगी। उनका कहना था कि इस Ph.D. में आपका जो topic है, उसको करने के लिए आपको दस साल लग जायेंगे।

आप मुझे बताइये कि इस museum में जो आपका काम है और research का काम है इसमें किस तरह से चीज़ें जुड़ी हुई है, किस तरह की कठिनाईयां हैं?

Museum में मेरी जो वर्तमान posting है वह Coastal Village Division में है। उसमें केरल के बहुत सारे आवास types है, अत: वहां से जो लोग आते हैं उनसे मेरी अच्छी dealings हैं और Public Relation पहले ही मेरा पुराना काम

था। इसके अलावा जो काम नहीं हो पाते वे काम अगर डिरेक्टर मुझको सौंपते है तो मैं उनको करने का प्रयास करता हूँ। यदि research में मुझको कहीं जाना है, तो मैं उस area में जाकर एक preliminary work करके आता हूँ और मैं यहाँ आकर अपने seniors को बताता हूँ कि मैंने यह देखा है। फिर उस काम पर दूसरे जाते हैं। होता क्या है कि पहली बार जाकर आप कुछ काम करके तुरंत objects नहीं ला सकते। अब जिस तरह से market में globalisation वाला काम चल रहा है, उसमें हर आदमी यह समझता है कि कोई आदमी आया है तो हमको पैसा देगा और research करने से इसको फ़ायदा होगा, इसको पैसा मिलेगा व हमको कुछ नहीं मिलेगा।

इसके पहले बस्तर में ही, विकास भट् साहब के साथ मैंने death songs के ऊपर काम किया था। मुरिया लोगों का मानना है कि जब उनके माँ या पिता का देहांत हो जाता है, तो उसके बाद जो funeral work करते हैं, उससे वह खत्म नहीं होता। funeral होने के बाद मुरिया customs के अनुसार पहले तो माता पिता living रूप में हमारे साथ थे अब मरने के बाद वो उस संसार में (मृत्यु संसार में) अभी भी जीवित हैं और उनकी अपनी ज़िंदगी है और वे अपने तरीके से वहां जी रहे हैं। जीवित रहते समय जिस तरह की activities करते थे, उसी तरह की activities वे मृत्यु के बाद भी कर रहे हैं। मुरिया में अंत में तर्पण करते है, उनके यहां यह काम पूरा गोत्र के हिसाब से चलता है। उसमें बहुत सारे लोग अपनी economical and social conditions के अनुसार बात करके इकट्ठा होते हैं। एक particular date fix होती है, उसमें वे पूरे गोत्र के लोग आते हैं और अपने पूर्वज के लिए एक पत्थर गढ़ाते हैं। उस पत्थर को गढ़ाने के लिए बहुत सारा process होता है। उसने जनम से लेकर मृत्यु तक जो-जो भी काम किया है, वो सब उस समय किया जाता है और उसके बाद जो मर गया उसकी आत्मा से पूछा जाता है कि आपने क्या क्या किया है, क्या क्या करना है। तो वह आदमी एक mediator के through transmit करके बताता है कि क्या क्या करना चाहिए और लोग वैसे वैसे करते जाते हैं। फिर उसके बाद एक पत्थर का घर बनाते हैं। जिसकी मृत्यु हो गयी है उस व्यक्ति लिए एक घर बनाते हैं, उसको हनाल्कोट कहते हैं। हनाल्कोट मतलब बहुत सारे अलग-अलग size के पत्थर। वहां जाकर पत्थर (घर का structure बनाने का पत्थर) को चुनते है। उसके बाद उस पत्थर को लाते हैं, कोटेकल (एक जगह जहाँ पर सारे पूर्वजों के पत्थर गड़े होते हैं) में अपने rituals पूरा करने के बाद उस व्यक्ति के पत्थर को गाड़ते हैं। और मृत व्यक्ति से विनती करते हैं कि ये आपका final departure हो रहा है आप इसमें आकर रह जाएं और हमको आप तंग न

करें। हो सकता है हमसे गलती हुई हो पर हम आपको याद रखेंगे, अगर इस final departure के process में कुछ गलती हो गयी तो रात को मृत व्यक्ति कुछ सपना देगा। या सपना नहीं दिया भी तब भी सुबह जाकर उस जगह को check करते हैं। किसी ने पत्थर को हिला तो नहीं दिया, पत्थर को कुछ दिक्कत तो नहीं है, वहां पर कुछ impression तो नहीं है, जिससे मृत व्यक्ति को तकलीफ़ हो रही हो। उसके बाद वहां पर एक अनुष्ठान करते है और यह मान लिया जाता है कि हमारे द्वारा process करने से हमारे पूर्वज का final departure हो गया है। अब हमको चिंता करने की कोई बात नहीं है और सारे लोग अपने अपने घर चले जाते है। final departure करने का process विशेष होता है कि यदि पिता का final departure करने का process कर रहा हूँ तो उसे मैं नहीं करा सकता। मेरी पत्नी के भाई हैं वे करेंगे या मेरी बहन के ससुर हैं वे करेंगे। वे पूरे process को करेंगे। वे हमारे घर आयेंगे हम उनको सारी चीज़ें उपलब्ध कराएँगे और उन्हें सारी चीज़ें बना करके खाना है और जो भी उनका खाना पीना कपड़ा सब काम वे करेंगे। हम कुछ नहीं करेंगे।

क्या मानव संग्रहालय से कोई पुस्तक निकली है, जिसमें ये चीज़ें described हों?

जी नहीं। मैं एक चीज़ बताऊँ, शुरू से मेरा माध्यम हिंदी रहा तो मुझे अंग्रेजी में लिखने में परेशानी होती है। हमारे यहाँ जो अधिकतर किताबें निकली हैं सारी अंग्रेज़ी में हैं। मैंने देखा है कि कई किताबें एक gist form में है कि Verrier Elwin ने क्या किया है। उसको पढ़ने में हल्का सा नयापन लगता है Verrier Elwin ने जो काम किया है मैं उसका parallel काम कर रहा हूं। मैंने जब बस्तर में काम किया तो मुझको एक कहानी बतायी गई। पालकी गांव में एक आदमी मर गया। उसके घर में कोई नहीं था। जब वह मर गया तो अचानक उसके आसपास के पड़ोसी लोगों को हल्का सा ऐसा लगा कि यह बुजुर्ग तो रोज़ निकलता था, पता नहीं क्या हुआ। सब लोग जुड़े तो उन्होंने देखा कि उनकी लाश पड़ी हुई थी। वे समझ नहीं पाए कि इसका क्या करें। उन्होंने गांव के सिरहा से पूछा, सिरहा को trance आया। trance आने का एक process होता है, उसके लिए थोड़ी पूजा करते हैं फिर धीरे धीरे उसको trance आ जाता है। तो trance में उससे पूछा कि यह आदमी मर गया है, इसकी आत्मा से पूछो कि क्या करना है। उससे पूछा गया। तो उसने कहा कि तुमको चिंता करने की कोई बात नहीं। मेरी जो लाश पड़ी है इसको पड़े रहने दो। मेरे घर पास के जो बर्गद का पेड़ है मैं उस पर बैठा हूँ। मैं कहीं नहीं गया हूँ। तो उससे यह पूछा कि भाई तुम्हारा तो पड़ोसियों को अंतिम संस्कार करना

है, वह कैसे करें। हम इसलिए पूछ रहे है कि यह लाश सड़ जायेगी और दिक्कत आएगी, गांव में बदबू फैलेगी उसने कहा तुम्हें चिंता करने की कोई ज़रूरत नहीं। यहाँ से अस्सी Kilometer दूर मेरा एक दोस्त है उसको मैंने inform किया हुआ है, telepathically। वह सब पैसा लेकर आ रहा है और वही सारा काम करेगा, आप चिंता मत करो। दूसरे दिन सुबह उसका दोस्त आ गया। उससे पूछा कि भाई तुमको खबर किसने की। वह बोला मुझे सपना आया, मैं सब लेकर आया हूँ। उसने अंतिम संस्कार किया। जब अंतिम संस्कार हो रहा था उस समय फिर उससे गायता के माध्यम से पूछा। मरे हुए आदमी ने कहा चिंता मत करो अभी। मैं बैठा हूँ। लाश को पूरी जलने दो, मैं बताता हूँ क्या करना है, मैं कहाँ रहूँगा। फिर लाश जल गयी, पूरा काम हो गया,.लोग दारु पी रहे हैं। उनके यहाँ जो दस दिन का काम तीन दिन पर खत्म हुआ उसके बाद फिर उससे पूछा भाई आपको कहाँ जाना है। हमारा काम तो खत्म हो गया। तो वह मरा हुआ आदमी बोला मैं इसी जगह रहूँगा, अपना काम करूँगा, अब किसी को तंग नहीं करूँगा। अब जिस जगह में वह रह रहा है, उस जगह में अगर कोई destructive activity होती है या कोई wealth activity होती है। तो माना जाता है कि वही कर रहा है।

जिस तरह की चीज़ आपने बतलाई है, इसका representation यहाँ संग्रहालय में mythological trail में या कहीं हुआ है?

अभी नहीं हुआ सर। मेरे ख्याल से हमलोगों ने इसको record किया है। उसका record और photographs भी है। मेरी Ph.D. पूरी करने के बाद यह काम होगा। कई चीज़ें ऐसे होती हैं जब आप कर रहे हों तो उन लोगों से पूछना पड़ता है। death song को उनकी भाषा में हानापाटा कहते है। हमने यहाँ पर अपने guest house में बुलाकर तकरीबन पचास songs की एक घंटे की recording करवाई थी। वे लोग आये थे और उन्होंने हानापाटा गाया। इसमें पूरी soul लगाकर गाते हैं। उसका record है। हमने उसके translation का काम भी करवाया पर naxalite activity के कारण वह काम पूरा नहीं हो पाया। Naxal problem बहुत ज़्यादा है। ज़ब मैं जाता हूँ, तो मुझको भी सोचना पड़ता है कि यह काम करूं या इससे बाहर निकल आऊँ।

थोड़ा सा मैं एक दूसरे विषय की बात कर रहा हूँ। यह है कि मुझे museum में visitors की categories पता लग रही हैं, स्कूल के बच्चे groups में आते हैं, दूसरे adults आते हैं, दूसरी जगह से आते हैं, कुछ विदेशी लोग भी आते हैं, reserach scholars भी आते हैं, यहाँ पर School of Planning and Architecture

है वहां के लड़के भी आते हैं, आपकी exhibitions होती है जिसमें general public आती है। आपके यहाँ workshops and seminars होते हैं, जिसमें विभिन्न भागों से लोग आते हैं जैसे दो लाख लोग हर साल आते हैं (मुझे एक rough figure मिली है)। उनको समझाने के लिए usually तो यहाँ पर एक guides system होता है। दूसरे Visitors के लिए जानकारी का dissemination/delivery कैसे किया जाता है?

यहाँ पहले हर शनिवार फिल्में दिखाई जाती थीं। जहाँ तक मैंने यहाँ लोगों को देखा है, उन फिल्मों को देखने और समझने के लिए लोगों में interest नहीं है। research scholars को इनमें interest आता है। पर वे एक pocket के रूप में आते हैं। कभी पांच, कभी दस और कभी नहीं आते हैं। general entry वालों को घूमने-फिरने से मतलब और बाक़ी से नहीं। यहाँ पर सब से बढ़िया काम हो सकता है जब स्कूल के बच्चे आते हैं। उससे फ़ायदे यह होंगे कि बच्चे जाकर अपने माँ बाप को बताते हैं और माँ बाप एक normal visitor के रूप में यहाँ आते हैं। कई बार यह होता है हमको बहुत कुछ समझाना होता है और हमारे पास शब्द नहीं होते। और जो शब्द होते हैं वे सामने वाले की समझ में नहीं आते। हम यदि कुछ इस तरह से बना दें कि वे देख कर ही अपने आप समझ जायें। पर अभी कुछ दिनों से भोपाल के बच्चे ही आते हैं, rural areas से बच्चे नहीं आ पाते हैं। यह बात भी है कि स्कूल का curriculum इतना ज़्यादा रहता है कि वे इन चीज़ों पर ध्यान नहीं दे पाते। एक particular समय पर जैसे दिसम्बर की छुट्टी में ही ध्यान देंगे, तो हमारी कोशिश भी होनी चाहिए कि हम दिसम्बर के महीने में ही ये चीज़ें organise कर दें। हमने लगातार सिहोर district के सारे स्कूलों को बुलाकर organise किया था एक volunteer को भी जोड़ा हुआ था और उसमें ये चीज़ें की गयी थीं। उससे यह impact हुआ कि एक पिता आकर कहने लगे कि मेरे बेटे ने आकर मुझको मानव संग्रहालय के बारे में बताया तो मैं देखने आया हूँ। इस तरह का impact हमने बहुत सारे लोगों पर देखा।

कारीगरी के विविध रूप

गरिमा आनंद

Are you Dr Garima? When did you join IGRMS and what are your qualifications?

I am not Dr I am simply Mrs Garima Anand. I am here since April 1993. I have done M.A. in Sociology and later in Ancient History, Culture and Archealogy after joining this institution. Later in 2006, I did M.A. in Social Anthropology.

Since you joined this institution, what work you have been doing?

Initially I was attached with Professor B.K. Roy Burman, who was doing a census project. So I was doing only data analaysis. After this project was over I went to the Director asking what to do now?

At that time Vikas Bhatt was the Director.

वे बोले, अच्छा हम कुछ काम सोचते हैं। We have craft in our educational program. He said you prepare something which says what is craft. और पहले से colleagues ने कुछ translation का काम दिया था। इस तरह से छोटे छोटे काम थे। फिर मुझे ख्याल आया कि pottery या tribal and folk arts पर काम करूं। Then I started going to the library और फिर, बाद में मुझे लगा कि मैंने कोई योगदान नहीं किया। यहाँ काम शुरू करने से पहले I was a school teacher. मेरी इच्छा थी कि मैं पुलिस में जाऊं, पर सेहत की वजह से मुझे कोई ऐसा chance नहीं मिला। मुझे तब लगता था कि मेरा कुछ personality development और vision कुछ clear नहीं था। After joining this museum I came in contact with public और फिर जो भी development मुझमें हुआ है for that I am thankful to this museum. The atmosphere, the people and everything was too good. Since then I am attached with the educational activities of the museum.

और उसके साथ technical correspondence, public relations भी चलता है। After joining as a regular staff as a museum assistant, field में थोड़ा बहुत काम करने को मिला। पर उसको मैं exactly field work नहीं मानती क्योंकि ये tour होते हैं। जैसे कोई camp organise करने आप कहीं चले गए। साथ में वहां कोई resource person है तो उसकी कुछ मदद लेकर थोड़ा पास के गांव में कहीं collection के लिए चले गए।

तो आप कहाँ कहाँ गयी हैं?

1998 में केरल में बीस दिन रुके थे। It was my first tour. उसके बाद में collection के लिए तमिलनाडू व सिक्किम गई थी, व जहाँ headquarter बनाया था, वहीं पर camp हुआ था व Sikkim Governement Department of Culture ने College Festival किया था। लोग वहीं सामान लेकर आये थे, उनसे हमने सामान collect किया था। उसके बाद फिर बीकानेर, राजस्थान में भी collection किया है। अभी हाल में पंजाब और हरियाणा में गए। हमने खुद ही जाकर लोगों के बीच contact किया।

जो आपने Social Anthropology पढ़ी और जो काम आपने यहाँ किया, उसमें क्या संबंध दिखता है या दोनों अलग-अलग चीज़ें हैं?

मुझे ऐसे महसूस हो रहा है कि practically पढ़ाई से संबंध नहीं हैं। मुझे लगता है कि बिना पढ़े जो कर रहे थे, वही पढ़ कर भी करते हैं और I think that anthropology is totally different. किताबें एक तरफ़ और काम दूसरी तरफ़ है।

अब आपको यहाँ इतने साल हो गए, आप एक स्कूल टीचर रही हैं, यहाँ भी visitors को बतलाती हैं, समझाती हैं कि क्या है, क्या नहीं है। तो उस अनुभव से आपको क्या लगता है कि यहाँ के लोग जो museum देखने आते हैं, क्या वे कुछ प्राप्त करते हैं? कुछ लोगों का ख्याल है कि सत्तर अस्सी प्रतिशत सिर्फ़ entertainment के लिए आते हैं। पर knowledge, education के लिए बहुत कम आते हैं। आपका क्या विचार है?

जब भी मेरा visitors के साथ contact होता है, I never let them feel that हम museum personnel हैं, और वे visitors only. कोई knowledge के लिए नहीं आया कोई बात नहीं। आप इंदिरा गांधी जानते हैं, museum जानते हैं, मानव संग्रहालय जानते हैं, जितना जानते हैं आप और कुछ चीज़ add करके ले जाईये। यह मेरी कोशिश रहती है कि मानव संग्रहालय उनकी जानकारी का हिस्सा

बन जाए। हमें उनके interest को जगाना होता है। Though I am not working as a full time guide, हम लोग पहले guide का काम भी किया करते थे, सिर्फ़ मैं नहीं, और भी लोग ऐसा करते थे। जब तक आप लोगों के साथ direct contact में नहीं आयेंगे, तब तक आप यही मान कर चलेंगे कि मानव संग्रहालय में लोग घूमने के लिए आते हैं या उनको interest कम है। interest जगाना होता है।

अपने सारे अनुभव में क्या आपको कुछ खास चीज़ें पता लगीं जो अलग हैं?

यहां का काम बिलकुल अलग ढंग का है। स्कूल में बच्चों को पढ़ा दिया और आप घर आ गए। वह अलग है। यहाँ पर हमारे ऊपर कुछ कहीं नहीं लिखा कि I am a museum personnel जब तक visitors को यह बताया नहीं जायेगा कि हम museum से हैं न वो आपकी बात मानेंगे, न वो आप से कुछ मदद लेंगे। जहाँ तक tribals और community के लोगों के साथ काम करने का सवाल है, कई बार हमारे program में artist आते थे, कहते थे हमको यहाँ रहने के लिए जगह दे दीजिए। यह हमारा लड़का है उसको काम पर रख लीजिए। आपने जो पढ़ा है उसको पढ़ा दीजिए।

संस्कृति की रक्षा करना और उसका सम्मान करना और उसको लोगों को दिखलाना और प्रदर्शन करना ये एक चीज़ है। पर tribal लोगों की livelihood क्या एक समस्या है?

livelihood की समस्या है। अब ज़्यादा develop हो गई है क्योंकि सभी को काम नहीं मिलता है। किसी ढंग का काम नहीं मिलता है। इस तरह की समस्या विकट है। अभी हाल में पिछले साल tribal बच्चों को museum लाकर पढ़ाने का एक program शुरू हुआ। उसको मैं और मेरी एक colleague हम दोनों देख रहे हैं। सबसे पहले बच्चे बेतुल district से आये। सबसे हैरानी की बात है कि बेतुल शहर से दूर नहीं है और वहाँ से आने वाले बच्चों ने बताया कि वे पहली बार train में चढ़े हैं। एक बार बाहर से कोई अठारह साल का artist आया था। किसी ने उससे पूछा कि वह क्या कर रहा है, उसने बताया कि वह नपाई का काम कर रहा है और उसके लिए उसे तीन सौ रुपये मिलेंगे। केवल कुछ दिन का ही काम है, फिर ख़त्म हो जाएगा और वह चला जाएगा। पूछने वाले को आश्चर्य हुआ और वह बोला अच्छा इतना तो हमारे बच्चों की सारी पढाई का खर्चा है। मतलब दस दिन या महीने की आमदनी हमारे बच्चों की पूरे साल की पढ़ाई का खर्चा है। तब मुझे एहसास हुआ कि कितनी ग़रीबी है, और tribal लोग अभी भी ग़रीबी के status

में जी रहे हैं। फिर उसके बाद, दूसरा एक और अनुभव हुआ, museum day पर उसी district से बच्चों को लाया गया था, पर group अलग था। हम उनके साथ बैठे बातें कर रहे थे, तो बच्चे बोले अच्छा इधर मोर को पाला है, शेर को पाला है। हम तो इन्हें मार कर खा जाते हैं। आप लोगों ने यहाँ इन्हें क्यों पाल रखा है? 10th and 12th कक्षा में आने के बाद भी उन्हें नहीं पता कि मोर national bird है या शेर national animal है। या ये Environmental Act है व हमें इन चीज़ों को बचाना चाहिए। अभी भी इन बातों की उन लोगों को awareness नहीं है।

आपके इस तरह के अनुभवों से मालुम पड़ता है कि स्कूल के बच्चों के लिए यहां बहुत scope है।

ज़रूर है लेकिन उनके curriculum के कारण उन्हें यहां आने के लिए समय ही नहीं मिल पाता है, कई बार teachers बहुत interested भी होते हैं। लेकिन संग्रहालय नौ बजे या साढ़े नौ बजे खुलता है और स्कूल सात बजे ही खुल जाता है। टीचर्स बोलते हैं कि अगर आप सात बजे permission दें तो हम बच्चों को ले आयें और पूरा दिन बच्चे enjoy कर सकें। बच्चों को एक बजे गाड़ी वापस ले जाती है। अत: संग्रहालय जल्दी खोलने की सुविधा होनी चाहिए ताकि ज़्यादा से ज़्यादा लोग, खास तौर पर बच्चे आ सकें।

tribal बच्चों को यहाँ आना चाहिए। इसका क्या कोई aim है?

cultural awareness बड़ों को दी जाती है पता नहीं कितने दिन रखेंगे। यदि बच्चों में awareness आये कि हमें हमारी culture को conserve करना है और ये conserve करने लायक है तो मुझे लगता है कि यहां आने वाले 1 प्रतिशत बच्चे भी follow up करें तो यह प्रोग्राम successful हो गया।

आप किस तरह की चीज़ें लिखती हैं?

कई exhibition folders लिखे हैं और students के लिए कुछ handouts बनाये थे। मेरे पास अभी सब ख़त्म हो गए हैं। हर craft के ऊपर एक introductory handout बनाती थी। उसे लोग बड़ा सम्भाल कर रखते थे, इसीलिए आते थे कि यह बहुत अच्छा लगता है। कहते थे कि हमें आपकी यह writing पढ़ने को मिलती है और उसके बाद ही हमारा उस craft में interest हो जाता है।

क्या आपके पास ये handouts यहाँ संग्रहालय में हैं?

सर, अब मेरे पास नहीं है। संग्रहालय में कहीं किसी file में अगर हों तो पता नहीं। At the time of my interview मैंने भूमंडल और शिल्प यात्रा के नाम से

एक presentation तैयार किया था। इसमें कुछ selective projects और बहुत technical process वगैरा डाले थे। उस पर मैंने एक documentation तैयार किया था और कई main crafts के पूरे process पर लिखा था। उसमें आंध्रप्रदेश का कलमकारी था। उड़ीसा का लैकर का काम था और भोपाल का ज़र्दोज़ी था। Students के लिए metal पर मेरे लिखे handouts बहुत काम आते थे। भोपाल में जहां जाती हूँ, लोग मुझे मानव संग्रहालय की क्राफ़्ट वाली मैडम कहते हैं। मधुबनी painting के लिए मैंने दो programs organise किये थे। Whenever I tried to organise such events, Yashoda Devi who is no more, was always there. एक तो कलाकारों के साथ ऐसा सम्बन्ध बना है कि अगर मैं एक फ़ोन करती हूँ तो कहते है कि मैडम आप कहेंगी तो हम आ जायेंगे। आप कभी भी फ़ोन कर देना हम आ जायेंगे। राजस्थान के पोखरन में मूनारामजी है, उनको pottery से इतना पैसा मिला कि वे landlord हो गये। उनको फ़ोन किया, उनके यहाँ शादी थी। नहीं मूनाराम जी आज सात तारीख है और हमको ग्यारह तारीख से प्रोग्राम शुरू करना है और आपको आना ही है। वे बोले ठीक है हम दस तारीख तक पहुँच जायेंगे।

अच्छा आपके प्रोग्राम में कौन कौन आते हैं?

ज़्यादातर Students होते हैं, ladies होती हैं। पहले लड़के भी आते थे, अब लड़के कम हो गये। ये महिलाएं housewives होती हैं। उसमें से बहुत सी ऐसी हैं

An Embroidery Expert

जो अपना खुद का क्लास चलाती हैं। यहाँ सीखने के लिए आती हैं। भोपाल में इन्होंने तरह तरह के courses शुरू कर दिए हैं। पर सभी महिलाएं कहती हैं कि जो यहाँ सीखने को मिलता है वह भोपाल के courses में नहीं मिलता है। पिछले साल से पहले मैंने Sindhi embroidery की classes लगाई थीं। हर्मी चौक embroidery सिंधी लोग करते हैं। सिंधी कला को कच्छी लोग भी करते हैं। Participation बहुत ज़्यादा नहीं था, केवल 20 से 30 लोग आये थे। उसमें से आठ students थे जो fashion designing institute से आये थे। उन्होंने बताया कि अपनी institute से हमने 72 stitches सीखीं पर उनमें ये stitches थी ही नहीं जो हमने यहाँ सीखी हैं। एक बार हमने Tie and Dye पर programme किया था। हमारे artists chemicals नहीं use करते हैं पर बहुत ही knowledgeable होते हैं। इतनी चीज़ें वे बताते हैं जो किताबों में नहीं मिलती हैं। ये Tie and Dye specialist राजस्थान से आते हैं।

अच्छा यह सारा जो network है, इन लोगों को contact करना, इन लोगों को बुलाना, इन लोगों का हिसाब रखना और फिर इनका जनता से संपर्क करवाना, क्या यह सब काम आप लोगों का अपना होता है?

जी सर, यह सब काम मैं ही करती हूँ। उसमें मेरे साथ supporting staff की तरह दो daily wage colleagues attached हैं। तिवारी जी के साथ मैं अठारह साल से attached हूँ। उनकी guidance में काम करती हूँ। जब मेला वगैरा लगता है तो हम लोगों से बातें करने जाते हैं।

artist लोगों के ठहरने का इंतज़ाम क्या guest house में है?

जी हाँ guest house में है। वैसे guest house यहाँ एक नहीं दो हैं। ठीक है, कोई भी problem नहीं। कुछ सुविधाओं की कमी होती है जैसे vehicles बहुत limited हैं।

यहाँ क्या कोई सुविधा नहीं है सिवा इसके कि एक जगह से दूसरी जगह लोग पैदल जाएँ?

साईकल है, पर हर आदमी साईकल नहीं चला सकता है। ऑफ़िस की गाड़ी है, पर अगर driver नहीं है और कुछ emergency है तो लोग क्या करें? Driver की fixed duties है। उसके बाद नहीं मिलेंगे। कभी engaged है, कोई दूसरा program चल रहा है और officially कहीं दूसरी जगह जाना है तो क्या करेंगे?

क्या यहाँ VIPs पर ज्यादा concentration होता है?

That I do not know क्योंकि मैं VIPs से दूर रहती हूँ। केवल तभी जाती हूं जब मुझसे कहा जाता है कि मैं जाऊं और उन्हें attend करूं। नहीं तो मैं public के साथ हूँ और मुझे उनसे interaction अच्छा लगता है। कई बार lunch time के बाद मैं ऐसे ही reception में बैठ जाती हूँ। वहां जो general visitors आते हैं उनके साथ interact करने में मुझे ज़्यादा मज़ा आता है। मैं बिलकुल संकोच नहीं करती, अगर मैं रास्ते में जा रही हूँ और किसी guide के साथ visitor का कुछ interaction हो रहा है तो मैं interfere करने में बिलकुल संकोच नहीं करती हूँ। मेरा सोचना है कि जैसे बैंक, रेलवे, हस्पताल में, जो बाहर से आ रहा है वह आपको काम दे रहा है। अगर आप उनको serve नहीं कर रहे हैं, तो बेकार है, फिर तो संग्रहालय एक जगह dump कर दीजिए और ताले लगा दीजिए।

क्या यहाँ security काफ़ी ठीक है या नहीं है? आपका क्या ख्याल है?

Security और होनी चाहिए। मेरे ख्याल से Security वाले सबसे पहले लोग होते है जिनसे visitors का पहले contact होता है। security guards gate पर बैठने वाले लोग हैं। सबसे पहले visitors उनसे ही मिलते हैं। तो security guards के nature में दो तीन चीज़ें होनी चाहिए Politeness, आप visitors को विश्वास में लीजिए। बोली भी ऐसे होनी चाहिए कि visitors के ऊपर impression पड़े। अब यहां स्थिति काफ़ी सुधर गई है। पहले थोड़े से security guards के ऐसे होते थे और कई बार interfere करना पड़ता था। पर थोड़ा इसमें अभी और सुधार होना चाहिए। मैं नाम तो नहीं लेना चाहूंगी, दो तीन दिन पहले की बात है। मेरी ही personal guest आईं और मैं छुटटी पर थी। उन्हें entry में problem हुई। मेरी इसके पहले भी इसी बात को लेकर बहस हुई थी। साथ में सुविधायें एक के बाद एक और होती जानी चाहिए। जैसे पहले रास्ते नहीं बने थे तो लोग चढ़कर जाते थे, रास्ते बन गये तो लोग आराम से जा रहे हैं। अब visitors की इच्छा है कि गाड़ी लेकर जाने दिया जाये। मैं सोचती हूँ यह हमारी कमी है कि हम गाड़ी allow नहीं करते। जब लोग expect करते हैं तो उनको सुविधा available कराना हमारी responsibility है। सबसे बड़ी चीज़ है timings। सरकार का टाइम चल रहा है और उस time में लोगों का visitation ज़रूरी नहीं। क्योंकि उनके लिए यहां की timings उनके working hours हैं। थोड़ा-सा time change होना चाहिए। shift basis हो सकता है। या कुछ contract basis हो जाए तो अच्छा है। Public amenities की कमी है जिनके पास vehicles है वे फिर भी ठीक हैं पर यहां तक public बस वगैरा नहीं आतीं। इतनी दूर आकर बच्चे देखते है कि यहाँ पेड़ ही पेड़ हैं। उनको attract करने के लिए कुछ होना चाहिए।

भले ही वो एक popcorn की दुकान हो। कैन्टीन में हमने vending machine लगाई। लेकिन यदि यह vending machine gate के पास होती तो अच्छा था। museum में आने वाले लोगों के साथ आस पास के लोग शाम को यहां से निकलते समय कह सकते हैं कि वहां पर जाकर कॉफ़ी पी लो यार या चलो घूमते-घूमते पैदल चलकर आये हैं तो coffee पी लें। कभी फिर ऐसे लोग म्यूज़ियम में अंदर आ सकते हैं, आज यहाँ तक आये हैं, कभी तो अंदर आएंगे और वे जब अंदर आएंगे और अच्छा महसूस करेंगे तो चार और लोगों को भी लेकर आएंगे।

जनसंपर्क और अन्य भूमिकाएं

सूर्यकुमार पांडे

आपका designation Assistant Keeper है। आपका काम क्या है, आपकी technical qualifications क्या हैं?

मैं यहाँ technical correspondence and public relations देख रहा हूँ। अभी एक दो साल पहले यह सब काम देखना शुरू किया है। उसके पहले जिन कामों में assist करता था उसमें field work एक हिस्सा था। सागर युनिवर्सिटी से मैंने 1992 में Anthropology में M.Sc. किया है। मैंने M.Sc.के previous year में मंडला में गोंड community पर काम किया था और Final year में मैंने वेस्ट बंगाल के विदिशा की Professor P.K. Institute में काम किया था। संग्रहालय का एक प्रोजेक्ट मैं देख रहा था। उसमें दो articles publish हुए थे, जो Humankind में हैं और एक दो articles बासा साहब के साथ भी लिखे हैं। मैं भीम्बेटका पर contemporary cultural studies के तहत् काम कर रहा था। Archaeological Survey of India ने एक buffer zone declare किया जिसमें 21 villages हैं। उन 21 villages की demographic study से काम शुरू किया और उसमें फिर detailed field work किया। इनमें धरोई गोंड का सबसे बड़ा ग्रुप है। उसके बाद tribal community में कोर्कू हैं। कुछ भील और भिलाला भी हैं। एक दो families प्रधान की हैं और बाकी फिर दूसरे ग्रुप हैं।

Museum और anthropology में आप किस तरह का संबंध देख रहे हैं।

इस particular museum और anthropology में तो connection है ही सर। यह एक Anthropological museum है और anthropology का जो कुछ भी हम करते है वो इस museum का एक हिस्सा ही है।

पर सवाल यह है कि जो museum के educational aspects हैं, जैसे recording, documentation, delivery, dissemination वे कहाँ तक पूरे हो

रहे हैं और किन-किन दिशाओं में पूरे हो रहे हैं?

Collection and development of the exhibition based on the documentation done in the field work—यहां का काम है। हमारा documentation textual form में होता है, हम कुछ audio और video documentation भी करते हैं और कुछ photography documentation भी करते हैं। इसको हम exhibition के form में display करते हैं। यहाँ पर एक कमी मुझे समझ में आती है कि textual form में documentation सामने नहीं आ पा रहा है। Books and research papers नहीं तैयार किये जा रहे हैं। इस museum का strongest aspect exhibition है। इसके अलावा कुछ इसकी activities ज्यादा important हैं, जैसे Do and Learn Museum Education Program, Performing Arts Presentation Program, Artists Camps, Selling Arts Program, Symposium, Museum Popular Lectures. इस

Performance in front of Vithi Sankul (Indoor Museum)

प्रकार की activities हैं, न केवल यहाँ बल्कि भोपाल से बाहर भी होती हैं। वे काफ़ी महत्वपूर्ण हैं। Mainly general public के लिए हम लोग अपने कार्यक्रमों को through press advertise करते हैं और हमारे जो भी activities और programs हैं, उसको electronic media और print media के through publicize करने की कोशिश करते हैं। संग्रहालय में आने वाले visitors सबसे

ज्यादा important हैं। एक तरह से उनके लिए ही इसकी स्थापना की गयी है। हर साल average दो लाख visitors इस meseum में आते हैं। Winter vacations व summer vacations में ज़्यादा आते है और अन्य holidays के साथ Saturdays और Sundays को भी अधिक visitors आते हैं। स्कूल की तरफ़ से groups आते हैं। Tourists स्वयं ही यहाँ पर आते हैं जो विशेष रूप से घूमने के लिए आते हैं। यहाँ international tourists में दो तरह के लोग हैं। एक तो साँची देखना चाहते हैं, जो usual circuit से जुड़ा international tourist spot है। दूसरी तरह के लोग भीमबेटका में interest रखने वाले हैं। यही दो खास तरह के international tourists इस museum में भी आते हैं। दो साल पहले हम भीमबेटका और साँची में अपना interpretation centre खोलना चाह रहे थे। किन्हीं कारणों से यह हो नहीं पाया। हमारा plan था कि दोनों जगहों में मानव संग्रहालय का interpretation centre हो और भीमबेटका देखने के बाद लोग भोपाल में मानव संग्रहालय आयें। मानव संग्रहालय में जो Rock Art paintings हैं, इनसे related भीमबेटका का जो interpretation है उसे भी समझें। पर ऐसा हो नहीं पाया। अभी केवल मझुली में हमारा एक interpretation centre काम कर रहा है, वहाँ नूतन कमलाबाड़ी में एक सत्र है। यह interpretaiton centre है। वहां पर एक आदमी भी contract पर रखा हुआ है। इस समय हमारी वहां पर काफ़ी सारी activities हो रही हैं। वहाँ के सत्र में ancient manuscript हैं। संग्रहालय ने इनमें निहित knowledge system के translation का काम शुरू किया था और आश्रम से जुड़े हुए resource person भी वहीं रुके थे। उन्हें भाषा की जानकारी है। हमने अंग्रेजी में, असमी में और हिंदी में translation कराने का काम लिया था। इस दौरान वहाँ पर बहुत सी activities भी हुई हैं। यह एक बहुत ही important work है। यह संग्रहालय का outreach प्रोग्राम है।

संग्रहालय की activities का सिलसिला बदलता रहता है। यदि director बदलता है तो priorities बदलती हैं। जब ऐसा होता है तो नये subject पर काम होना शुरू हो जाता है और पहले वाले काम में एक break आ जाता है। मुझे इस संग्रहालय में सोलह साल हो गये हैं। मोटे रूप से जब संग्रहालय का प्लान बना था उसमें तीन बातें मुख्यतः थीं—i) infrastructure, ii) development, iii) education outreach and operations. यह तीनों schemes बहुत open हैं। तो इन schemes के तहत् जो programs बनाये जाते हैं, उनमें भी बहुत liberty है। छोटे-छोटे changes होने की बहुत संभावना रहती है। Broadly हम देखें तो काम वही हो रहा है, लेकिन उसके अंदर काफ़ी बदलाव हो चुका है। Development of open air exhibition में कहीं पर है river valley culture, कहीं पर forest villages. इस प्रकार की कुछ चीज़ें incorporate की गई हैं। यदि senior persons का interest river valley culture में है तो वह काम होने लगता है। फिर कभी कोई और area हो सकता है। उसमें बहुत ज़्यादा काम होने लगता है। कहने को काम open air exhibition का होता है। लेकिन area बदल गया है, communities बदल जाती हैं। इसके साथ साथ इस संग्रहालय में सभी चीज़ें खुले आकाश के नीचे प्रदर्शित हैं। लोगों का इन चीज़ों के साथ interaction होता है, उसमें भी उनको बहुत liberty है। ये मत करो, वो मत करो, Don't touch, यहां पर यह सब नहीं है। Visitors को guide करने के बारे में मुझे लगता है कुछ कमी है। हमारे पास में trained guides नहीं हैं। जब भी कभी इस प्रकार की ज़रूरत होती है, तो हम लोग खुद करते हैं। आज मुझे आपके पास बारह बजे आना था लेकिन suddenly director साब का फोन आया कि एक VIP आ रहे हैं। तब मुझे उसमें involve होना पड़ा।

मानवशास्त्र और संग्रहालय कार्य

राकेश भट्ट

राकेश जी, आप बतलाइये कि आपका अनुभव यहाँ पर कब से हुआ और कैसे शुरू हुआ?

मैं यहाँ पर service में 1987 में आया था। यहाँ पर मैंने as a museum assistant शुरू किया था। आपको यह museum का open air जो दिख रहा है तब नहीं था, सिर्फ़ एक hut सा बना हुआ था। उसके अलावा यहाँ पर कुछ नहीं था। जब मैंने join किया था, तब हमारे seniors ने एक या दो मकान बनाये थे। लेकिन वो भी public के हिसाब से नहीं थे। न proper road थी, न कुछ था। इस कारण से इसका ऑफ़िस तो विट्टल मार्केट पर था। मैंने जब join किया तो सीधा यहाँ पर आया और काम देखा। काम tough था क्योंकि आने जाने के साधन नहीं थे।

आप कहाँ के रहने वाले हैं?

मैं सागर का रहने वाला हूँ। जब भोपाल आया और मैंने यहाँ काम शुरू किया, उस समय यहाँ के route पर कोई बस भी नहीं आती थी। एक साल तक हम लोगों को कभी tempo पकड़ कर आना पड़ता था, या कुछ और या हम लोग पैदल आते थे। नीचे depot से पैदल आना पड़ता था। जाते समय पहाड़ी से होते हुए निकलते थे, काफ़ी दूर पड़ता था। हर रोज़ करीब सात या आठ kilometer site पर भी visit करते थे, क्योंकि काम देखना पड़ता था कि कहाँ क्या करना है, huts बनना है। जब मैंने पहले join किया व पहले tour पर मैं और तिवारीजी छत्तीसगढ़ गये। यही मेरा पहला experience था। यह अलग तरह का museum एक concept पर आधारित है। इस तरह के museum का किसी के पास कोई experience नहीं होता है। जो कुछ भी हम लोगों ने gain किया है, यहां काम करते हुए ही सीखा और develop किया और उसी को लोगों ने appreciate किया। क्योंकि इस तरह का museum कहीं था नहीं। कहीं experience के लिए हम न ही गये और न ही

पहले देखा था। यहाँ का माहौल इतना अच्छा था कि जो भी हमने अपने seniors से सीखा या बोला, वे बोले ठीक है तुम बेफ़िक्र हो जाओ और जो भी field में देखा है वही चीज़ें यहाँ बनाओ। ऐसे 'देखने' (observation) के practical काम के लिए हम field में गये।

सबसे पहले मैं मण्डला गया फिर बिलासपुर गया, जहाँ छत्तीसगढ़ का खास तरह का metal work होता है। फिर वहाँ से बिलासपुर होते हुए रायपुर गया। अशोक तिवारी और मैं गये थे। उस समय बैगा का कुछ collection किया था। प्रधान, बैगा और पनका के कपड़ों का कुछ collection किया था। दूसरी बार मैं 1988 में फिर गया। इस बार अकेला ही खुद जसपुर गया। पहाड़ी कोर्बा और उसके आस पास की communities का collection किया। यह अनुभव बड़ा कठिन था, क्योंकि वहाँ पर गाड़ी की सुविधा नहीं थी व field में जाना था। कई बार गांव में ही कहीं खाने के वास्ते रुक जाते थे। गांव का रहने वाला न होते हुए भी मुझको कुछ भी अलग सा नहीं लगा। यह विचार था कि उनके साथ नहीं रहे तो न वे हमको समझ पायेंगे और न ही हम कुछ चीज़ collect कर पायेंगे। उनसे लेना है तो यदि उनके साथ उठेंगे बैठेंगे नहीं तो मुश्किल है। ऐसा नहीं है कि वहां दुकानें नहीं हैं इसलिए हम उनके पास गये। ऐसा नहीं है। हम गए क्योंकि हमारा museum basically living culture का museum है। जितने भी museum आप जायेंगे, या हमने नौकरी में आने के पहले देखे, वे सारे mostly applied museums हैं। उसमें एक बार आदमी जाता है दूसरी बार कभी नहीं जाता। क्योंकि यह जो setup है जिसमें एक showcase में मूर्ति रखी होगी, कुछ बर्तन होंगे, कुछ कपड़े होंगे, लोग लौटकर आ जायेंगे। दूसरी बार कोई guest आयेंगे तो आप नहीं आयेंगे guest को भेज देंगे। लेकिन यह museum इस तरह का है जो contemporary culture से जुड़ा हुआ है और anthropological museum का एक बड़ा अच्छा गुण यह है कि आदमी जानी पहचानी चीज़ों से थोड़ा सा अलग कुछ चाहता है और यहां उसे कुछ नया मिलता है। इधर हम आये व हमने काम किया। 1998 में छः महीने हम लोगों ने रात दिन काम किया और tribal habitat के मकान बने। घर से सुबह आठ से पहले पैदल आना और शाम को आठ के पहले हम नहीं निकलते थे। workforce थी, artist भी काम कर रहे थे, labour भी काम कर रहे थे, सब से काम कराना। उन artist से बोलना, यह जगह है, इसमें से आप select कर लो। उसके बाद material provide करना। उन चीज़ों को जैसे हमने field में देखा था या उन्होंने देखा होगा वैसे ही सब बनवाना होता था।

यह बतलाइये कि इस सब के पीछे motivation क्या था? आप लोगों को कैसे यह हुआ कि इतना काम करें?

उस समय हम लोग सब young थे। सब तेईस, चौबीस, पचीस की age के थे। और हमारे seniors की age भी इतनी ज़्यादा नहीं, सब चालीस के पास ही थे। जब वो इतना काम कर रहे थे, हम लोग तो रुक ही नहीं सकते थे। Secondly हमारे एक senior विकास भट्ट थे, उनका ऑफ़िस शाम छ बजे के बाद ही शुरू होता था। ऐसा होता था, कि हम सुबह ऑफ़िस आ गये और उन्होंने हमको आज काम क्या करना है बता दिया कि आज ऐसा करना है, वैसा करना है और हम लोग field work पर चले गये और वे शाम को छः बजे के बाद field पर आते थे व आकर देखते और कहते क्या क्या करना है, कैसे करना है। अतः रात को हम आठ बजे लौटते थे। अगर अगले दिन की planning हो गयी तो अगले दिन सुबह से ही हमको काम करना है। Labour आठ बजे आते थे तो हम लोगों को भी जल्दी आना पड़ता था। एक तरह से बहुत अच्छा लगता था, हमारा एक familiar माहौल था। एक brother जैसा ही हाल था। कोई आये भी तो ऐसा नहीं लगता था, कुछ ऊँच नीच हो गयी। कोई कुछ बोल भी दिया, कुछ डाँट भी दिया तो कुछ नहीं लगता था। एक यह भी बात थी कि हमें training मिल रही थी। कह दिया जाता था कि आप जाओ, आपका यह field work है, आपको bus से जाना है, collection करना है। आप वहां जाकर हमें फ़ोन कर लेना कि वहां पर क्या problems आ रही है। वहां से ही बता दो, हमसे वहीं से ही फ़ोन पर sanction ले लो। आपको जो भी करना है, आप लोग सब करके आना। एक freedom भी थी। यह नहीं कि हम कागज़ कबूतर बैठे हुए हैं। यह माहौल था। एक government office जैसा हाल नहीं था। बहुत familiar लगता था, ऐसा नहीं लगता था कि हम museum में सहायता करने आये हैं। एक अलग तरह का experience था। जब museum develop कर रहे थे, तब मैंने बस्तर से मुरिया tribe का एक temple यहाँ बनाया। उसको माता चौकड़ी कहते हैं और मुरिया लोगों का घोटुल भी बनाया। उसके लिए artist वहीं से मिट्टी लेकर आया था। वहीं से पूरी लकड़ी खरीदी। जो बड़े बड़े wooden planks थे, और खंभे थे, सब वहीं से लेकर आया। पहली बार जाकर उनको लेकर आना, मुरिया लोगों को लेकर आना, कैसे संभव हुआ मैं नहीं जानता। वहां जाकर उनके गांव में रुका। उनके होटल में रुका। वहां पर उनके जैसा खान पान किया। वे लोग जब थोड़ा familiar हो गये, तब अपने साथ बारह तेरह लड़कियां, आठ दस लड़के, बीस बाईस लोगों को उनके utensils के साथ लेकर आया। पहले उनके material को देखा, क्या materials चाहिए। फिर

government का पूरा process किया। वहां जो काष्ठागार थे, वहां से पूरी लकड़ियाँ transport करके यहाँ लेकर आया। फिर artist को लेकर आया। हम तो बहुत used to जैसे हो गये, उन्होंने हमारा कुछ नाम रख दिया था, मेरा नाम था लहरदार। आदमी की nature पर और उसकी activities के ऊपर उन्होंने नाम रखे थे। मुरिया में मेरा नाम लहरदार रख दिया। कई महीनों तक उनके साथ काम किया। उस समय मैं उन्हीं के साथ ही खाना खाता था। उनके साथ ऐसा हो गया कि वे कहते थे कि हमारा एक घर भोपाल में है। मुरिया के जो भी ritual हैं, चाहे वो बकरा चढ़ाना हो, मुर्गा चढ़ाना हो या शराब चढ़ाना हो जो भी हो—सब करते थे। उनको यह लगता कि यहाँ पर हमारा एक घर है और जब भी भोपाल आते यहाँ मिलने के लिए आते, देखने आते। यह एक feeling जुड़ गयी थी कि यह government की चीज़ ही नहीं, हमारी भी है।

यह तो बहुत ही important है। ऐसा तो किसी museum में नहीं है।

किसी museum में नहीं है। जब भी उनकी चीज़ें जैसे ornaments या drums हैं, जो भी हैं collect हो रही हैं और transport हो रही हैं, उनके लिए पैसा इतना महत्वपूर्ण नहीं था। उन्होंने देखा कि हमारीं चीज़ें सही जगह जा रही हैं। उनको सही लगा। जितनी भी उसकी कीमत हम लगाएंगे हज़ार रुपये या सौ रुपये लगाएंगे, इस बाबत हम सदा उनके हिसाब से करेंगे। सोचेंगे कि यदि अगर उनको नया लेना हो तो मार्केट में जायेंगे और नयी चीज़ लेंगे। अत: हमने उनको बाज़ार का दाम दिया। यह देखा कि कहीं ऐसा न हो कि वे किसी तौर पर ठगे जाएँ।

यह बड़ी responsibility का व बड़ा sensitive काम था।

बहुत ज़्यादा, जहाँ मैं काम कर रहा था उस area में naxalites थे। वहां के लोगों ने naxal लोगों को बताया कि यह लोग social activist नहीं हैं और ये forest department के नहीं हैं, केवल हमारे साथ बातें करने आये हैं। यह हमारे साथ रुकनेवाले हैं। कई गांवों में जहाँ naxal meeting चलती होती वहीं मैं रुका हूँ। ऐसे खतरे में हम गए लेकिन हमें कोई दिक्कत नहीं पड़ी क्योंकि हम लोगों की feelings अलग थीं, motives अलग थे, कोई इस तरह का नहीं था कि हमें कुछ खरीदना है उसी के लिये जाना है। नहीं। बल्कि हमारा ज़ोर नैतिक मूल्यों पर होता है, यह simple society है और हम से ज़्यादा developed है। उन चीज़ों को हमने हमेशा यहाँ महसूस किया। जब भी यहाँ आयेंगे उसी नाम से बुलायेंगे। बात करेंगे। मैं अगर वहां जाऊँ तो सभी लोगों को जानता हूँ।

इसी तरह से मैंने राजस्थान, गुजरात व केरल में काम किया। जब मैंने गुजरात

में काम किया, तब भट्ट साहब ने मुझसे कहा कि 1991 में हमको coastal area के घर भी बनाने हैं अत: आप field में जाईये। वहां जाकर बात करेंगे कि यहाँ पर हमको house type बनाना है, कुछ collection करना है। आप field में जाकर वहाँ पहले अच्छी तरह से देखें, बाद में हम असली काम की बात करेंगे। हम लोग field में गए व मलयालम भाषा के area में पहुँच गए। केरल बहुत अच्छा state है। communication की कोई problem नहीं। भाषा की कोई दिक्कत नहीं क्योंकि हर family से एक आदमी north में काम करता है। हर गांव से दस बीस आदमी आपको army में काम करने वाले मिलते। हर घर से आदमी विदेश में काम करनेवाला मिलता। जिनको हिंदी नहीं आती वे gulf में जाकर सीख आते। Army वाले सीख ही लेते हैं। north में काम करनेवाले सीख लेते हैं अत: हमको ऐसा कहीं नहीं लगा कि हम कहीं और हैं। पता नहीं लोग मेरा nature जानते हैं या क्या है, जिस field में भी गया, लोग बोलते होटल में मत रुकिये, हमारे घर में रुकिये। केरल में एकदम अलग culture थी। जब हमने मकान तलाशा, एक नालिकेट्टू house type वहां से collect किया। यह छोटा मकान होता है। करीब चार सौ साल पुराना मकान मैंने देखा। बहुत सस्ता था, with cowshed केवल 33500 or 35500 रुपये का था। उनकी tradition में मकान लकड़ी का बनाया जाता है, क्योंकि coastal area में बिजली बहुत कड़कती है। इसलिए environment के हिसाब से लोगों को अपना मकान इस तरह का बनाना चाहिए जो बहुत दिन तक चले और नुकसान न हो। इस हिसाब से वहाँ लकड़ी के मकान थे जिसकी खासियत यह है कि लकड़ी के मकान में nails का use नहीं होता।

जब मैं मकान के लिए बात करने गया तो सवाल उठे कि कहाँ से आये, क्यों आये। हमने उनको museum के बारे में बताया, अपना objective बताया। तब उन्होंने गांव के लोगों को बुलाया। लोगों में बात हुई कि सही है कि नहीं है। बहुत चर्चा हुई। फिर उनको सब ठीक लगा। By chance केरल के कुछ लोग मुंबई से shift हुए थे, उनकी family का एक मकान था, उनको थोड़ा interest हुआ कि हिंदी में बात करनेवाला मिला। उसका birth place मुंबई था, मलयाली था, पर वह respected मलयालम बोल नहीं पाता था। जब भी कोई उससे बात करे तो उसको लगेगा कि कोई पत्थर मार रहा है। जब मेरी उससे मुलाकात हुई तो बोला अरे यह तो हमारे हैं। मेरे साथ वो गया गांव में। बात हुई। नालिकेट्टू का उनका एक मकान बेचने का था, उसने local support से बात किया कि बेचने के लिए ठीक है। मैंने भट्ट साहब को बुलाया क्योंकि उस समय वे डिरेक्टर थे और committee वगैरा करना था। local experts को बुलाया। Historians को बुलाया। बात हुई। मकान

तय हो गया कि इस मकान को ले आयेंगे। सवाल था कैसे ले जायेंगे। हम इसको पूरा खोलकर ले जायेंगे। वे लोग तैयार हो गए। वहां system है कि carpenters या आचारी मकान की पूरी astrology बताता है कि मकान की कितनी life है, कब खुलेगा, कब बनेगा, और इसमें रहने वालों का नुकसान हो सकता है या फ़ायदा हो सकता है वह उसके बारे में सब बतायेगा। मकान को खोलने की कोशिश चालू की। भट्ट साहब भी आये। उनको दो तीन महीने उधर रुकना पड़ा। जब वह मकान खुलने लगा व हम उसको truck पर load कर रहे थे तभी उस लड़के के अस्सी साल के दादाजी ने कहा कि वे नहीं चाह रहे थे कि मकान खुले। लेकिन वह छोटा मकान था, उनको बड़ा मकान बनाना ही था। जब वह truck में load हो रहा था, तो उस लड़के के मामा बोले कि हमारा आचारी सही बोल रहा था कि यह मकान पूरी जिंदगी ऐसा ही रहेगा। यह मकान museum जा रहा है और वहां ऐसा ही रहेगा। जब हम उसको खोलकर भोपाल लाये, वहीं से carpenters, masons और आचारी, कल्लन लोहे का काम करने वाले को बुलाया। हमने उनको जगह, particular direction व facilities दिलवाईं। वहाँ चट्टान थी उसको तोड़ने के लिए हमको ज़्यादा खर्च करना पड़ा। Coastal area का घर बनना था, तालाब था जो sea का backwater लगता। मकानों में वहां पर environment की वजह से humidity अधिक होती है इसलिए खराब न हो व तालाब के कारण यहाँ भी humidity बनी रहे इसीलिए उनको ऐसा location दिया। नारियल के पेड़ भी लेकर आये। सुपारी का पेड़ भी लेकर आये। वो सब वहां पर लगाने के लिए कोशिश की। यह process है और फिर उसमें नारियल के बुने हुए पत्ते लगते थे। तो उनको भी हम वहीं से लाए। हमको पूरा environment बनाना था। वहां के मकान तो एक farmhouse type के ही होते हैं। आस पास पूरी ज़मीन है। नारियल के पेड़ लगे हुए हैं और बीच में उनका घर है। उनको कोई दिक्कत नहीं पर हमको पत्ते वहीं से लाने पड़े। हमको वहां continuously जाना पड़ता था, artist को लाना पड़ता था, पत्ते के लिए जाना पड़ता था, maintenance के लिए बुलाना पड़ता था। मुझे दो साल तक अक्सर जाना पड़ा था। जब भी मैं गया जिनका मकान था, उन्होंने मुझे होटल में नहीं रहने दिया। आप हमारे घर पर रहिये, सामान यहीं रखिये। खाना भी यहीं खाइये, सब कुछ करिये। आप हमारे घर के लड़के समान हैं। यह एहसास museum से ही हुआ। उनका लड़का जो मुंबई में था, पांच साल पहले वह भोपाल आया, इधर देखा तो बोला, हमारा मकान तो हमारे यहाँ से अच्छा इधर maintain हो रहा है। उसने अपनी माँ को फ़ोन लगाकर यही कहा। इस तरह यह community से जुड़ने वाली बात है।

Community से जुड़ रहे हैं और साथ में ये है कि ये national intergration

का एक उदाहरण है। आपने ऐसे लोगों को चुना, जो मुंबई से आये थे, और वहां के रहनेवाले थे, उनकी भाषा कुछ वहां की थी, कुछ हिंदी में भी बात की। बहुत unique है ये experience।

अब जब मुझको collection लेना है, तो पूरे area में इतनी publicity हो गयी कि मन्नाडी से भोपाल में मकान गया है। एक वीरुबनडी थी जिसमें नायर लोग revenue collect करने आते थे। आज केरल के लोग भी इसे नहीं जानते, आज कल नयी generation भी नहीं जानती है। आप को भले ही फिल्मों में देखने मिलती पर अब उसका मिलना बहुत मुश्किल है। मैं उसको collect करने गया। एक petrol pump के मालिक नायर थे मैं उनसे मिला। उनकी पत्नी की property थी। वे बोले हमारी पत्नी दे देगी। फिर मुहूर्त निकला व जन्माष्टमी के दिन उनके यहाँ मुझे खाने को बुलाया। तब मैं गया। उन्होंने पूछा कि आप इसका कितना दे पायेंगे। मैंने कहा, मैं तो इसकी कीमत नहीं बोल सकता, और जितना मेरा अधिकार है उससे ज़्यादा मैं दे नहीं सकता। वे तो बहुत पैसेवाले थे। उन्होंने पूछा कि कितना दे पायेंगे। मैंने कहा दस हज़ार से ज्यादा मैं नहीं दे पाऊँगा। ठीक है। जब कि उनको उतने दाम की भी कोई ज़रूरत ही नहीं थी। उनके परिवार से जुड़े हुए लोग भी थे, वे बोले, ऐसे ही दे दो, यह चीज़ museum में जा रही है। अभी भी उनके यहाँ से लोग कई बार यहाँ आते है। देखते हैं कि मन्नाडी के मकान में वीरुबनडी लगी हुई है। वहां के उनके folk dancers को बुलाया। ऐसे ही हम लोगों ने उन लोगों को जोड़ा। आपने यहाँ मणिपुर festival देखा, उस तरह का केरल का भी हुआ था। हमने राजस्थान का ethnic food festival किया। केरल से हम एक नाव भी लेकर आये। वह एक सौ दस फुट लंबी नाव है जो सिर्फ ओणम के समय boat race में निकलती थी। पम्बा नदी में race होती है। मैंने जो नाव खरीदी वह fishing boat थी। वह नाव ओणम के दिन 31 or 32 days में by road भोपाल आई थी। कोचीन तक sea से आई फिर वहां से special trailer में भोपाल लेकर आये। भोपाल के रहनेवाले मलयाली लोगों ने उसका पूरा welcome किया।

जब मैंने दूसरी fishing boat खरीदी, तो मैंने वहां के fisherman को contact किया और मैंने उनका मकान यहाँ भोपाल में बनवाया। तो वे allepey district में अरद्गपाल्य से artist को लेकर आये। वहीं से मैंने नाव खरीदी। जब नाव खरीदी तो मुझे यह मुसीबत हो गई कि हमको उसे तीन महीने tender के लिए रखना पड़ेगा। क्योंकि ऐसा करना पड़ता है। जब transportation में लगेंगे 91 days, मुझे भी ये problem हो जायेगी। तो मैंने इसे खरीद लिया, पच्चीस हज़ार की नाव थी वो। 65 feet long। उस समय जो डिरेक्टर साहब थे, वे बोले, क्या

करोगे, खरीद तो ली, कैसे transport करोगे। तीन महीने के बाद तो मुश्किल पड़ेगा, tender करना और छोड़ना। बोले, तुम जैसा कहो वैसा कर लेते हैं। मैंने वहां artist से बात की। बोले, हम इसको खोल सकते हैं तो खोल लेंगे। पूरी नाव उन्होंने dismantle करा दी। नहीं तो कम से कम डेढ़ लाख रुपया लगता transportation पर। और मुझे तीन महीने के बाद जाना पड़ता। फिर रुकना पड़ता। तो मैंने उसको पूरा dismantle किया और उसका copper wire जो उसमें लगता मैंने कुछ purchase किया। Dismantling की पूरी videography भी करा ली। उसका पूरा documentation भी किया। Ordinary truck में आ गया पूरा नाव जिसमें मुश्किल से दस पन्द्रह दिन लगता था, transport के लिए। उसमें आ गया। और भोपाल में पूरा उसका reassembling करके, fisherman village में उसका display करा दिया। तो उसको पुनः बनाने की हमारी कोशिश भी पूरी हो गयी अब public के लिए देखने के लिए develop भी हो गया और उससे हमको इतना हर्जाना भी नहीं लेना पड़ा।

इसी तरह जब मैं राजस्थान गया, तो हम लोगों का राजस्थान के desert के घर बनाने का plan था। हमारे यहाँ desert and coastal दोनों तरह के घर बनाये हुए हैं। Artist सब यहाँ आते थे और हम सब बैठकर काम कराते थे। हम दिसम्बर में सोडा गए थे। वहां पर मैंने उनके मकान देखे, जो आधे रेत में थे। यहां उनके घर बनाने के लिए सब बात कर ली, मकान और design सब select हो गया, material सब वहीं से लाना था। बनाने का artist वहीं से लाना था। मैं border में गया। उसमें खैर की लकड़ी होती है। वह बहुत प्रसिद्ध है। मैं लकड़ी लेकर वहां से आ रहा था। रास्ते में पीने का पानी खत्म हो गया। बड़ा tough था, सैंतालीस temperature था। दिन में सैंतालीस और रात में दो और तीन। रात में बहुत ठंडा। वह मेरा पहला experience था, 1994 की बात है। जो पानी ले गए थे, वह खत्म हो गया। वहां तो tanks चलते रहते हैं, लोग दो साल तीन साल पुराना पानी पीते रहते हैं। बारिश में गिरा पानी store कर उसे पीते रहते हैं या बहुत दूर से पानी लाते हैं। जब मैं वहां गया, मेरा बहुत tough अनुभव था। दिन भर truck से लकड़ी लेकर आये तो पानी खत्म हो गया। पानी के लिए और दो घंटे लगेंगे, समय लगेगा। पानी के लिए इतनी दूर जाना पड़ेगा, कैसे काम करेंगे। वे बोले tube में पानी है साहब। मैंने बोला लाओ कैसे भी कुछ प्यास तो बुझानी है। तो वे लाये एक दम yellow पानी। मैं देखते ही दंग रह गया। ये लोग कैसे जीते हैं। उन्होंने क्या किया लोटे में कपड़ा लगाया और पी लिया। मैं नहीं पी सकता। मैं तो मर जाऊँगा। मैंने क्या किया, कपड़े में गीला करके गले से लगाया था। दो घंटे के बाद रात को गांव

में truck रोका। रात को वहां खाना खायें या न खाएं। राजस्थान का खाना इतना rich है, इतना काम करने के बाद हजम भी हो जाता। डेढ़ सौ दो सौ ग्राम देसी घी का खाना एक दिन में हजम हो जाता। खाना खाकर मैं वहां पर रात को सोया। मैंने सोचा ये कैसे लोग हैं कि कह रहे हैं कि सर आप अंदर जाकर सो जाईये। मैंने कहा गर्मी है मैं बाहर सो लेता हूँ। बाहर उन्होंने cot डाल दी, दो तीन चद्दर बिछा दी। रजाई रख दी। मैंने सोचा कैसे पागल लोग हैं, दिन में इतना temperature है और रात को इतनी गर्मी है और रज़ाई रख कर चले गए। रात को ग्यारह बारह बजे इतनी ठंड लगी कि मैंने गांववाले का दरवाज़ा खटखटाया। उसने कहा कि साहब मैंने पहले ही कहा था कि आप अंदर सो जाइए। रात में उसने थोड़ी चाय पिलाई और मैं फिर अंदर सो गया। यह मेरा राजस्थान का experience है।

वहीं एक और जगह मकान select करने के लिए गया। पांच kilometer रेत में जाना था, वहाँ कोई गाड़ी या jeep नहीं जाती। यह भी एक experience बताना था। जाने के लिए एक ऊँटवाली गाड़ी मिली। एक बार मुझे बगैर काटलीवाला ऊँट मिला जिस पर बैठकर मुझे जाना था, उसमें इतनी तकलीफ हुई थी क्योंकि उसमें seat नहीं होने से हड्डी पसली एक हो गई और गांव वाले बैठे तो उनको कोई problem नहीं। ऊँट के ऊपर के बाल को पकड़कर मुझे बैठना था, इतनी कष्टदायक घड़ी थी। लेकिन उस सवारी पर बैठकर किसी तरह पहुंचा। लौटकर भी फिर मुझे आना था। जब मैं दो दिन बाद गया, जिस ऊंट गाड़ी पर जा रहा था, उस पर tyre वाले टंगे रहते थे, और वे रेत में ऊंट चलाकर ले जाते थे। इसमें मेरा एक experience हुआ। मेरा उद्देश्य था कि museum में मकान बनाना है, community के साथ जुड़ाव पैदा करना है, house type develop करना है। तो मैंने tyre वाले से बात की, उसने बोला ठीक है साहब मैं उसी रास्ते मंदिर जा रहा हूँ। पास में पहाड़ी मंदिर है, मैं वहां जा रहा हूँ। चालीस kilometer कुडी है, कुडी से दस बारह kilometer और जाना है। तो मैंने कहा ठीक है, उसने कहा कि आप चलते हैं तो चलिए। मैं चला गया। उसको पैसे देने पड़े थे, मैंने पैसे दिये। मैं ऊँट गाड़ी पर बैठा। उस में एक बकरा भी बैठा हुआ था। उस आदमी ने कोई मन्नत मानी हुई थी और वह बकरे की बली देने आया था। एक ही गाड़ी में दो लोग जा रहे थे जिनके उद्देश्य अलग थे, और बकरे को मालूम नहीं था कि उसकी बली चढ़ने वाली है और वह बहुत आराम से बैठा हुआ था। मैंने कहा, मेरा उद्देश्य अलग है, तुम्हारा उद्देश्य अलग है, पर हम दोनों का रास्ता एक ही है।

केरल में काफ़ी काम किया व बहुत collection किया। मैंने केरल के लोगों को भी काफ़ी पसंद किया। ऊटी भी गया। मैंने गुजरात में भी काम किया। कच्छ में

काम किया। वहां रबाड़ी के बीच गया। खास कर सौराष्ट्र और काठियावाड़ गया। भट्ट साहब का यह plan था कि काठियावाड़ का house type यहाँ बनाना है। उसके लिए काम करना है। हम लोगों ने survey करके पता किया कि वहां एक मकान था। एक तरह से वह मकान जैन लोगों का था लेकिन वे लोग स्वामी नारायण धर्म में convert हो गए थे। उस मकान में इस धर्म के संस्थापक नारायण स्वामी कुछ समय के लिये रहे थे। हमारा उद्देश्य था कि एक traditional house type हमारे यहाँ बने और चर्चा में यह बात भी निकल आई। यह काफ़ी बड़ा मकान करीब चार हज़ार square feet वाला तीन level का मकान था। जैन परिवार से बात हो गई थी, पर उनके ऑफ़िस के funds की problem होने से यह बात materialise नहीं हो पायी। उन्हें किसी और को देना पड़ा फिर मैंने उस area से मकान के elements का collection किया pillars, doors, panels को कहीं कहीं से हमने खरीदा। हमारे museum में आप देखेंगे कि सात नंबर gallery में कुछ पिटारा, पेटियां रखी हैं। वहीं से यह collection किया हुआ है। ये objects धरवा लोगों के हैं। यह राजपूत community है। इनके यहाँ से मैंने collection किया। कपड़े में उनका beads work बहुत अच्छा होता है जिसको औरतें करती हैं और इन कपड़ों को दहेज में लड़कियों को देते है।

आपने तो हमें काफी अच्छी information दी और अपने अनुभव भी बताए हैं। क्या आपने कुछ लिखा भी है?

Museum में एक बड़ी दिक्कत है। कुछ हमारे newsletters में नालिकेट्ठू के बारे में लिखा था। बाक़ी हम लोगों को लिखने का इतना अभ्यास नहीं था। अब बताइये, 1988 में दो सौ labour काम करते थे। उनको भी देखना है, काम कराना है, road develop करना है, कहाँ pillar sign पर क्या आयेगा। पत्थर कहाँ से लाना है। खास तरह के पत्थर एकदम से लेकर आना है। ये एक museum assistant का काम नहीं है। पर हम लोगों ने यह सब काम किया। मैंने पाया कि जो communities यहाँ आती हैं, हम उन सब communities से हम इतने जुड़े हुए हैं। हम लोगों को अच्छी तरह से जानते है। वे अब आते हैं, रुक जाते हैं। वे सोचते हैं कि हमारा घर यहां है। बगैर बोले ही इतना कर जाते हैं। नए लोग जब आते हैं वे नहीं जानते हैं कि कब कौन आ गया। लेकिन हम लोग उनको जानते हैं, हम लोग उनको रोक लेते हैं। चलो आये हो तो कुछ काम करके जाओ, कुछ maintain करके जाओ। हम उस समय कुछ program organise करते हैं इसमें उनको कुछ पैसा भी मिल जाता है और communities जुड़ी रहती हैं। कोई painting बनाकर लाते जैसे वार्ली के लोग workshop में आये तो एक painting बनाकर लाये व

हम लोगों ने उसको museum shop में ले लिया। यह सब तो हमारा उद्देश्य नहीं है। परंतु यह सब उनको support करने के लिए व एक market देने के लिए करते हैं।

यह तो एक बात है कि इन लोगों की livelihood के लिए problems हैं, लेकिन साथ में इन लोगों को इतना लगाव हो जाता है, एक अपनापन हो जाता है। ये एक खास चीज़ है।

आप विश्वास नहीं करेंगे कि जितनी भी इनकी traditions हैं, वे खत्म होने के खतरे पर आ रही हैं। पहले समय में tribes का पूरा bare area था, आज हज़ारों industries आ गयी हैं। दस दस करोड़ से ऊपर वाले units हैं। आज एक होटल में रुकने की जगह भी नहीं मिलेगी और ज़मीन जिसकी कीमत बीस हज़ार रुपये एकड़ की थी, अब लाखों में है। लेकिन वहां पर उनकी traditions खत्म हो रही हैं क्योंकि इन areas के लोग आज gulf में काम कर रहे हैं। रबाड़ी लोग embroidery work करते थे, एक market में कुछ लोग purchase करते थे। अब उन्होंने एक bill पास करा लिया कि हम उन चीज़ों को नहीं बेचेंगे। अब बनायेंगे नहीं। बनायेंगे तो खुद के लिए बनायेंगे। इस तरह ये चीज़ें खत्म होने लगीं हैं। इन चीज़ें को बचाने के लिए हम लोगों ने एक exhibition लगाई। वहां रबाड़ी लोगों को ले आते हैं ताकि उनके mirror work को आम public जानें तथा सीखें। एक community की चीज़ मात्र न रहकर यह tradition चलता रहे। कच्छ में भी कई संस्थाएं काम कर रही हैं जो उनकी चीज़ों को market भी provide कर रही हैं और उनको अच्छी service भी provide करते हैं। अच्छा प्रयास है। Government level पर हमारी एक सीमा है। कई बार आदिवासी चिट्ठी लिखते हैं कि हमारे गांव का थोड़ा विकास कर दो पर यह हमारा काम नहीं। लेकिन वे यह सोचते हैं कि हम उनको support करने आयेंगे। उनकी feelings इस तरह भी जुड़ जाती हैं। वे हमको अपने से अलग नहीं मानते हैं। यह जुड़ाव ही हमारा प्रयास है। हमारा अलग तरह का museum है यह बेजोड़ है। हर Museum की working अलग होती है, सीमायें होती हैं। यहाँ हमें autonomy मिली इसलिए हम लोग काम कर पाए। Field में गये, हम लोगों ने collection किया, डिरेक्टर ने अपने अधिकार के अनुसार committee बनायी और उसको approve किया। तभी काम हो पाया। एक ही दिन में हम लोग tour पर निकल जाते थे, ये आप विश्वास नहीं करेंगे। आप सोच भी नहीं सकते। field में जाना है तो लोग दस दिन पन्द्रह दिन पहले तैयारी करते हैं, planning करते हैं। परन्तु IGRMS में आप बैठे हैं, मैं बैठा हूँ, डिरेक्टर साहब बैठे हैं, यह तय हुआ कि जाना है, केरल से सब

कुछ लाना है। ठीक है तो आज निकल जाओ। हम लोग जवान थे, चले जाते, ऐसा सब हो जाता था। Record सब submit किया, note sheet सब यहीं है, sign किया, advance के लिए दिया, वहां cashier को दे दिया और पैसे same day मिल गये और अगले दिन हम field पर निकल गये। जाना south में, पास में जाना नहीं कि लौट कर आना है। तो ये एक cooperation था, कि आप जाओ और आप को कहीं भी problem आये तो फ़ोन पर बता देना। हम सब कुछ करेंगे। इस तरह का एक माहौल था। और लगातार इस तरह के डिरेक्टर के साथ चार पांच साल कोई आदमी रहे तो उसका motivation बढ़ जाता है। Actually क्या है इस museum के बारे में, paper में experts ने दे दिया कि ये एक pattern है और हमें diverse cultures को दिखाना है या genetics में करना है। इन चीज़ों को लिखना अलग बात होती है, और वास्तव में execute कर दिखाये और public उसे समझे उसको visually प्रदर्शित करे इसके लिए बहुत बड़ा visualization चाहिए। विकास भट्ट के बराबर कोई नहीं है क्योंकि जो vision उन्होंने रखा है, उसकी वह स्वयं planning करते थे और कई stages में उसको रोक भी देते थे। कई नयी चीज़ें add भी करते थे। कई बार ऐसा होता है कि हमने कोशिश की और अगर हम दूसरी चीज़ लाते तो वह add नहीं हो पाती। लेकिन उनके plan में कुछ chapters खुले होते हैं जिससे ऐसा लगता है कि हमारी कोशिश उसका ही एक हिस्सा है। उनके vision में total museum of life style है, इसमें खाने से लेकर, music, उनके kitchen garden, उनके house-types सब शामिल होते हैं। तभी तो लोग जुड़ते हैं। हमने classical music का जो program किया, उसको भी public ने appreciate किया। हर महीने की पूर्णिमा के दिन यह प्रोग्राम करते थे। राजस्थान से fold dance थे। ट्राइबलहैबीटाट में बने उन्हीं के dance और songs को उनके घर के आस पास किया तो पूरा environment lively हो गया। Desert village में भी हमने वही किया। वहां background में नीम के पेड़ के नीचे मकान बनाया था और उसके आगे कुछ dance किया, सबने नीचे बैठकर देखा। ऐसे ही हमने केरला के मोहिनीअट्टम व कुच्चिपुडी भी किये। तमिलनाडु का प्रोग्राम भी किया। हमारी कोशिश है कि ये परम्परायें ज़िंदा बनी रहें।

आप लोगों का उत्साह और आप लोगों का committment हमें मिलता रहे तो बहुत है।

यह support कहीं कहीं थोड़ा रुक जाता है, इसलिए रुकता है कि लोगों की अपनी channel आगे नहीं बढ़ती है उसी जगह लोगों का stagnation है, तो problem है। फिर भी ठीक है, government एक salary देती है उसके लिए

काम करना है और museum अपना मानकर ही लोग काम करते हैं। otherwise आप विश्वास नहीं करेंगे, जब यहाँ पूरा barren था, कुछ huts बनी हुई थी, और हमारे लिए आने जाने की travel का टिकट बन गया था। दस बारह ट्राइबल मकान बन गए थे पर सब जगह तो यहाँ घास थी, आग लग जाती थी। तो हमको रात को बारह बजे घर से आग बुझाने के लिए आना पड़ता था। क्योंकि यहाँ सिर्फ दो चार labour लोग ही रहते थे, बाकी सब बाहर रहते थे। तो आकर साथ में यह सब भी करना पड़ता था। हमारे लिए कोई सुविधाएँ नहीं थीं लेकिन जगह को अपना मानकर करते थे, यह नहीं है कि पुलिस आयेगी, fire brigade आएगा। जिस दिन पहला open air exhibition उद्घाटन था, छब्बीस जनवरी को था, 1998 में रात को दो बजे हम लोग यहाँ से पैदल गए। कुछ साधन नहीं था। रात को कोई गाड़ी नहीं थी। जब senior आते थे, तो साथ में हम को भी आना पड़ता था। वे कहते थे, यह किया है, इसको ऐसे भी कर सकते हैं तो हम लोग करते थे।

A View of Public Participation at IGRMS

एक program चरैवेति हुआ। उसमें हम लोगों ने काफ़ी काम किया। आप विश्वास नहीं करेंगे, इस museum में उस समय इतने लोग आये थे कि सड़क पर खड़े रहने तक के लिए जगह नहीं थी। यहाँ से लेकर lake side तक समारोह रहा। यह समारोह तीन दिन के लिए हुआ था। उसमें international exhibitions लगाई थीं, जिसमें बाहर से काफ़ी लोग आये थे। उसमें हम लोगों ने उस दृश्य को

देखने के लिए ऊंट, घोड़े, टांगे की facilities provide की थीं। यह हमारा सबसे बड़ा program था। उसमें यहाँ पर इटली के objects की exhibition भी हुई थी। वहां तो Rock painting के लिए केवल एक site है। हमारे यहाँ तो rock paintings भरी पड़ी हैं। गोंड paintings भी थीं। गोंड art का जो relation Australian aboriginal communities से है उस पर भी हमारे यहाँ exhibition हुई थी। Australia से लोग आये थे। उनके सामान यहाँ पर display हुए थे, museum ने कुछ purchase भी किये थे। उसमें उनकी aboriginal community का leader भी आया था। उसने बताया कि यहाँ के गोंड लोगों की art और उनकी aboriginal art की painting में क्या common है। दोनों doors का use करते हैं, हम लोगों ने दोनों की combined exhibition की थी। उन्होंने दिखाया कि कैसे Australian aborigines दीवार पर हाथ रखकर अपने मुंह में लाल वाला गेरू भर लेते हैं और फिर उससे spray करते हैं।

Anthropology to Museum: A Journey

Shakmacha Singh

I joined Oriental College, Imphal, for my graduation with a combination of subjects—Botany, Zoology and Chemistry. As I was very poor in Chemistry, I started exploring the better combination of subjects with Botany and Zoology. I remember even today when I first attended the class of Anthropology without registering my attendance in it. The lecture was on *Man's Place in Animal Kingdom* given by Dr. Kamlabati Devi. The lecture was so interesting that I could not but shift over to the subject of Anthropology. Soon after the completion of B.Sc. Honours (Anthropology) in 1997, I worked in NHPC at Loktak in Manipur as a typist on contract basis to earn money to support my family. I could not continue my onward study owing to the poor financial condition of the family. All the same, I gained some experience in official noting, drafting and technical correspondence, which were frequently placed on my table to type for presentation to the concerned officer. I also used to take tuitions for students from Class IV to X, especially in Science subjects in two batches one in the morning and other in the evening after returning from the job.

One day at the office when I was typing a letter of correspondence in the office of the Senior Manager, I saw a copy of *Employment News*, left near my table by the officer. A job for the post of Museum Assistant in the Indira Gandhi Rashtriya Manav Sangrhalaya (IGRMS), Bhopal, had been advertised in the *Employment News*. I was pleased to find myself eligible for the post as the minimum qualification required was an M.A./M.Sc. in anthropology or a B.Sc. Hons. in anthropology. Without further delay, I applied for the post.

Fortunately, I was selected for the post of Museum Assistant in the Other Backward Classes category.

Truly speaking, I had barely visited museums. It was only after seeing the advertisement I made up my mind to visit Manipur State Museum. Museum for me at that point of time was nothing more than a place where antiquities are preserved and exhibited on four walls with attractive blaze of lighting to make the people curious. With some theoretical concerns of anthropology in my background and some knowledge of a museum, I joined Indira Gandhi Rashtriya Manav Sangrahalaya on July 26, 2000. It was after joining IGRMS, I broadened my interest in subjects of anthropology and museology. The interface between anthropology and the museum became gradually clearer to me through the activities of this museum.

First Official Fieldwork

I was very fortunate to get my first official tour to my homeland of Manipur. Our team of four members, led by Shri Ashok Kumar Tiwari, Curator, visited the village of Lunghar of Ukhrul for collection of objects and their documentation. The programme was organized in collaboration with the Manipur State Museum. Dr. K. Sobita Devi, the then curator, and other officials of the State Museum accompanied us to the field.

It was very refreshing to find myself in the midst of a remote tribal village and heartening to see a traditional rich man's house *Ran-Shak-Shim* (house of merit). Beautiful carvings on the frontal face of the wooden wall and a symbolic horn symbolized his high status and preserved these objects as a living museum in the village. Our team spent one night in the village that was lighted up with torches of pine trees in every family. Lunghar village at that point of time was out of the reach of electricity. The dark and cool night we spent together with the villagers near a fireplace is still cherished in my mind. Documentation in the field during the day proved quite fruitful and we were able to engage ourselves in constant interaction with the villagers. It was after our field work at

Lunghar village that IGRMS planned the construction of a traditional Tangkhul house in the museum's Open Air Exhibition premises. A prototype of *Ran-Shak-Shim* was constructed with the active involvement of the people from the Lunghar village after collecting and transporting all the housing materials from the village. The house-type is now preserved in the museum as one of the important exhibits of the Tribal Habitat.

Field Memoirs

Memorable incidents encountered in the field situation are still fresh in my mind. I remember my Sikkim and Arunachal tour in 2003 and 2004. In 2003 our team had visited Gurudungma Lake in the high mountains of the Himalayas. Places, in certain parts of North Sikkim, especially around the Sacred Gurudungma Lake are restricted for the tourists. However, with the accompaniment of officers from the Department of Art and Culture, Government of Sikkim and after obtaining permission from the military personnel as a special case, we ventured on a memorable journey to this lake. In the rugged terrain of the high Himalayas capped with snow and glaciers on one side, we carried out fieldwork among the Bhotia tribal group of this area. On account of constant exposure to the extreme environment which we were not accustomed, one of our team was afflicted with severe cold leading to a state of unconsciousness. I still remember the moment when I rushed to the nearest household to find *Petromatch* (petrol lamp). It was very kind that the family helped us out by lighting up the lamp to provide maximum possible heat to our officer. Finally, we were safe.

Further, in 2004 our exploration for collection and documentation programme continued in the East, West and South Sikkim. In Tashiding Monastery we found a master craftsman who was working on stone in the eastern corner of the monastery. When we heard the sound of hammer and chisel, we rushed to him. Our team was fascinated by the incredible work he had done on stone. Some beautiful images of Lord Buddha, Guru Padmanasambhawa chiselled by him lay in his workshop. After a long spell of interaction and discussion with the artist, we were able to acquire a stone idol with his great workmanship for IGRMS. The problem then was of transporting the idol from the top of the hill to the land below (about 2-3 kilometres) in the darkness of the evening. I remember how the heavy stone idol was carried on shoulders even when it was completely dark. Our officer lit his torch to guide us on the path of the steep hill and I still feel that we were fully blessed to carry the idol successfully up to the motorable road.

Next, we had the opportunity of conducting extensive field work at different locations of Arunachal Pradesh. It was in Apatani villages of Hapoli and adjoining villages that we carried out collection and documentation work. We sought the help of the Directorate of Research, Government of Arunachal Pradesh. The then Keeper of Zero District Museum, Mr. Tabin, who himself belonged to the Apatani tribe, extended help in carrying out fieldwork in Apatani villages. Despite the process of rapid social change among the people of this beautiful tribal group, we found some elements of cultural continuity, like nurturing of Bizu bamboo by every household, building of houses in cement and concrete without losing the pattern of their traditional pinewood dwellings, age-old food habits and dressing and design patterns of their woven textiles. The linear pattern of settlement across the two sides of main village roads with bamboo groves in each household, and cluster of granaries on the outskirts of the villages made us more curious to go into their details. The village, which we documented, experienced four incidents of fire when many houses caught fire and were burnt to ashes. But the pattern of settlement with dwellings built close to one another has remained unchanged even today. Mr. Tabin told me that, "Owing to frequent occurrence of incidents of fire we construct our granary on the outskirts of the village. We do not keep our valuables inside the house. Rather, it is safely placed in the granary and one member of the family has to live in the granary to keep a watch over it at night." Incidentally, this proved to be true as we saw with our own eyes when we visited the granary.

Further, we were able to move to the Siang district of Arunachal Pradesh. I had an old friend from Lugum Geni village about 6 kilometres from Alo, the district headquarters. This fieldwork was quite memorable for all of us in the team from IGRMS. Lugum Geni village, at that point of time had a very elegant look with a cluster of traditional Galo houses over the backdrop of dense green vegetation. Palm trees in abundance added a riot of colours to the habitat of this population. We had carried out photographic and textual documentation of house type, village court, and granary of the village. Places of entry into the house, sitting places for the boys, girls and head of the household and even for the guests are well demarcated in a Galo house. To some extent it is mostly gender-specific. Later on a prototype of the traditional Galo house was constructed in the Tribal Habitat Open Air Exhibition of IGRMS, with the help of our Galo friends from Lugum Geni village.

I recall our work in Assam. It was in Kakopathar, traditionally known as the Samarpith area where larger concentration of Moran people of Assam is found. This area comes under the administrative jurisdiction of the Tinsukia district of Assam. Once a princely state, the Samarpith area is known as the place of Moran and their elephants. We also carried out our work at Rabha inhabited areas in Gwalpara district of Assam where we experienced a constant fight between the Rabhas and wild elephants. Morans according to the colonial writers were the expert hunters of elephants. But, my long association with the Moran people in several villages of Samarpith forced me to rethink that they were not hunters but the caretakers of elephants. It is so because many aspects of their culture, both material and immaterial, assign a place of importance to elephants. Even in their folk sayings, proverbs and riddles elephants and their behaviour are depicted in a positive light. For example, an old man says "grandchildren are dear but child elephants are dearest." Moran people have good knowledge about elephant behaviour and the structure of their houses and granaries reflect an ecological and cultural association with elephants. They respect the natural habitat of elephants and never spoil it and live harmoniously with this animal. As a result of this fieldwork, the Moran habitat was successfully put up in IGRMS with the participation of the villagers.

I undertook field study of traditional salt-makers of Manipur. I visited Ningel village each time I did fieldwork in Manipur. Ningel is the only surviving village where traditional salt cake is manufactured.

Visit to a Museum Abroad

Under the sponsorship of the British Council, as a part of the Museum Exchange Programme, I had the opportunity to visit the National Museum of Scotland in Edinburgh. There I learnt about the collection management system and conservation issues in relation to a museum. I expressed my views about the Indian collections, especially the Naga Collections of the National Museum of Scotland. I also visited the National Museum of Rural Life, which is a unique open air museum located in Glasgow.

Field Encounters

In my experience museum work can only be achieved through extensive field work by reaching out to the people in villages and remote areas. There are several instances of dreadful moments we faced that linger in the mind though I do not wish to recall them ever again. Our team was returning by an auto-rickshaw from Arunachal University after meeting the people whom we were asked to meet. On the way, the driver perhaps took the short-cut route, we had to cross an old suspension bridge of about four feet wide hanging above hundred feet from the river. We were assured that they were used to cross the bridge and nothing would happen and we did cross it without any mishap. But on the way from Itanagar to Naharlagun the auto-rickshaw suddenly rolled over three or more times and I could not believe that we were alive. We found the driver lying with blood either alive or dead I do not remember. Immediately we went to the hospital as our officer was injured in the accident. I had some scratches on my arm.

In Manipur, when we were returning from a field tour, on the way to Imphal and Khoirentak, our vehicle was stopped at an outpost. It was around 7 pm, we saw about six to seven commandos at the outpost. We were asked to come out of the vehicle and stand by raising our hands. I can still remember the smell coming out from the Commandos. I knew they were drunk. We were taken to different sites and asked several questions. I gave a graphic account of my field tour and showed my tour order and official identity card. I suddenly heard the sound being beaten up. It came from our driver who was crying and begging for help. When I spoke to the officer, he shouted 'keep silent'. I told him that, we were on official duty and I showed my identity card which was thrown away and we were asked to lie down without any reason. One young commando got so angry that he was about to pull the trigger on the head of the driver and the resource person whom I had accompanied. Thanks to an old Havildar who asked me some questions. He helped us to escape from unwanted incidents that could break out from the drunken acts of the Commandos. When we were asked to leave, I asked the driver, "Why did they beat you?" He said, "They asked my name and the names of my parents. My father happens to be Nepali and my mother a Maring. Instantly, they asked me to speak the Maring language which I didn't know. They thought, I was lying and they started beating me." It was an example of a disgraceful act of someone who is supposed to protect the law.

Relations with the Villagers/Artisans/ Personalities

I still have cerdial relations with the villagers and people whom I came to know while working for the museum. This I think is one of the biggest rewards I cherish. People in my study area know me not merely as a kind of government servant but they like me as their own friend. When I joined this museum, I did not even have proper knowledge of our own land and people in a true sense. I did not even know the meaning of Loktak (the famous lake). It was from the study and seminar that this Museum hosted, I was completely astonished to learn about the genesis of the lake sung in the narrative of the Moirang-Kangleirol. Many of the elders whom I recorded during the course of documentation, they are no more. But, their voices and past memories shared have rejoiced every one of the younger generation. I am still part of the learning process, and feel delighted that I am working in a Museum, a Museum which is truly anthropological in nature.

The above information was supplied by Mr. Shakmacha Singh in a written form; what follows is part of a brief interview.

When you do your fieldwork, do you find that being a Maite yourself is an advantage or a disadvantage? Supposing I went to that area and try to study the ceremonies and rituals, would it be very difficult to do that?

Being a Maite it is difficult. That is what I find, because there are those who discourage you. But as an anthropologist our motive is to be a part of the people in a special sense. If villagers are with you nothing happens.

Where else have you done fieldwork and collected objects?

We did fieldwork in Sikkim in 2006. Around 15,000 ft in the Himalayas in Shardukpen areas. We collected a huge box. A huge one, to my surprise, it was tools which were used for their mortuary practice for disposal of their corpse. It aroused a kind of enthusiasm among us. We said anyhow we have visited such a height and we should collect this one. They were not ready to part with it or give it to us. But we tried our level best to motivate them. Ultimately we got success.

Do they need monetary inducement?

Yes. They are very much in need of money. If we go through the snow-capped area, it is very interesting and great fun for us. It is only for a few days for us. But they lead a very hard life. They are in need of money. In this challenging modern situation, they need it. Because every commodity that reaches them they want to buy it, they want to own it. So they need money.

Any interesting incidents?

When we crossed the slopes, we found Bhotia people. We have collected some textile items from them as well. The tribals said that the different kind of textiles were like the number plate of our car. Married women wear a thick red apron over their heads. This they said was their number plate!

I remember there was a festival on foundation day, where people from Manipur arrived in large numbers. Do you think it was a successful thing that Manipur festival?

To some extent.

What do you think should have been better?

Manipuri performance at IGRMS

It should have been better; I say it to some extent for the fact that we were not successful in making them happy. In the sense, that travelling from Manipur or other north eastern states to Bhopal is a long journey. It is a hard journey. So nobody knows when the bandh will be imposed. Owing to the sudden imposition of bandhs, more than 200 artists they missed the programme and our museum could not do anything. I tried to discuss matters with the director. But our financial rules do not permit us to give them extra remuneration or something else. But they spent money from their own resources. They have to fend for themselves there since the train had already left. Without any reservation they had to come here. So these are the problems.

Tell me what is the motivation of these people to travel to Bhopal? Why do they want to even when they know the difficulties involved in travelling, etc.? What motivates them?

It is their culture. They want to see other cultures. They also want to expose others to their culture. Furthermore, most of the people in their area are unemployed. Though unemployed they are good artists. They are PG holders from the Jawaharlal Nehru Dance Academy and many of the cultural organizations. Because there is no industrial development, they are not employed. According to our tradition, as Dr Kapila Vatsyayan once said, the verandah of every Maite family is the universe of culture performance. Since in the verandah itself our young boys and girls start learning dance and music. When they come of a certain age, they get a platform in some cultural organization, they get some gurus. After that the only means of their livelihood is as artists. They do not practise any kind of agriculture or some other mix. So it becomes very important for them to get programmes like this, one in which they can perform and deliver in any part of the country. So that is the motivation. Sports and culture. There is nothing, other than that there is nothing except agriculture. There is no industry. Small-scale industries are there. They are picking up. But in the marketplace they are not going up to any appreciable extent. It cannot give much employment.

I met some of the people who had come here to this Manipur festival. One was guru. Is he well known in that area?

He is well known there.

Is he also Maite?

No sir he is from the Khom tribe.

What is his role basically?

Actually, because it is one and a half decades ago that the Khom tribe had converted to Christianity completely. The way of life and living standards flourished as Christians and missionaries come to their place. But on the other hand, they are losing their language and many facets of their culture. So Achonkhom is one of the pioneers and one of the well known personalities among the Khom tribe.

Is he able to converse in English?

Yes sir.

So if we invite him to a seminar is it all right, will he be able to participate?

Yes. The Department of Culture recognizes him as a guru. And the Guru title is awarded by the Department of Culture.

Who are the other Manipuri people here associated with the museum?

There are several people like Hipomucha Maite, Dr K. Shobita Devi, Dr L. Ganapathy Devi. They are PhDs Even our Padmasri Ratan Thiyam is associated with the museum.

Do you think that there should be more outreach programmes?

Right sir. Last time, we had conducted two workshops. One in the Querentak village. Querentak is where Guru Achonkhom lives. I proposed the programme only for the fact that for the last twenty years there is no proper road. There has been a proposal given to the state government several times. I thought we should go for another kind of approach, what we say applied anthropology. Why should we not host a programme and invite the concerned MLA, who will participate in the programme, who will promise and who will deliver. We did that once. And we invited the MP, he promised and now it is going ahead, the proposal is going ahead and the road is going to be constructed.

Very good, that is excellent. That is really doing applied anthropology in your own area. On a different sort of a track, when you go to the field, do you have a cameraman and people who will make video recordings and so on?

We have our own unit here. Because of some engagement, if they did not accompany our unit then we have to hire people.

Are they available to hire?

Yes in some areas. It is available in some urban areas and some towns.

Like which towns?

In Imphal, there are some people who make documentary films, who are documentary film makers. We used to approach those people. In Assam also it is available. But if we go to some remote village we find it very difficult. We have to engage prior to our approaching the village. Otherwise, we ourselves carry some handycam or some small cameras or recorders.

I was thinking, it is a long shot from what you collect in the villages and then delivery and demonstration here in the museum. My impression is, I may be wrong, that lots of video tapes have been made, materials have been collected, but it is not being used for display. Even the classification has not been done, nor has the commentary been done. Production and script writing is not done. Do you think that is a problem?

This is very much needed here, since we need to undergo training, writing scripts based on our archival collections, based on our experiences.

Your commentary, your own voice which will be given to people who visit the museum. Because there is no use in collecting so much material without its dissemination, without its circulation. That is one problem I am trying to think about because I think there is money from the tribal sub plan to make packages for display purposes. Because you see when you enter the museum here, people come and go, they are not interested in viewing what films are being screened since it has not been thought out clearly. How packages should be done, how timings should be given that for half an hour or 15-20 minutes at a particular time the film about the the mortuary ritual or about the wedding ritual or something about a festival like Laiharomba would be shown. I think this is really needed.

A systematic and well organized form of display is required.

What are your suggestions? How can we do it here?

One important thing is regeneration of information. Because our early collections lacka lot of information but they are very good collections. So we need to collect information. It is the right time when in villages there are elderly people who have preserved this valuable information in their memories. We need to invite them to the museum to regenerate the text through some of their experiences of the past. This would be really fruitful.

And then these regenerated experiences should be made available to people who come to the museum in a certain systematic manner not casually, something is going on and they wander about aimlessly. I think this is very true. I think we have had a good discussion.

मैं और मानव संग्रहालय

शम्पा शाह

शहरी कोलाहल व आपाधापी से कोसों दूर मानव संग्रहालय तब हमारे लिये एक जादुई टापू के मानिंद था। हम (मैं और मेरी बहन राजुला शाह) अक्सर यहां आते और पूरा दिन यहीं बिताते, थोड़ा घूमते-घामते, देखते-जानते और फिर कोई अच्छी सी जगह चुनकर चित्र बनाने में या किसी किताब में डूब जाते। अक्सर इस पर हैरान होते रहते कि ऐसा अदभुत संग्रहालय बनाने की संकल्पना किसके दिमाग में आई होगी। किसने यह स्थान चुना होगा। फिर इसका तमाम अन्य संग्रहालयों से इतना भिन्न स्वरूप चुना होगा आदि-आदि। हमें इस संग्रहालय की हर चीज़ चकित करती थी। बारिश के बाद पूरे परिसर में हज़ारों की संख्या में खिलने वाले ज़ीनिया के रंग-बिरंगे फूल, दर्शकों के बैठकर आनंद लेने के लिए जगह-जगह लगाई गई बेन्चें, आदिवासी आवास-प्रकार और इस सबके ऊपर दर्शकों के लिये एक खुला वातावरण। तब सिक्योरिटी गार्ड्स नहीं थे, केवल कुछ चौकीदार हुआ करते थे जो दर्शकों की निजता में किसी तरह का कोई हस्तक्षेप नहीं करते थे। हम कभी किसी घर के बरामदे में ही बैठे सारा दिन गुज़ार देते या किसी शैलाश्रय में बैठ कर चित्र बनाते रहते, पर हमें टोकने, हमारी शांति में खलल डालने कोई नहीं आता था। लोग छू-छू कर आवासों में रखे गये सामान को देखते तो भी चौकीदार मना नहीं करता, हां इतना खयाल रखता कि उसे कोई नुकसान न पहुंचे। इस तरह संग्रहालय में बने हुए आदिवासी आवास और उनसे जुड़ी हुई वस्तुओं से हमारा सीधा संवाद और गहरी आत्मीयता बिना किसी गाइड और बिना किसी कर्मचारी से मिले स्थापित हो चुकी थी। उन्हीं दिनों कभी संग्रहालय की लोक रुचि व्याख्यान माला के बारे में पता चला। श्री वैद्यनाथ सरस्वती का व्याख्यान था। उन दिनों संग्रहालय के कार्यक्रमों के अवसर पर बाकायदा शहर के प्रमुख हिस्सों से घूमकर और दर्शकों को लेती हुई एक बस आती थी। पालीटेकनिक चौराहे से इसी बस सुविधा का लाभ उठाकर हमारा पूरा परिवार ही इस व्याख्यान को सुनने आया था। सरस्वती जी ने पारंपरिक

कुम्हारों द्वारा प्रयुक्त की जाने वाली विभिन्न तकनीकों और उनकी कला, उनके औजारों आदि से जुड़ी कई कथायें भी सुनाई थीं। उन दिनों मैं भारत भवन के सिरेमिक्स विभाग में बतौर फ़्री-लान्स कलाकार काम कर रही थी। सिरेमिक्स कला संबंधित खासी विदेशी जानकारी होने के बावजूद स्वयं अपने देश की पारंपरिक पॉटरी कला और खास कर उससे जुड़ी कथाओं से मैं बिलकुल अनजान ही थी। व्याख्यान के बाद मैं सरस्वती जी से मिली और उनसे बहुत सी बातें हुईं। तभी मेरी मुलाकात श्री विकास भट्ट से भी हुई थी, जो उस समय संग्रहालय के प्रभारी निदेशक थे।

1992 में श्री विकास भट्ट जी ने इच्छा ज़ाहिर की कि मानव संग्रहालय में भी एक सिरेमिक सैक्शन होना चाहिये जो पारंपरिक व आधुनिक कलाकारों के बीच सेतु निर्मित करने का काम करे। उन्होंने यह भी बताया कि वे मिट्टी की एक देशव्यापी कार्यशाला का आयोजन करना चाहते हैं जिसमें देश के तमाम प्रांतों से कुम्हार आमंत्रित हों। इसी काम के लिये मैं संग्रहालय से जुड़ी थी। मिट्टी में काम की परंपरा के विस्तृत डाक्यूमेन्टेशन के लिये श्री विकास भट्ट और श्री अशोक तिवारी के मार्गदर्शन में एक लम्बी प्रश्नावली तैयार की जिसमें कलाकार के सामाजिक, आर्थिक, कलात्मक पहलुओं तथा कला-कलाकृतियों से जुड़े तकनीकी, धार्मिक, आनुष्ठानिक, मिथकीय आयामों को हर कोने से टटोलने की कोशिश की गई थी। देश भर से आये कुम्हारों की 'पड़ाव-92' नामक वह लम्बी कार्यशाला एक अविस्मरणीय अनुभव था। उसमें इतना कुछ देखने, जानने को मिला और इस सबसे ऊपर उन कलाकारों से ऐसे आत्मीय और चिरस्थाई संबंध बने कि जिनके चलते जीवन में अपनापे और सहजता के नये द्वार खुले और खुलते चले गये।

1994 में डॉ. के.के. चक्रवर्ती संग्रहालय के निदेशक बने। फ़ील्ड वर्क अथवा कलाकार शिविरों के दौरान डाक्यूमेन्टेशन करते हुए मुझे कई अदभुत गीत-कथाएं सुनने को मिलतीं, जिनका साझा मैं डॉ चक्रवर्ती से करती थी। एक बार कथा सुनकर उन्होंने मुझसे कहा "क्या होगा इन कथाओं का, ज़्यादा से ज़्यादा आप इनको किताब के रूप में संकलित कर देंगी और फिर वे लाइब्रेरी में रखी किताब में क़ैद हो जायेंगी, पर उन लोगों को कुछ नहीं मिलेगा जिनकी ये कथायें हैं।... फिर कुछ रुककर सोचते हुए बोले 'आप इन कथाओं के इर्दगिर्द एक प्रदर्शनी क्यों नहीं विकसित करतीं?' इस वाक्य ने पहले तो मुझे बेहद डराया किन्तु बाद में यही वाक्य इंदिरा गांधी राष्ट्रीय मानव संग्रहालय, भोपाल में मिथक वीथी नामक मुक्ताकाश प्रदर्शनी के विकसित होने में निर्णायक रहा। इस प्रदर्शनी में देश के विभिन्न आदिवासी समुदायों के मिथकों पर आधारित प्रादर्श प्रदर्शित हैं जिन्हें मिटटी, पत्थर, रंगों,

From the Mythological Trail

टेराकोटा, लोहा, पीतल आदि माध्यमों में उन्हीं समुदायों के कलाकारों द्वारा निरूपित किया गया है। ये मिथक प्राय: संसार की रचना कैसे हुई? क्यों हुई? हम कहां से आये? आदि महत्वपूर्ण प्रश्नों का उत्तर हर समुदाय ने अपनी-अपनी तरह से

मिथकों को गढ़कर दिया है। इसलिये इन मिथकों को जानना उस समुदाय की जीवन दृष्टि को समझने के लिये अत्यंत आवश्यक होता है। जैसा कि मैंने पहले कहा था यह काम शुरूआत में अत्यंत दुरूह जान पड़ रहा था क्योंकि मिथक-कथायें, गीत आदि किसी भी समुदाय का अभौतिक और एक तरह से अमूर्त पक्ष होते हैं। उन्हें भौतिक, मूर्त रूपाकारों में कैसे प्रस्तुत किया जाये, किया भी जाये अथवा नहीं आदि महत्वपूर्ण प्रश्न थे। गौर से देखने पर मैंने पाया कि हर समुदाय का जैसे अभौतिक पक्ष है वैसे ही भौतिक, मूर्त पक्ष भी है। हमारे देश के संदर्भ में यह भौतिक पक्ष प्रायः कलात्मक अभिप्रायों के साथ है।

अधिकतर आदिवासी अथवा उनसे जुड़े लोक-समुदाय किसी न किसी कला माध्यम में निपुण हैं और सदियों से अपने को उसमें अभिव्यक्त करते आये हैं। इसी तथ्य का लाभ उठाते हुए मैंने सबसे पहले मध्यप्रदेश के मण्डला जिले के अगरिया समुदाय के लौह शिल्पी श्री पनकूराम अगरिया तथा श्री रामजी राम अगरिया को संग्रहालय में काम करने हेतु आमंत्रित किया। मैं इनसे पहले कभी संसार की उत्पत्ति की अगरिया की कथा सुन चुकी थी। पिता और पुत्र पूछने लगे कि क्या बनाना है? मेरे यह कहने पर कि इस बार उसी कथा को बनाना है जो पिछली बार सुनाई थी, पनकूराम जी जिनकी उम्र कोई पैंसठ बरस होगी, साफ़ मुकर गये। कहने लगे, ''यह कहानी-वहानी बुजुर्ग लोगों को आती है, हमें नहीं आती!'' मैंने हतप्रभ रहते हुए कहा, ''ठीक है, फिर आराम करिये क्योंकि कुछ और तो बनाना नहीं है। अगली सुबह पिता-पुत्र नौ बजे ही आ गये और बेटा यानी रामजीराम बोले–''ठीक है, मैडम जल्दी से हमें लोहा दिलवाइये, बहुत सारा लोहा लगेगा...पूरी धरती और उसकी उत्पत्ति की कहानी जो बनानी है। दोनों बाप-बेटे लगभग एक माह तक रात-दिन लगे रहे और इस तरह मिथक वीथी का पहला प्रादर्श निर्मित हुआ जिसकी लम्बाई-चौड़ाई 10×14 फ़ीट थी। इसका आकार अगरिया लोगों के पारंपरिक लामन दिये जैसा था और इसमें बड़ी सी धरती, धरती को लोहे, पीतल और ताम्बे की कील ठोक कर सिथर बनाते हुए पनकूराम और रामजीराम के पूर्वज भी बने थे। पहला प्रादर्श इतना सार गर्भित और सुंदर बना कि हिम्मत जुटी और मिथक वीथी प्रदर्शनी को बनाने का क्रम चल पड़ा। इसके बाद फिर एक एक कर छत्तीसगढ़, गुजरात, उड़ीसा, बंगाल, महाराष्ट्र, मणिपुर, आंध्रप्रदेश आदि से कलाकार आते रहे और अलग-अलग माध्यमों से अपने अपने मिथकों, अनुष्ठानों को रूपाकार देते गये। इन सभी कलाकारों के साथ ऐसा घरोपा स्थापित हुआ कि बिना किसी अतिश्योक्ति के कह सकती हूं कि आज देश भर में कोई तीस-चालीस घर-परिवार हैं जो मेरे परिवार का हिस्सा हैं और मैं उनके परिवार का हिस्सा हूं।

मानव संग्रहालय के पास सौभाग्य से पर्याप्त जगह है इसलिये प्रदर्शनी को विस्तार देने की अभी भी बहुत गुंजाइश है। कुछ वर्ष पूर्व इस प्रदर्शनी का हमने एक घुमंतू स्वरूप भी तैयार किया है तथा इसका प्रदर्शन अलग-अलग शहरों में लोगों द्वारा सराहा जा रहा है।

जब इस संग्रहालय में आई थी तब मैं मिटटी में काम करने वाली एक आधुनिक सिरेमिक आर्टिस्ट थी जिसे पारंपरिक कुम्हारों व अन्य कलाकारों के बारे में नहीं के बराबर जानकारी थी। इसी संग्रहालय से जुड़ने पर सोशियोलोजी में एम.ए., म्यूज़ियोलॉजी में डिप्लोमा आदि किया ताकि संग्रहालय के बेहतर काम आ सकूं। किन्तु, इस सबसे बढ़कर एक सिरेमिक कलाकार या स्कल्प्टर होने के नाते यहां मैंने पारंपरिक कुम्हारों के रूप में नये गुरु पाये। बस्तर के श्री सहदेव राणा, कच्छ की श्रीमती सारा इब्राहिम और इब्राहिमभाई, मणिपुर की श्रीमती नीलमणि देवी, उड़ीसा के श्री लोकनाथ राणा, तमिलनाडु के श्री रंगास्वामी आदि मेरे लिये गुरुस्थानीय हैं। इस संग्रहालय से जुड़कर मेरे व्यकितत्व और कृतित्व दोनों में ही आमूल-चूल परिवर्तन आया। बी.एन. सरस्वती जी का वह लैक्चर और अपनी बहन के साथ बीस वर्ष पहले के संग्रहालय के उद्देश्यहीन फेरे जीवन में इतनी दूर ले जायेंगे तब इसका धुंधला अहसास भी नहीं था।

Memories in Museum

P. Sankara Rao

In July 1998 I joined Indira Gandhi Rashtriya Manav Sangrahalaya (IGRMS) as a museum assistant. To begin with, I familiarized myself with the museum work through practical exposure particularly in the exhibition galleries and also visited the library regularly to refer to books and journals in anthropology and museology. My professional journey at IGRMS started in its Rock Art Heritage Open-air Exhibition-cum-periodical Gallery, where I worked under a senior officer. I learnt slowly how to maintain a periodical gallery and carry out its day-to-day maintenance work. During the regular interaction with visitors to the gallery I explained about the exhibition and guided them to the prehistoric rock cave shelters.

Rock art engraving at IGRMS

Within the first year of my service at IGRMS, there was a two-day international seminar on shared social ecology of Seven Himalayan

Countries on its premises from November 26-28, 1998. At this seminar I presented a paper on "Bio-diversity, traditional systems of eco-management and futuristic perspective of Himalaya". This was my first museum related professional experience of participation in a seminar which included eminent scholars of disciplines such as Anthropology, Museology, Archaeology and Geology. The seminar provided me with a broad perspective to expand on cultural ideas in the museum profession. Later with my senior officer I went for fieldwork to interior places of Vizianagaram district in Andhra Pradesh and made collections of objects pertaining to different arts and crafts in materials like metal, wood and pottery (terracotta). During the fieldwork I learnt on the job how to establish a close and harmonious relationship, which we called 'rapport' with the informants in anthropological fieldwork of our student days. I came across diverse craft traditions. Even though I belong to this district, I did not know earlier that such an incredible heritage of arts and crafts existed in this area. I perceived through my new lens of museum work the quality of people, their arts and crafts and wealth of information they possess.

In May-June, 1999 IGRMS organized a national festival comprising workshop-cum-cultural performances for a period of ten days at Bobbili, a small historical town in Vizianagaram district, in collaboration with Raja Sahib of Bobbili, Shri R.V. G.K. Rangarao, popularly known as "Kumar Raj of Bobbili". He was a statesman as well as a great lover of arts and crafts. He extended full cooperation for making this event a grand success. The ten-day event was celebrated under the title of "Alikidi" (congregation of rural and tribal folk). Alikidi is a local vernacular folk word and refers to "something good happening". In this sense the word 'Alikidi' fitted the theme and the programme as well as it caught the attention of the local folk. I will never forget this ten-day programme as it was such a wonderful experience and became a permanent memory in many ways. On the one hand it was a huge gathering of cultural spectrum and on the other hand it was a meeting of skilful artists with whom I interacted and shared a few moments. Each artist I met broadened my views about the rural and tribal crafts of the area. This was an unforgettable and amazing experience in the early part of my life as a museum professional.

After one year at IGRMS, I became Museum Associate in July 1999, and moved from rock art heritage exhibition to specimen store. Here I worked under another senior officer. My duty was to assist the senior officer in various assignments given to him. These were mainly related to museum activities like exhibitions, seminars and collection of ethnographic objects. I assisted the senior officer in addition to regular care and maintenance work of the specimen store. In this section of IGRMS I encountered a large collection of ethnographic objects and here I learnt how to do accession, indexing, issuing and receiving back the objects. This experience exposed me to procedures of setting up different exhibitions and complexities of storage of different kinds of objects. Often when I issued objects to experts for photography and slide documentation I closely observed the working process of very senior and experienced photographers. In essence what I have so far learnt in this section of IGRMS relates to careful handling and proper upkeep of its collection of objects. I have learnt to handle them as I would handle an infant. This is a different kind of experience with memories of a complex nature.

Almost one and a half years later in December 2000, I went to Ooty in Tamil Nadu for a seminar that was jointly organized by the Tribal Cultural Research Institute of IGRMS and a local NGO. This was the first time I came face-to-face with the tribes of Nilagiri (Blue Mountains), mainly the Toda, the Kota and the Kurumba. Here I saw their habitat, settlement and observed their way of life along with the natural beauty of the terrain. The honey collection of the Kurumbas from canopies of large trees on hill cliffs in the forest, melodies and meanings of songs of the Todas, pottery, musical instruments and agricultural implements of the Kotas have been etched in my memory forever. Many objects related to these themes were displayed at "Thamijigam Guest House", the venue of the seminar. The guest house, a wonderful architectural heritage building, is worth seeing. The landscape with its forest, tea gardens dotted with small and simple tribal settlements makes this region a unique sight to behold. This is the kind of visual education medium to understand the people in their local context and has helped in making me a museum professional.

Later in 2000 I went to Mysore for a six-week long field work along with a team of museum people. The purpose of this fieldwork was to start a Southern Regional Centre and to develop an exhibition in the Heritage Building of Wellington House on the ground floor. Professor Shankho Choudhury, a renowned artist, and many other eminent personalities attended the inauguration of the Southern Regional Centre. For me it was an opportunity to work in a new place. After the inauguration, as per the instructions and guidelines of my senior officer, we invited a reputed academician and historian, Dr. Ramachandra Guha, who accepted our invitation to come and deliver a lecture on "Verrier Elwin's Works" as part of the IGRMS series of popular lectures. His lecture was mind blowing, very informative and educative. This kind of strong dose of experience is an unforgettable event of my life at Mysore. How academicians enlighten others through their speeches!

In terms of my work at IGRMS, after a short span of one and a half years in the specimen store, I went back to the rock art heritage exhibition where I worked from 2001 to 2008. In this section of IGRMS, I worked under senior officers and received their instructions for regular and routine museum exhibition work, care and maintenance of museum objects and guidance to visitors particularly students, scholars, artists, etc. Apart from making arrangements for different programmes and workshops in the rock art heritage department of IGRMS, during this period, I undertook fieldwork in different parts of Andhra Pradesh, Orissa, Maharashtra and Manipur mainly for collection and documentation of ethnographic objects among the folk and tribal communities with particular reference to their traditional and technological knowledge systems of handicrafts, handlooms and textiles. One such textile tradition is in "Ponduru", an old popular cottage handloom, textile village of Srikakulam district in Andhra Pradesh. It is a classic example. Another textile handloom tradition is at Sambalpur near Bargad village in Orissa, which is well-known for its weaving techniques. Both are examples of handloom villages with skilful craftsmen. These simple weavers produce beautiful textiles from their hands by working for long hours on their looms.

During this period, I also organized a number of seminars and workshops in collaboration with universities, research institutes and museums. I planned and held a photographic exhibition on "Rock Art of India and World" along with "Stone Age India Tools" in different places of Madhya Pradesh, West Bengal and Goa. Experience of carrying out intensive documentation of rock art in Orissa gave me an opportunity of working in a group and sharing my ideas with museologists, anthropologists and archaeologists.

Simultaneously I also presented a research paper on 'Tribal Development, Continuity and Change: A Case Study of Tribal Sub-plan Area in Vijayanagaram District of Andhra Pradesh' at the National Seminar on Current Trends in Ethnographic and Ethno-archaeological Researches on Tribes of Chhattisgarh and Neighbouring States, held on February 25-27, 2004 at the Department of Anthropology, School of Social Sciences, Pt. Ravishankar Shukla University, Raipur, Chhattisgarh. Another research paper presented by me was on 'Material Culture and Cultural Identity: An Anthropological Perspective' at the National Seminar organized by IGRMS, Bhopal on A Gendered Approach to Material Culture: Representations and Practices, held from March 26 to 27, 2011.

Ethnographic material collection by me among the Gadaba, Kondadora and Jatapur tribes and folk populations of Andhra Pradesh added to my appreciation of the link between material culture and ecology. Field visits to Bondo, Khond tribes and folk populations of Orissa provided me an indepth understanding of their material cultures and environment. Later I did fieldwork among the "Jatapu" tribe in

Vijayanagaram district of Andhra Pradesh and carried out a detailed ethnographic documentation. As a result of this work, IGRMS acquired all the raw materials of their traditional dwelling, locally known as "Purillu". The acquisition work was facilitated by the village tribal headman and other leaders of their community and concerned government officials of the department of tribal development. After delivering raw material to the museum, a few weeks later around ten Jatapu tribal people including two women came to IGRMS. They stayed here and re-constructed their traditional tribal house. For the first time they carried out house-building activity outside their village. This was the first time that a life-size dwelling of the Jatapu tribe was displayed in the national museum. In the entire process, we faced several obstacles, like getting permission, inviting the tribals and local officials to communicate the purpose of this acquisition by IGRMS and arranging transportation of raw material from this small remote village to the national museum in Bhopal. Dealing with these problems was quite a difficult task. But with patience and perseverance we could slowly build a rapport with the local people and carry out our mission successfully. This experience remains in my mind as an unforgettable memory and I still remember the interaction with simple, friendly and loveable people who treated me as their kinsman.

By God's grace and all my senior officers' guidance, co-operation and blessings the museum (IGRMS) has given me an immense opportunity to see and study Indian culture in a different perspective. One of my most precious memory relates to the Bicycle Expedition I took from Bhopal to Vishakhapatnam in 2010, on the eve of the International Year of Biodiversity. It was a a fantastic cultural journey of 1350 kilometres. The ride was to see and study at close range the living cultures across the five states of India and it personified for me the elements of unity and diversity in the country. I will never forget this experience of my life.

The present Director, Prof. K.K. Mishra allotted me a wonderful project "Island Cultures" as a novel idea. For this project some of my colleagues and I at IGRMS visited

Andaman & Nicobar Islands. This was our first visit to these far-flung Islands, dotting a small human habitation in the waters of the Bay of Bengal. It was an entirely new experience for us to study these strange populations, particularly the Nicobarians of Andaman. They appear to possess good survival skills against the natural disturbances. I was immensely impressed by simple people with such outstanding capabilities. I recently visited the River Islands of Andhra Pradesh. Godavari and Krishna rivers of Andhra Pradesh have islands with human settlements and found the livelihood patterns of these island communities of great interest to me as a museum professional.

बंगाल से भोपाल तक

सोमा कीरो

सोमा जी आपने पढ़ाई कहाँ से की है?

मैंने B.Sc. तक तो कलकत्ता में ही की, फिर M.Sc. सागर University से किया है और Ph.D. भी सागर University से ही Professor Chowbeji के under की थी, B.Sc. Anthropology में सभी mixed ही था, फिर सागर में आकर choice मिली। पहले साल में तो पूरे सभी general topics थे। दूसरे साल में specialisation मिला था। मैंने 1990 में M.Sc. किया। यहाँ पर just passout होने के बाद मैंने 1991 में join किया...

आप के husband पहले से ही यहाँ पर थे?

जी पहले से ही थे। शादी तो मैंने अभी दो हज़ार में की।

आप assistant keeper हैं। आप किस section की in-charge हैं?

मैंने यहाँ museum में पहले assistant की तरह ही काम शुरू किया था, फिर promotion में associate हो गई। शुरू से मैं specimen section में ही थी। 16-17 years मैंने specimen में ही काम किया है। हाल में ही मुझे rock art तथा traditional technology के areas दिये गये हैं, museum shop and exhibitions में भी मैंने काम किया है। अभी सिर्फ rock art exhibition में मेरा काम है।

तो आप museum object collection वगैरा में नहीं गयीं या कहीं गयी हैं?

गयी हूँ सर। मैंने mostly Bengal ही cover किया है। North Bengal, South Bengal करके पूरे बंगाल में ही किया है। हां, मैंने हिमाचल में भी collection किया है। Mr. Shom जब यहाँ के curator थे, तब उनके साथ गयी हूँ। फिर पंजाब, हरियाणा में भी मैं एक और madam को लेकर गयी हूँ। एक बार Kurukshetra भी गयी हूँ। इसके बाद South में मैं Tamil Nadu गयी हूँ।

आपको collections में काफ़ी experience है?

हाँ जी, काफ़ी field work किया है। West Bengal में मैं अकेली ही गई थी। और उसके बाद दार्जिलिंग, सिक्किम वगैरा मैं तिवारी जी के साथ गयी थी, शोम साहब के साथ भी गयी थी। Dr. Chakravarty के साथ भी दार्जिलिंग गई थी।

तो आपके अनुभवों में सबसे ज्यादा interesting कौन सा है?

जब group में गई, तब उतना feel नहीं किया। अकेले थोड़ा ladies type का problem face करना पड़ता है। पहली बात तो यह है कि आपको लोगों को समझाना होता है, rapport बनाना होता है। एक पुराने सामान के collection की बात को लोग थोड़ा अजीब ढंग से लेते हैं। बिना resource person के काम करना बहुत मुश्किल है, क्योंकि उस community में घुसना है तो उनका ही आदमी आपको चाहिए। जहां मैं गई लोग अपनी ही भाषा में बोलते जा रहे, हँसते जा रहे, एक छोटी सी टूटी झाड़ू लेकर आ गये कि हमारे पास यह है। फिर जब मैं deeply उनके बीच घुसी, उनसे बहुत बातें कीं। उसके बाद जब एक जन ने देना शुरू किया, फिर बाकी लोग आना शुरू करते हैं। धीरे धीरे ही यह काम होता है। थोड़ा-सा वक्त लगता है। शुरू में लगता है कि इतनी मुश्किल से तो आये और यहां काम नहीं हो पा रहा है। हर जगह पर ऐसे ही होता है। हाल में ही मैं पुरुलिया और मथुरा जाकर आई हूँ। वहाँ पर गयी तो कहाँ मिलेगा क्या मिलेगा पता नहीं था। बहुत दिन पहले एक बार मैं पुरुलिया गयी थी। Mask वगैरा collect करके लायी थी। इस बार जब मैं गयी तब माँ सीतादेवी ने अपने ही technique से कुछ basket वगैरा बनाना सिखाया और museum shop के लिए मैं उनके कुछ products लेकर आई हूँ। कुछ कुछ जगह पर आपको लगता है कि कुछ हो नहीं पा रहा है, नहीं निकल रहा है। लेकिन धीरे धीरे उनसे बात करिये और उनसे थोड़ा close हो जाइए, तब काम बन जाता है। मैंने तो ऐसा ही किया है, उन्हीं की hut में रहती हूँ। महिला होने के कारण होटल वगैरा में रहने में थोड़ा uncomfortable लगता है। तो उनके घर में रहकर उनके साथ मित्रता करके काम करना पड़ता है।

As a lady anthropologist, do you find your work to be difficult or easy?

कहीं कहीं पर थोड़ी सी परेशानी आती ही है। हम लोगों को objects की packing वगैरा में बहुत परेशानी होती है। मैंने खुद बैठकर packing, stiching वगैरा की है। हम लोग ही बेहतर जानते हैं कि object कैसे packing करके

transportation में भेजना है। अगर labour involve हुआ तो उसमें भी हमको ही involve होना पड़ता है। पंजाब में होटल में रात बारह बजे तक मैंने packing की है। मेरे साथ एक मैडम आई थी, वो भी आपसे मिलेंगी। उनको इतनी practice नहीं थी, मैं इतने दिन से कर रही हूँ तो पूरी रात भर उसको बिठाकर ड्रम व पंजाब की folk art को कैसे भी करके packing किया था। उस समय थोड़ा difficult लगा। पर enjoy भी करते हैं। अच्छा लगता है जब भी एक piece जो हमारे यहाँ नहीं था और मुझे मिला। शोम साहब भी बंगाल के हैं और वह भी इसके लिए काफ़ी दिनों से कोशिश कर रहे थे। मुझे अच्छा लगता है कि कुछ अच्छी चीज़ें मैंने collect कीं।

बीरभूम में तो बंगला ही बोलते हैं?

हाँ, बंगला ही बोलते हैं। इसीलिए मुझे इतनी दिक्कत नहीं हुई कोई problem नहीं हुई। पर resource person फिर भी ज़रूरी है। नहीं तो, लोगों के बहुत सवाल होते हैं कि आप क्यों आये। फिर सब समझाना पड़ता है कि हम government से हैं। हमारा motive क्या है, आपकी चीज़ों को preserve करना है। धीरे-धीरे ये चीजें लुप्त होती जा रही हैं। एक बार हम हरियाणा गए थे। वहाँ कांसे के बरतन अब steel में बनने लगे हैं और कांसे का बरतन मिलना बहुत मुश्किल है। हमें यह लुप्त होते हुए बरतन ढूंढने थे।

तो आप लोग price वगैरा कैसे fix करते हैं?

Price का यह है, कि मैं 5000 रुपये तक purchase कर सकती हूँ। उस सीमा के अंदर object देखती रहती हूं, कभी-कभी एक basket आपको दस, बारह रुपये में मिल जाएगी और आप उधर पचास साठ रुपये दें तो ज़्यादा लगेगा। यदि objects की uniqueness और उनका पुरानापन और साथ में इतने दिन की मेहनत को count करें तो उस हिसाब से सही लगता है। कोशिश रहती है कि उन लोगों ने जितनी क़ीमत बताई है उसको देखें और फिर उसको थोड़ा आगे पीछे कर के ही दाम तय करें।

इसमें experience बहुत count करता है न?

बहुत count करता है। दरअसल store में मैंने बहुत काम किया है। पंद्रह साल से ऊपर store में ही काम किया है। वहाँ पर बहुत objects आते रहते थे, price का पता चल जाता था।

आपको क्या लगता है कि collection यहाँ इस museum में पिछले पांच साल में ज्यादा accelerate हुआ है या कम हुआ है? कैसे हुआ?

Collection तो यहाँ पर regurlarly होता ही रहता है। Ministry से communication आता रहता है कि इतना percent का collection करना है। Collection तो हर साल अच्छा होता ही है। बीच में शायद एक साल, शायद 1992 में, बहुत कम हुआ था।

अच्छा आपका क्या अनुभव है, जो visitors आते हैं, उनको बतलाने के लिए संग्रहालय में adequate arrangement है या नहीं है?

पहली बात यह है कि शुरू में enter करने से ही आपको guide map मिलना चाहिए। फिर जगह-जगह में folders वगैरा की बहुत कमी है और guide भी होना चाहिए। कोई special व्यक्ति आता है तभी guide को रखते हैं। मुझे लगता है एक ऐसा information centre होना चाहिए जहाँ पर एक guide भी उपलब्ध हो। इतनी बड़ी जगह में आकर लोगों को पता नहीं होता है कि कहाँ जाना है, कैसे करना है। और visitors facilities तो बहुत ही कम हैं। Proper drinking water का इंतज़ाम नहीं है, proper toilets नहीं हैं।

क्या स्कूलों से बच्चे आते हैं?

वो तो summer vacation में आते हैं। उन लोगों को फिर भी इतनी दिक्कत नहीं होती क्योंकि उनके teachers साथ में आते हैं, उनका फिर भी इंतजाम हो

School Children at IGRMS

जाता है। आज कल स्कूल के बच्चे सीखने से अधिक entertainment के लिए आते हैं। छोटे-छोटे बच्चों को लाकर नाश्ता करा दिया और संग्रहालय देखना हो गया। यह ठीक नहीं है मैं देख रही हूँ। स्कूल के बच्चे बहुत ज्यादा ऐसे ही करते हैं। हम ने बीच में एक बार एक tribal स्कूल के बच्चों को visit कराने के लिए TRI (Tribal Research Institute) के collaboration में इंतजाम किया। उसमें तो हम लोग थोड़ी कोशिश करते हैं कि बच्चों को थोड़ा-सा सीखने के लिये मिले। बाकी जो भोपाल के स्कूल के बच्चे आते हैं वे तो coming just for entertainment। बहुत कम ही लोग हैं, जो particularly museum को ही देखने आते हैं। उनको सिर्फ आना है, बैठना है। इसीलिए कॉलेज के students भी कम आते हैं। भोपाल में तो बहुत लोगों को मालूम भी नहीं कि यहाँ पर एक museum है। एक तो इतनी दूर ऐसी जगह पर है। आने जाने का साधन नहीं है। सबके पास गाड़ी नहीं है। इसीलिए बिलकुल ऐसे ही रह जाता है। भोपाल शहर में ही बहुत लोगों को इसके बारे में मालूम नहीं है।

आपने कहा कि guides की कमी है।

Guide तो होना ही चाहिए और जो visitors के लिये सुविधाएं होती हैं, उनकी भी बहुत कमी है। Proper toilets होना चाहिए, drinking water होना चाहिए और दो चार cafetaria भी होने चाहिए। ऊपर में एक canteen है। लोग वैसे ही इतना थक जाते हैं, कि उतना ऊपर चढ़ नहीं सकते। Parking place में चाहे छोटा ही सही, कम से कम चाय पानी या biscuit कुछ तो मिलना चाहिए। आप अगर खुद नहीं कर पा रहे हो तो मुझे ऐसा लगता है कि एक दो private stall को ही दे देना चाहिए कि आप कुछ token amount दो और रोज आकर parking पर stall लगाओ। यह चीज़ रहने से आपको भी थोड़ा पता चलेगा कि stall लगा है व कितना profit आ रहा है। चाय का stall। आज कल आप किसी को भी बोलिए तो यह इंतजाम हो जाएगा। जब भट्ट साहब हमारे डिरेक्टर थे, हमने एक visual store बनाया था। वह बहुत बढ़िया बना और उसमें बहुत visitors आए। जब exhibition में at a time research room में पूरा संग्रह देखने को मिलता है, collection की variety मिलती है। तो बहुत ज्यादा visitors भी आते हैं। फिर बाद में सामान को इधर से निकाल कर उधर करके कुछ का कुछ कर दिया। इससे हम लोगों का काम करने का मन भी धीरे-धीरे चला गया है। आजकल ज्यादा politics चलती है कि कौन क्या करेगा। आजकल एक काम करने के लिए पांच बार सोचते रहते हैं। अभी collection में भी जाने के लिए अपने को ऐसा ही लगता है कि कोई issue न बना दे, कुछ नुकसान न करा दे। हमारा संग्रहालय थोड़ा अलग

है सर, इसको और भी develop करना पड़ेगा। चक्रवर्ती साहब ने इसको इतना बड़ा बनाकर इतनी ऊंचाई पर पहुंचाया। फिर उसको नीचे कर दिया गया। यह बात सही नहीं है। इसको और ऊंचा कर पायें। ऐसा करने के और भी तरीक़े हैं। यहां अच्छा leader होना चाहिए, साथ में video का भी प्रबंध हो। इतना पैसा लगाकर अपना video section बनाया गया है पर इसमें वह चीज़ नहीं है कि इससे संग्रहालय और बढ़िया हो। जनता तो फिर भी आती है, कुछ program होता है तो उसमें काफी rush भी होता है। Advertise करने के लिये paper में देते हैं, TV में भी देते है, कई programs में public आ जाती है। Sunday में तो visitors बहुत होते हैं। Saturday and Sunday में काफ़ी rush रहता है। Working days में इतना ज़्यादा नहीं होता। ऐसे ही student type कुछ आ जाते हैं। Research scholars और foreigners भी काफ़ी आते हैं। Audio visual की clipping को तैयार करने में यहां थोड़ी कमी है और उसका organisation अधिक ठीक नहीं है। Package बनाकर उसका presentation करना ज़रुरी है। छोटे छोटे clipping को तो तैयार करते हैं, पर proper presentation की यहां पर कमी है। बहुत कमी है। आज अन्य संग्रहालयों में इतना बदल गया है यहां कुछ नहीं बदला है। हमारे senior लोग शुरू से जो trained हो उसे बदलना नहीं चाहते। पहले वालों की तरह ही करते रहो। आप अगर कोई suggestion दें तो उसको follow करना ही नहीं है। मतलब शुरू में उन्होंने गोबर मिट्टी से शुरू किया तो आज तक वही चलता आ रहा है। आप पहले store में जाकर देखिये कि क्या सामान है जिससे पहले जैसा ही collection दुबारा न हो। जिस area में collection नहीं हुआ, उसको cover करिये। यहाँ पर ऐसा है कि जो जिस area का है वह उसी area में collection के लिये जा रहा है। इतने सारे tribes हैं कि हर tribe को cover करना चाहिए। यहाँ पर यह हो रहा है कि एक ही चीज़ का collection हो रहा है। ऐसे ही हो गया है। परंतु इस तरह तो आप कुछ कर नहीं सकते। ऊपर के इतने बड़े-बड़े अफ़सर हैं और वे लोग हम सब को कुछ नहीं समझते हैं। हममें से अच्छे-अच्छे लोगों को भी वो कोई महत्व नहीं देते हैं।

एक महिला क्यूररेटर

सुदीपा रॉय

डॉ. सुदीपा रॉय। आप यहाँ कब से हैं व किस डिपार्टमेंट में हैं?

सर, 1995 से मैं यहां हूं। अभी मैं Tribal Habitat में बैठती हूँ।

Tribal Habitat में आपका काम क्या है?

Tribal Habitat में मेरी post तो assistant की थी पर वहाँ जितने Tribal houses से जुड़े हुए जिस भी काम की ज़रूरत है, जैसे Tribal लोग आते हैं, उसका maintenance होता है, workshop करते हैं। यह सारी चीज़ें देखने का मेरा काम होता है।

आप जब से यहाँ आईं, तब से आपने क्या-क्या काम किया?

कुछ तो सर, field work किया है। कुछ collections किया है। कुछ outreach program में senior officer के साथ काम किया है। स्वयं भी collections के लिए field areas में गई हूँ। बाकी यहाँ पर जो program चलते हैं, जैसे north east culture पर program चल रहा है, यह celebrating regional cultures से जुड़ा है। जो कलाकार आते हैं, उन लोगों की जो भी ज़रूरतें हैं, वे कहाँ रहेंगे, क्या करेंगे, यह सब काम और उसके साथ जो food festival होता है उससे जुड़े सारे कामों को देखना होता है।

आपका field work वह कहाँ-कहाँ हुआ?

पहली बार field work, के लिये मैं शिल्पारामम, हैदराबाद गई थी, वहां IGRMS का program हुआ था। वहाँ cultural performance के लोग संग्रहालय से गए थे। यह culture performance हम लोगों ने organise किया था। यह संग्रहालय का out reach program होता है जो जगह-जगह संस्थाओं के साथ collaboration में किया जाता है। वहां rock art व craft पर exhibition लगाई थी। उसमें painting के लिए वार्ली बनाने वाले कलाकार हमने संग्रहालय की

Warli Style Wall Painting

तरफ़ से भेजे थे और cultural performance के लिए भी हमारी तरफ़ से कलाकार गए थे। शिल्पाराममम में लगातार मैं तीन साल program में जा चुकी हूँ। उसके बाद, सर, गुमला, झारखंड में एक outreach program organise किया था। वहाँ उरांव community के लोग अपनी material culture से related objects का एक museum बनाना चाहते थे। वहां एक स्कूल है व एक NGO है जो एक क्रिश्चियन फ़ादर चलाते हैं। उन लोगों के पास काफी objects थे। इस प्रोग्राम के coordinator के पास भी कुछ collection है, उन सबको रखने के लिए वे लोग वहाँ पर museum खोलना चाहते थे। वहाँ पर उनके collections की हम लोगों ने एक exhibition लगवाई थी। हमने वहाँ पर बताया कि वे लोग objects को कैसे रख सकते हैं, कैसे करना चाहिए है वगैरा। उसके बाद सर, हम असम गए थे। वहाँ alternative literature के ऊपर एक program हुआ था। जैसे अलग-अलग कम्युनिटी का अलग-अलग भाषा में उनका जो literature है, उसके ऊपर एक exhitbition लगवाई थी, वहाँ पर जो लोग आये थे, उनके लिए एक seminar भी organise किया गया था। यह सब सोम साहब के समय पर हुआ था। यह सर, 1999 या 2000 की बात है। उसके बाद, हमने West Bengal में भूमिज tribe पर कुछ काम किया था। हमारे यहाँ लगभग सब area से सब tribes का habitat बनाया गया है। परंतु भूमिज का नहीं था। अब सर। यहाँ पर

भूमिज लोगों ने ही भूमिज लोगों का मकान बनाया। हम लोग भाकुड़ा district जाकर कुछ collection लाये थे। भूमिज लोगों के मकान मिट्टी के doubled storyed होते हैं। उसमें वे लोग लकड़ी का उपयोग करते हैं। उनके घर बनाने में जो भी सामान लगता है वह सामान हमने यहाँ पर transport करवाया। फिर यहाँ उन लोगों को बुलवाया गया था, वे लगभग एक महीना तक यहां रहे और अपना घर बना कर गए। शुरू में थोड़ी बहुत खाने पीने की मुश्किल हुई, बाद में उन लोगों ने कहा कि हम खुद अपना खाना बनायेंगे। यहाँ पर कुछ लोग आते हैं, उनको कुछ tribal habitat के घर पसंद आते हैं और वे कहते हैं कि हमको यहाँ पर ठहरने दीजिए। हम उनका सब इंतज़ाम कर देते हैं। मेरे ख्याल से, खाने पीने की कुछ समस्या होती है, बाकी कुछ नहीं। Communication तो हो ही जाता है, टूटी फूटी हिंदी तो बोल ही लेते हैं। कुछ समस्या नहीं होती।

घर बनाने का उनका जो system होता है, पहले कौन सा काम कब शुरू करना है। कब-कब पूजा करते हैं, फिर छत का structure हो जाने के बाद एक बार पूजा करते है। वो जैसी पूजा करते हैं वो सारी चीज़ें हम follow करते हैं। घर के सामने कौन-कौन-सा पौधा लगाना पसंद करते है, घर के सामने क्या-क्या लगाते हैं। उनके सब rituals का हम video documentation करते है। Photography व videography दोनों कराए जाते हैं।

Video documentation का क्या use होता है? यह रखा रहता है या कुछ और होता है?

अभी तो ऐसे ही चल रहा है, क्योंकि museum के पास बहुत सारे collections हैं अत: सभी tribes के ऊपर एक अलग से gallery बनाने का विचार चल रहा है। एक छोटी documentary film टाइप बनाई गई है। अभी इसी साल मकर संक्रांति पर हम West Bengal गये थे। West Bengal में मकर संक्रांति पर बड़ा सा मेला होता है। इतिहासकारों के अनुसार खेंधूली में मकर संक्रांति का मेला इंडिया का सबसे पुराना मेला माना जाता है। खेंधूली गीत गोविंद के रचयिता जयदेव भूषण का birth place है। वे वैष्णव थे। वहाँ पर उनका देहांत होने के बाद एक मेला लगता है, जिसमें वहाँ के सारे वैष्णव लोग और बाउल सम्मिलित होते हैं। इस मेले का नाम अन्नधान मेला है। सबको वहाँ पर खाना मिलता है। उस मेले का हमने एक बार video documentation किया था। वहां जाने वाली team में video section से मैं परिहार जी को लेकर गई थी। यह एक documentary film है। हमने सब लोगों का interview भी लिया है। उन्होंने बताया कि यह मेला क्यों कर रहे हैं, उनको कैसा लगता है। वे किस टाइप का गाना गाते हैं।

Accounts वगैरा कौन रखता है?

जिसके नाम पर advance होता है वही accounts देखता है, इस बार परिहार जी ने लिया था, कुछ-कुछ program में accounts section वाले भी जाते हैं।

आपको यह लगता है, कि आपकी anthropology की training useful है कि नहीं।

मेरी anthropology की training काम की नहीं है। यहां तो काम बिलकुल अलग है। यहां पर practical experience बहुत मिलता है। लोगों के साथ मिलना-जुलना होता है, बाकी इस museum का काम बहुत अलग है, जैसे अधिकतर संग्रहालयों में सामान लाकर रख देते है। परंतु IGRMS में जो भी हम लोग सामान लाते हैं, उनसे जुड़ी हुई जो community है, उनको भी हम यहां बुलवाते हैं। वे यहां पर आते हैं, अपना सामान देखते हैं। उनसे एक attachment और relation महसूस करते हैं। जब भी कोई program होता है, हम उन लोगों को बुलाते हैं। उन लोगों का एक ऐसा attachment हो जाता है कि जब उनको लगता है कि संग्रहालय में उनके घर की maintenance की ज़रूरत है। तो वे लोग स्वयं फ़ोन करते हैं। एक मंगला दादा थे जिनका अब देहांत हो गया है। उनको बुलाना नहीं पड़ता था। जब बारिश होती तो वे खुद आ जाते थे और कहते थे। 'मैं तो आ गया हूँ। यहां के घर की maintenance करनी है।' इस तरह का संग्रहालय के साथ लगाव हो जाता है। मैंने देखा है कि लोग बहुत सारी जगहों में जाते हैं, पर यहां पर वे लोग बेहद खुश रहते हैं। कुछ भी program हो या workshop है तो आयेंगे, यदि उनसे पूछें तो पता लगता है कि अन्य जगहों के सब programs से अधिक यहां पर उन्हें बहुत अच्छा लगता है।

यह बतलाइये, कि इन लोगों का यहां से जो लगाव है, उनको लगता है कि उन लोगों का घर भोपाल में भी है और एक महीने तक आकर रहते भी हैं, । यह contact आप लोगों का लगातार रहता है? और उन लोगों की livelihood की जो मुसीबतें हैं उनका क्या आप लोगों को कुछ अंदाज़ा रहता है? क्या वे बात करते हैं कि हमारी चीज़ कितनी बिकती है, नहीं बिकती। हमें कितना काम मिलता है, नहीं मिलता। Agriculture में कुछ फ़ायदा है, नहीं है। और कोई व्यवसाय मिल सकता है, या नहीं?

जी contact लगातार रहता है। Livelihood की बातें होती हैं। कुछ लोग ऐसे है जिनको संग्रहालय के कारण कहीं और काम भी मिला है। जैसे अगरिया लोगों को पहला काम संग्रहालय में ही मिला था। अभी रायपुर में museum बन रहा है।

इन लोगों को वहाँ भी काम मिल रहा है। फिर दूसरा-दूसरा कहीं और भी होता है। वार्ली लोग जो पेंटिंग दीवार में बनाते हैं, उसको आज कल कपड़े में भी करने लगे हैं, दूसरी चीज़ों में भी इस्तेमाल करने लगे हैं। उस तरह से देखें तो, थोड़ा बहुत उनका improvement हुआ है।

यहां की वजह से उनका livelihood थोड़ा extend हुआ है। जो लोग factories में काम करते हैं, उनके काम में और इन लोगों के काम में क्या कुछ फ़र्क है?

फ़र्क है। इन में perfection होता है। जब तक एक चीज़ सही ढंग से नहीं होती है, लगे रहते हैं उसमें। छोड़ कर चले जाने वाले type के नहीं हैं।

पर कुछ modern और traditional का combinations हो सकता है, जैसे यहाँ भोपाल में School of Planning and Architecture के students हैं, जो vernacular architecture की बात करते हैं। आज के मकान में air conditioner fridge इत्यादि हो लेकिन उसकी आकृति या form traditional हो। School of Planning and Architecture के लड़के-लड़कियां क्या museum से कुछ सीखकर जाते हैं?

हाँ। वे लोग वास्तु से related चीज़ें देखते हैं जैसे Tribal लोगों के सब घर पूर्वमुखी हैं। अधिकतर south east में ही उनका kitchen बनाया जाता है। उनके घर में ventialtion का जो gap बनाया हुआ है, उससे सिर्फ हवा ही नहीं, रोशनी भी आती है। और उनके छत पर जो slope बनाया हुआ, उससे घर में पानी भी नहीं गिरता है, और घर भी बहुत ठंडा रहता है। यह कुछ, यहाँ से लोगों ने apply किया है। जो लोग शहर से आते हैं, वे कुछ लेकर जाते हैं। यहाँ पर जो exhibitions वगैरा होती हैं उनसे लोगों को यह प्रेरणा मिलती है कि हम भी ऐसा घर बनवायें। दूसरे यहाँ पर हमने tribal food festival किया था। उसमें हर tribe का अलग अलग खाना होता है। और उसमें अपनी-अपनी जगह में जो available होता है और उसमें जो पौष्टिक गुण होता है सबको दिया जाता है। इस विषय पर मैंने काफी data collect किया है। कितने लोग आये थे, किसी चीज़ का क्यों इस्तेमाल करते हैं, आदि।